Studies of
DYLAN THOMAS
ALLEN GINSBERG
SYLVIA PLATH
AND
ROBERT LOWELL

Other Books by Louis Simpson

POETRY

The Arrivistes: Poems 1940–1949

Good News of Death and Other Poems

A Dream of Governors

At the End of the Open Road

Selected Poems

Adventures of the Letter I

Searching for the Ox

PROSE

James Hogg: A Critical Study

Riverside Drive

An Introduction to Poetry

North of Jamaica

*Three on the Tower: The Lives and Works of
Ezra Pound, T. S. Eliot, and William Carlos Williams*

Studies of

DYLAN THOMAS
ALLEN GINSBERG
SYLVIA PLATH
AND
ROBERT LOWELL

LOUIS SIMPSON

M

*First published in the United States of America 1978
under the title* A Revolution in Taste
First published in the United Kingdom 1979

Published by
THE MACMILLAN PRESS LTD
*London and Basingstoke
Associated companies in Delhi
Dublin   Hong Kong   Johannesburg   Lagos
Melbourne   New York   Singapore   Tokyo*

Printed in Great Britain
by Unwin Brothers Limited
Old Woking Surrey

British Library Cataloguing in Publication Data

Simpson, Louis
    Studies of Dylan Thomas, Allen Ginsberg,
    Sylvia Plath and Robert Lowell
    1. Ginsberg, Allen – Criticism and interpreta-
    tion
    2. Plath, Sylvia – Criticism and interpretation
    3. Thomas, Dylan – Criticism and interpreta-
    tion
    4. Lowell, Robert – Criticism and interpretation
    I. Title
    811'.5'409   PS3513.I74Z/

    ISBN 0–333–27396–6

Acknowledgements

The author gratefully acknowledges permission to reprint excerpts from the following works.

Kingsley Amis, *A Case of Samples*. Copyright © 1956 by Kingsley Amis, by permission of Curtis Brown Ltd.

W. H. Auden, *Collected Poems*. Copyright © 1976 by Edward Mendelson, William Meredith and Monroe K. Spears, executors of the Estate of W. H. Auden, by permission of Random House, Inc. and Faber and Faber, Ltd.

T. S. Eliot, *Collected Poems, 1901–1962*. Copyright © 1970 by Esme Valerie Eliot, by permission of Harcourt Brace Jovanovich, Inc. and Faber and Faber, Ltd.

Allen Ginsberg, *Empty Mirror*. Copyright © 1961 by Allen Ginsberg, by permission of Corinth Books.

Allen Ginsberg, *The Gates of Wrath*. Copyright © 1972 by Allen Ginsberg, by permission of Gray Fox Press.

Allen Ginsberg, *Howl and Other Poems*. Copyright © 1956, 1959 by Allen Ginsberg, by permission of City Lights Books.

Allen Ginsberg, *Kaddish and Other Poems*. Copyright © 1961 by Allen Ginsberg, by permission of City Lights Books.

Allen Ginsberg, *Planet News*. Copyright © 1968 by Allen Ginsberg, by permission of City Lights Books.

Allen Ginsberg, *Journals*. Copyright © 1977 by Allen Ginsberg, by permission of Grove Press, Inc.

Ted Hughes, *The Hawk in the Rain*. Copyright © 1956, 1957 by Ted Hughes, by permission of Harper & Row, Publishers, Inc. and Faber and Faber, Ltd.

Robert Lowell, *Day by Day*. Copyright © 1975, 1977 by Robert Lowell, by permission of Farrar, Straus and Giroux, Inc. and Faber and Faber, Ltd.

Robert Lowell, *For the Union Dead*. Copyright © 1956, 1960, 1961, 1962, 1963, 1964 by Robert Lowell, by permission of Farrar, Straus and Giroux, Inc. and Faber and Faber, Ltd.

Robert Lowell, *Imitations*. Copyright © 1958, 1959, 1960, 1961 by Robert Lowell, by permission of Farrar, Straus and Giroux, Inc. and Faber and Faber, Ltd.

Robert Lowell, *History*. Copyright © 1967, 1968, 1969, 1970, 1973 by Robert Lowell, by permission of Farrar, Straus and Giroux and Faber and Faber, Ltd.

Robert Lowell, *Life Studies*. Copyright © 1956, 1959 by Robert Lowell, by permission of Farrar, Straus and Giroux, Inc. and Faber and Faber, Ltd.

Robert Lowell, *Land of Unlikeness*. Copyright 1944 by Robert Lowell. Copyright renewed © 1972 by Robert Lowell.

Robert Lowell, *Lord Weary's Castle and the Mills of the Kavanaughs*. Copyright © 1944, 1946, 1947, 1950, 1951 by Robert Lowell, by permission of Harcourt Brace Jovanovich, Inc.

Robert Lowell, *Near the Ocean*. Copyright © 1963, 1965, 1966, 1967 by Robert Lowell, by permission of Farrar, Straus and Giroux, Inc. and Faber and Faber, Ltd.

This book is dedicated to
Robert Levine
and
Robert S. Liebert,
who, with their friendship
and advice, helped me to write it.

Contents

There can be no interpreting the masterpieces of the past unless one judges them from the standpoint of those who wrote them, and not from the outside, from a respectful distance, and with all academic deference.

—PROUST, *Contre Sainte-Beuve*

Foreword

THE AIM in writing is to convey a feeling—by creating an illusion, said Ford Madox Ford, "the sort of odd vibration that scenes in real life really have," giving the reader the impression that he is witnessing something real, that he is passing through an experience.[1] "You attempt to involve the reader amongst the personages of the story or in the atmosphere of the poem. You do this by presentation and by presentation and again by presentation."[2]

Modern writing in America begins with this idea. The Imagist movement of the years immediately preceding the Great War took its impetus from Ford's insistence on presentation and T. E. Hulme's insistence on writing with images. This tendency has prevailed with American poets ever since. Not with all: there are some who are content to describe and make statements about life, but those who have given American poetry a character, who have made it possible to speak of American as distinct from English poetry, have followed in the steps of the Imagists.

English writers use poetry as a means of discourse; they are conscious of the weight of the past and of their place in a literary tradition. Americans believe, as Wallace Stevens put it, that "poetry is not a literary activity; it is a vital activity."[3]

For a time, however, the movement I have described as American appeared to have come to a stop. This was largely due to the influence of W. H. Auden, who emigrated from England to the United States on the eve of the Second World War, established himself at the center of literary power, and exerted an influence for more than a decade. The nature of the influence was not clear at first, for Auden arrived in New York with a reputation as a rebel—many even thought him a poet of the Left. But as time passed he revealed himself to be a mainstay of tradition. As long as Auden set the fashion—and this he was able to do, for he was a brilliant literary journalist as well as poet—the stream of experiment that had begun with the Imagist poets, especially that kind of writing of which William Carlos Williams was the chief exponent, receded into the background. Auden ruled with wit and a knowledge of verse forms; in comparison, the American poets who looked to Williams, or to a poet thought to be even more rudimentary, Walt Whitman, appeared to be fumbling provincials—certainly not worth the attention of readers who had been trained by the New Criticism to look for shades of irony and multiple, ambiguous meanings.

But something was missing in Auden's concept of poetry, and what this was became evident when the Welsh poet Dylan Thomas began his American tours. The missing quality was passion. In Thomas this was expressed in music, the sound of the words, over and above what they might be saying. A poem by Auden was an exercise in reason, listening to a poem by Thomas was an experience. At the boom of his voice from the platform the Audenesque façade began to crack, and a few years later Allen Ginsberg brought it tumbling down. The poet moved to the center of the stage and spoke his mind freely. This became the common stance for poets in the years that followed. "Most artists and critics," said Susan Sontag, writing in the sixties, "have discarded the theory of art as representation of an outer reality in favor of art as subjective expression."[4]

The change was brought about by other poets as well, notably those who were associated with Charles Olson. I have not written about Olson, however, because I do not feel the sympathy that would enable me to enter into the process of his work. In writing about Dylan Thomas, Allen Ginsberg, Sylvia Plath, and Robert Lowell I was involved, but I feel an antipathy for Olson's ideas. He believed that poetry should be based in science and that the humanist traditions of the West were a mistake. He was for "objectism," which he explained as "getting rid of the lyrical interference of the individual as ego, of the 'subject' and his soul, that peculiar presumption by which western man has interposed himself between what he is as a creature of nature (with certain instructions to carry out) and those other creations of nature which we may, with no derogation, call objects. For a man is himself an object . . ."[5]

I have not been able to reconcile this with the feelings of Thomas, Ginsberg, Plath, and Lowell, or with my own. I love the humanist traditions of the West, and see no reason to be afraid of the ego or soul. In any case it is unavoidable, we are born into it, sink or swim. I am with

Conrad's Stein who said that we are in this life as in a dream, and that the secret is to immerse oneself in the destructive element, let the deep sea keep you up.

Olson had many useful things to say about the art of writing. He was not as original as he has been said to be, but originality is not everything; it can be just as important to be useful. Olson's theory of "projective verse" can be traced back to Coleridge's theory of organic form, and to other nineteenth-century writers. Emerson said, "It is not metres, but a metre-making argument that makes a poem—a thought so passionate and alive that like the spirit of a plant or animal it has an architecture of its own, and adorns nature with a new thing."[6] In the twentieth century D. H. Lawrence and William Carlos Williams had stated the ideas brought forward by Olson. But he did bring them forward—that was his usefulness. Olson said:

> Let me put it baldly. The two halves are:
> the HEAD, by way of the EAR, to the SYLLABLE
> the HEART, by way of the BREATH, to the LINE[7]

The clearest explanation of this I have seen is Denise Levertov's:

Head (intellect) and ear (sensuous instinct) lead to syllable, which has intrinsic meaning but has not rhythm. It is when heart (emotion, feeling) influence the operation of breath (process) that we are led to the line (the phrase, the rhythmic, emotive grouping of syllables) . . .[8]

Olson encouraged poets to write what Lawrence called "poetry of the present," making poetry out of their experience. His "associationism," the idea, going back to the eighteenth century, of one thought leading to another, was also useful until his followers made it into a dogma. But though I respect Olson as a teacher I do not have the sympathy with his views that would enable me to present them with warmth and understanding.

At one time I thought of writing about Wallace Stevens who had a considerable influence in the fifties and, in recent years, has been called our greatest modern poet. He is frequently mentioned by reviewers—I wonder, however, if they have tried reading his later, "philosophic" poems. I find them impenetrable, a slippery, meaningless surface of words, and cannot believe that I am alone in having this reaction. Critics of the old Symbolist school are fond of saying that poems are made of words. There is a great difference, however, between words that point to things and words that point to themselves. My liking for the first kind, the poetry that is an "imitation of life," prevents me from liking the poetry of Wallace Stevens. A man cannot walk in two different directions at once—the poetry I like has a connection with the world we perceive through our senses. It is always calling us back to the heat and drama of human contact.

John Dewey shared my point of view. He said that "The abiding struggle of art is to convert materials that are stammering or dumb in ordinary experience into eloquent media."[9] William Carlos Williams saw poetry as "lifting to the imagination those things which lie under the direct scrutiny of the senses."[10] And the greatest of American poets, Whitman, summed up the matter in a line:

> Behold, the body includes and is the meaning, the main
> concern, and includes and is the soul . . .[11]

The poets in this book created art out of the confusion of their lives. The Ginsberg in *Kaddish,* the Lowell in *Life Studies,* the Plath in *Ariel,* are self-portraits, not literal representations. There is hardly any need for mirror images of life. The poets, however, were not always selective, and at times they lapsed into merely stating what they had seen and felt. Now, in order for a man's feelings to be important in themselves he must be a kind of saint. Attention shifts from the work to the life, and the lives of most poets won't bear inspection. So the poet works up his feelings, his occupation now is seeming to be sincere, and the fabric collapses. The mixture of life and poetry has been fatal in some cases. But there are signs that the vogue for confessional writing may be coming to an end. "We are tired of looking in mirrors. Every year there is a new style in personalities, we try to draw attention to ourselves . . . and soon, what does it matter? No one is listening."[12]

In spite of the pitfalls, the greatest of which is vanity, there is a continuing need for poetry that expresses the individual. There have been other movements in our time but none has captured the attention of the public as much as this—and, I believe, deservedly. Thomas, Ginsberg, Plath, and Lowell, though their poems were intensely personal— perhaps because they were—have seemed to speak for many others. Paradoxically, two of these poets, Ginsberg and Lowell, who might have been expected to have nothing to do with public life, found themselves compelled by some inner necessity to take a stand on political questions, and their opinion carried weight. This is the reverse of what happens when writers set out to convert others to a point of view: they deal in expedient ideas, address themselves to the largest possible number, and end by convincing no one.

In writing this book, my method, like the subject, has been somewhat personal: to immerse myself in the writings of the poets, seize upon what seemed vital, and convey my impressions to the reader. I have referred to other men's opinions when they seemed better than my own, or in order to give a sense of the literary atmosphere. At times I have tried to imagine what the poets thought—not substituting my ideas for theirs but imagining what it would have been like to be in their place. There is no danger that the reader will be misled in these passages: they are clearly imaginary. The reader will see that I am interpreting the facts, which is not always the case with books that appear to have a more objective, academic approach.

Once again I wish to thank Merridy Darrow and Jean Carr for their painstaking work on the manuscript and their valuable suggestions.

The
Color
of
Saying

Once it was the colour of saying
Soaked my table the uglier side of a hill . . .[1]

*D*YLAN MARLAIS THOMAS was born in 1914 in Swansea, South Wales. "Marlais" was the name of an uncle of his father who had been a poet and who took the bardic name "Marles" from a stream that ran near his birthplace. The name "Dylan" came from one of the medieval prose romances in the *Mabinogion*. As a noun the word means "sea" or "ocean." In the *Mabinogion* Dylan makes a brief appearance when Math the son of Mathonwy challenges Aranrhod, who claims to be a virgin, to step over his magic wand. "A fine boy-child with rich yellow hair" drops from her as she does so. Math son of Mathonwy calls him Dylan, and the child makes for the sea, his natural element.[2]

Dylan Thomas's mother, Florence, came of a family named Williams in Carmarthenshire. They were farmers, but Anna Williams married George Williams who was employed by the railway. They moved to Swansea, and in the course of time George Williams rose to be an inspector. They had seven children, of whom Florence was the youngest.

Dylan's father was a schoolmaster. He, too, had come up in the world: his father had been a humble railway employee known as "Thomas the Guard." But D. J. Thomas made the hard climb out of the working class into middle-class respectability. The poet's wife Caitlin speaks of his making the transition from "farmhouse and railwaymen standards, to schoolmaster in a semi-detached suburban matchbox." The Thomases had moved up to "penny-pricing gentility," and this required constantly keeping up appearances though they could scarcely afford to. "No blue-blooded gentleman," says Caitlin Thomas, "was a quarter as gentlemanly as Dylan's father." There was a strong streak of puritanism in Dylan himself that his friends never suspected but of which she got "the disapproving benefit."[3]

Florence Thomas, however, was no puritan. Paul Ferris in his biography of the poet says that she liked "to kiss and cuddle," and suggests that all this physical contact made Dylan sexually precocious. His cot was placed in his parents' bedroom—a common enough practice among families with limited means, "though it can set a psychiatrist's teeth on edge." All his life, says Ferris, Dylan Thomas "hankered after the warm beds and mother-love of his childhood." He liked to be looked after, and he was very skillful at getting people to look after him. He would be disgusted with himself for doing it, but this did not stop him. He was particularly helpless when it came to food and drink. Psychiatrists would say that Dylan Thomas was a man with powerful "oral traits." He depended on being fed: by his mother, his wife, his friends, and the people he called "silly ravens," who had money they might be persuaded to part with.

Ferris suggests that Florence Thomas's doting on her son brought about the classic Oedipal situation in which the son competes with the father for the mother's love, and succeeds in ousting the father. But this brings guilt and a fear of punishment. Dylan Thomas's poems and stories contain references to mutilation of the sexual organs; references to tailors and scissors remind one of *Struwwelpeter*, especially the story of Little Suck-a-Thumb in which a child is punished by having his thumbs cut off by a tailor with flying hair and an enormous pair of scissors.

The fear of retribution may lead to impotence and the loss of other powers as well . . . for example, the ability to write. In later years Thomas showed a desperate need to assert his masculinity, drinking heavily and trying to get women to go to bed with him, and writing had become a difficult, almost impossible task.

However, Ferris observes that if Thomas's early experiences had bad effects, they were also "part of a process that helped produce a poet of Thomas' uniquely morbid self-interest."

"My horrible self," Thomas wrote to the poet Henry Treece, "would not be itself did it not possess the faults."[4]

Attempts to psychoanalyze artists and their works are never quite satisfactory—there is a gap between life and the work of art. Knowing what a poet's childhood was like cannot explain why he turned to poetry or why he wrote in a particular form and style. On the other hand, psychoanalytic criticism can help us to understand the poet's attitudes, and these have a demonstrable relationship to the content of his work. It is only when we expect too much of psychoanalysis, when we try to make it take the place of aesthetic criticism, that it is plainly inadequate.

Dylan Thomas does appear to be a case of the Oedipus Complex. But it is not straightforward: one would expect Little Suck-a-Thumb to grow up hating his father, but Dylan respected his—in fact, had a great deal of affection for him. Daniel Jones, who went to school with him, says that Dylan avoided D. J. Thomas, who was one of the masters. But it can be embarrassing to be at a school where one's father teaches, and D. J. was very unpopular. According to Jones, Dylan stayed out of his father's way at home as well as at school. This, too, is understandable—D. J. was cranky and easily moved to anger. "However," Jones adds, "it was equally clear that he respected his father and was proud of him, and that any would-be detractor would be wise to remain silent about him in his presence."[5]

When Dylan was a grown man his famous poetry-reading voice was patterned on his father's way of reading poetry aloud to his students. And he wrote poetry in praise of his father.

The young D. J. Thomas won a scholarship that took him to the University College of Wales at Aberystwyth. He graduated four years later with a first-class honors degree in English. But then something went wrong—instead of pursuing an academic career at one of the more prestigious English universities, he lapsed into a schoolmaster. According to Mrs. Thomas he was offered a traveling fellowship but did not take it because he was "tired." But there is no record at Aberystwyth of D. J. Thomas's having received a fellowship. It seems more likely that he got Florence Williams pregnant and had to marry her, and then found that he had to earn a living as best he could, by teaching English in a grammar school. It was commonly said that Florence Williams was pregnant before she was married. The child either was stillborn or died shortly after birth.

The Thomases started married life together in Sketty, a village to the west of Swansea. A girl child, Nancy, was born in 1906. Eight years later they moved to a bigger house in Swansea, in the Uplands. They were always short of money for they were living beyond their means. Mrs. Thomas used to pay the tradesmen in rotation, and D. J. did extra work, teaching Welsh in evening classes, a job he must have hated for he was never heard speaking Welsh at any other time.

When he was a boy D. J. Thomas had wanted to be a poet—Dylan Thomas told this to Ruthven Todd. But his efforts had been rejected, and his love of poetry found its only outlet in reading aloud. It is said that he read Shakespeare aloud to Dylan before the child could speak. Whether or not this is true, he did read Dylan nursery rhymes and some

rhymes of his own making. Dylan Thomas once said that the first poems
he knew were nursery rhymes: "I wanted to write poetry in the beginning because I had fallen in love with words. The first poems I knew
were nursery rhymes, and before I could read them for myself I had
come to love just the words of them, the words alone. What the words
stood for, symbolised, or meant, was of very secondary importance;
what mattered was the *sound* of them as I heard them for the first time
on the lips of the remote and incomprehensible grown-ups who seemed,
for some reason, to be living in my world. And these words were, to me,
as the notes of bells, the sounds of musical instruments, the noises of
wind, sea, and rain, the rattle of milkcarts, the clopping of hooves on
cobbles, the fingering of branches on a window pane, might be to
someone, deaf from birth, who has miraculously found his hearing.
I did not care what the words said, overmuch, nor what happened to
Jack & Jill & the Mother Goose rest of them; I cared for the shapes
of sound that their names, and the words describing their actions, made
in my ears; I cared for the colours the words cast on my eyes. . . ."[6]

This was said in 1951 in answer to five questions asked by a student,
and published ten years later in the *Texas Quarterly* under the heading,
"Poetic Manifesto." Thomas made similar observations from time to
time, insisting that sound, "the colour of saying," was of the first
importance in his poetry, and that the meaning of words, and what the
symbols might be said to stand for, had little importance. If Thomas's
view of his poetry is correct, then much of the criticism of it has been
mistaken. Critics have chosen to ignore his statements—perhaps on the
assumption that what a writer thinks he is doing is not to be taken
seriously—and have proceeded to show, line by line and symbol by
symbol, the logic in his verse.

D. J. Thomas knew and quoted the Bible, and this may have helped
to form the Biblical phrases and images that are found in the works
of his son. But D. J. was not religious—he had the same contempt for
the Creator that he had for everyone else. There were moments when
D. J.'s unwillingness to be pleased lifted him from the ruck of humanity
to the sublime. Once the Thomases were staying at a house in the
country. "Father," Dylan told Daniel Jones, "is still as bitter as ever.
He got up the other morning and looked through the window to the left,
to the right, and straight ahead. He sneered, and, putting every ounce
of venom into the words, said, "*Grass! Grass!* everywhere—nothing but
grass!"[7]

The Thomases lived at Number 5, Cwmdonkin Drive, a semi-

detached villa like hundreds of others in Swansea, furnished for respectability with flowered wallpaper, a clock on the mantelpiece supported
by horses of mock ebony, willow-pattern china, and tea cosies. No
doubt there was also an aspidistra.

D. J. had a study lined with books to which he would often retire.
Sometimes at the dining table Mrs. Thomas would be talking about the
children, or clothes, or some other of the foolish things women talk
about, whereupon D. J. would throw down his napkin, rise in a rage,
and stalk off to his study.

The house was on a hill; from the upper windows you could look
down a slope of slate roofs to the bay and harbor, with the Mumbles
Head lighthouse to the west. There was a school across the way, with
a playing field sloped so that the ball ran downhill . . . a crazy game,
like something in *Alice*. Then there was the thick growth of trees that
marked Cwmdonkin Park.

His nurse took him there almost daily in his pram to listen to the
pigeons and feed the gulls that were blown over in windy weather. The
nurse, Addie Elliott, remembers that the first word he spoke was "bird."[8]

He grew up thin and active. A young woman who baby-sat for the
Thomases when Dylan was five recalls that he was "an absolute tartar,
an appalling boy. I remember him grabbing for oranges. He never
asked."[9]

At seven, wrapped in thick sweaters and layers of underclothes, he
was sent trudging off to day school. There he soon was teacher's pet.
He had shimmering curls and a cherubic face, and he was mischievous . . . an irresistible combination.

The discipline at the "dame school" was firm and kind. He would
recollect a smell of galoshes . . . the sound of a piano drifting downstairs
to the schoolroom where a small boy sat alone, doing penance for
unfinished sums or for pulling a girl's hair or kicking a shin.

There was a lane behind the school where the oldest and boldest
gathered to throw pebbles at the windows and to boast and tell fibs
about their relations. As a grown man he would dream that he went
from school into the lane and that he said to his classmates, "At last,
I have a real secret." The secret was that he could fly, and when they
did not believe him he flapped his arms and went flying over the school,
the trees and chimneys, the docks, masts, and funnels, over the streets,
the men and women, the children, idlers and cripples, "over the yellow
seashore, and the stone-chasing dogs, and the old men, and the singing
sea."[10]

Dylan and his friends played in Cwmdonkin Park. It was approached by crawling under a wire for there was no entrance from the main road. Then they would be among the giant firs, palmettos, yuccas, and monkey puzzle trees. It was their African jungle. There was a lake which had formerly been a reservoir, and a fountain where Dylan sailed model boats. There was a rookery and "the loud zoo of the willow groves." It was the park where the Hunchback sat.

> Like the park birds he came early
> Like the water he sat down
> And Mister they called Hey mister
> The truant boys from the town
> Running when he heard them clearly
> On out of sound[11]

Dylan was a town boy. But his mother's sister had married a farmer named Jones, and they had a farm in Carmarthenshire. Fernhill stood on a rise above a wooded valley shielded from the road by trees. The farm building made three sides of a square around a small courtyard. There Ann and Jim Jones kept a few cows and pigs and chickens. The place was dirty and run down—Jim Jones was shiftless, known throughout the district as "a terrible man." It was said that he drank. Ann Jones did most of the work, making the butter they sold. She has gained another kind of life as the Ann Jones of Dylan Thomas's "After the Funeral."

At Fernhill the town boy received his impressions of the country. "About the countryside in general," Ferris remarks, "Thomas always seemed in two minds. He needed to break away from urban life, but he soon tired of rural retreats. It was part of his inability ever to settle anywhere for long."

The countryside around Fernhill fed his sense of the macabre. As a child he dreamed of ghosts and vampires and he seems to have taken a perverse delight in frightening himself with them.[12] "The Peaches," one of his autobiographical stories, includes a demon with "wings and hooks, who clung like a bat to my hair." When he arrived at the farm with his uncle, at night, he imagined that "nothing lived in the hollow house at the end of the yard but two sticks with faces scooped out of turnips."[13]

In the autumn of 1925, shortly before his eleventh birthday, Dylan entered the Grammar School where his father was a master. According to Jones, while Dylan was at school his relationship with his father was "strained," and no wonder, for the boys feared D. J. Thomas. He was ironic and sarcastic—"The whip-lash of D. J.'s tongue," Jones says, "held us in terror." And he was capable of rage. Jones recalls an occasion when D. J. was reading aloud a poem by Wilfred Owen and one of the boys giggled. D. J. gave him a savage beating. Jones says, "We all thought he really was going to kill the boy. . . ."[14]

D. J. despised his job—with his superior abilities he should have been holding a chair at Oxford or Cambridge. He had hoped for the chair in English at the new Swansea University College, but it went to a W. D. Thomas whom he thought less qualified than he. And a fellow student from Aberystwyth, T. J. Rees, had been made Director of Education at a higher salary than his.[15] D. J. had nothing but contempt for his fellow masters who were satisfied with their humble place in life, chasing schoolboys to their tasks. He had been intended for better things, but Destiny had thrown an obstacle in his path, in the shape of Florence Williams, and chained him to Cwmdonkin Drive.

He was extremely fastidious. A coarse remark would make him angry; words that were sexually suggestive had an alarming effect. On the good side, he was an effective reader of poetry—Dylan said that it had been grand, all the boys thought so. It was D. J.'s reading that made them, for the first time, see that there *was*, after all, *something* in Shakespeare and all this poetry.[16]

It has been said that D. J. had great hopes for Dylan—his son was to have the academic career that he had been denied. But in this, too, he was disappointed—Dylan had no inclination at all for study; he was absent from class as often as not. The surprising thing is that D. J. did nothing about it. One would have expected him to be enraged, but this was not the case: Dylan was allowed to do as he liked at the Grammar School, as he had done ever since he was a child.

It has been said that Mrs. Thomas stood between Dylan and his father's anger, pleading his poor health. But Dylan was not in poor health—he was "indecisively active, quick to get dirty."[17] Here, from *Portrait of the Artist as a Young Dog*, are some of his activities.

I let Edgar Reynolds be whipped because I had taken his homework; I stole from my mother's bag; I stole from Gwyneth's bag; I stole twelve books in three visits from the library, and threw them away in the park; I drank a cup of my water to see what it tasted like; I beat a dog with a stick so that it would roll over and lick my hand afterwards; I looked with Dan Jones through the keyhole while his maid had a bath; I cut my knee with a penknife, and put the blood on my handkerchief and said it had come out of my ears so that I could pretend I was ill and frighten my mother . . .[18]

At Grammar School Dylan showed a surprising ability for long-distance running; on Sports Day in his first summer term he won the one-mile race for under-fifteens, and for years he competed successfully in school races and cross-country runs. Jones tells us that he could also fight like a wildcat, scratching and biting. Nevertheless, in the Thomas family it was understood that Dylan's health was not strong and that he had to be indulged—a belief he accepted willingly and traded on all his life.

But his poor record in the classroom cannot be attributed to Mrs. Thomas's coddling. After all, D. J. was on the spot and it was within his power to see that Dylan got an education. But he did not—on the contrary, he abetted his misbehavior. Dylan refused to observe discipline and was absent from classes as often as he pleased, and the masters did not dare to punish him because they feared a confrontation with his father. As a result Dylan, "if recorded at all," was listed at the bottom of the class in all subjects except English, and even in English he came close to the bottom. He did not pass any examination and left school as soon as possible. As Jones puts it, his appearances in class became more and more sporadic until they ceased altogether.

By bringing up his son in this way, D. J. Thomas showed his contempt for the world and, at the same time, bound Dylan to him for life. He encouraged him to be the rebel he himself could not be, permitting him to avoid all dull and dreary tasks; as a result Dylan knew nothing but poetry, which he got from his father, and only fine-sounding poetry at that. He would have to be a poet, and when the early lyric impulse was played out he would have no way of making a fresh start—lacking all discipline, he would not be able to submit himself to philosophy, religion, or any intellectual system. Like his father he despised all systems, or pretended to despise them—"He had," says Caitlin Thomas, "the ... dislike, amounting to superstitious horror, of philosophy, psychology, analysis, criticism; all those vaguely ponderous tomes; but most of all, of the gentle art of discussing poetry. . . ."[19] He was uncomfortable in the company of people who seemed to know about philosophy, psychology, and so on. These occasions would bring out his rudest behavior, and, of course, his drinking. D. J. Thomas, a tyrant to every other boy, was the most permissive of masters where his son was concerned, and the result—Dylan locked into the narrow round of his own immediate consciousness, his poetry restricted to a view of the world as an extension of himself, literally, his flesh and blood and bones—was disastrous.

When Dylan Thomas went to school "modern poetry" meant:

> When I was but thirteen or so
> > I went into a golden land;
> Chimborazo, Cotopaxi
> > Took me by the hand . . .[20]

It meant:

> From troubles of ·the world
> I turn to ducks,
> Beautiful comical things
> Sleeping or curled
> Their heads beneath white wings . . .[21]

It did *not* mean:

> 'My nerves are bad tonight. Yes, bad. Stay with me.
> 'Speak to me. Why do you never speak. Speak.
> > 'What are you thinking of? What thinking? What?
> 'I never know what you are thinking. Think.'[22]

The poets whom Americans think of as the masters of twentieth-century verse in English—Yeats, Pound, and Eliot—were not taught in British classrooms. Yeats's "The Lake Isle of Innisfree" was taught, but not his later, more difficult poetry. A rare teacher might show his students one of Eliot's poems, but usually if Eliot were mentioned it was as an example of "this modern verse." Eliot was a hoax . . . the fellow was obviously pulling the public's leg.

The Georgian poets—Masefield, Drinkwater, Abercrombie, W. H. Davies, Walter De La Mare—were the fellows to read. Schoolboys were required to memorize and recite Robert Bridges's "London Snow," or:

> Lord Rameses of Egypt sighed
> > Because a summer evening passed;
> And little Ariadne cried
> > That summer fancy fell at last
> To dust; and young Verona died
> > When beauty's hour was overcast . . .[23]

The Georgian poets wrote about a passing mood induced by the contemplation of nature. Sometimes they wished with James Elroy Flecker to be on a golden journey to Samarkand, or with W. J. Turner to be hunting velvet tigers in the jungle; usually, however, they were content to be in the Home Counties.

> God! I will pack, and take a train,
> And get me to England once again!
> For England's the one land, I know,
> Where men with Splendid Hearts may go;
> And Cambridgeshire, of all England,
> The shire for Men who Understand;
> And of *that* district I prefer
> The lovely hamlet Grantchester . . .[24]

Recently there had been a disruption of the natural order, the Great War that had taken the best of the nation's youth, sixty thousand on the first day of the Somme alone. The names of battles in France and Flanders were sacred. Each name evoked the same landscape, acres of mud laced with barbed wire through which lines of men wound hopelessly. Photographs of the trenches showed white, strained faces with eyes that looked beyond the camera, beyond all observers, at some private vision of Hell.

English poetry had encouraged the nation's youth to go to war. In "The War Films" Henry Newbolt wrote:

> O living pictures of the dead,
>   O songs without a sound,
> O fellowship whose phantom tread
>   Hallows a phantom ground—
> How in a gleam have these revealed
>   The faith we had not found . . .[25]

He wished that he could have taken the place of the "lads" whose death he was mourning. Other poets, however, who had seen active service, had a different view: they found nothing noble in a death by high explosive, machine gun, or gas. Siegfried Sassoon condemned the war in satirical lyrics, heaping sarcasm on the General Staff and patriots and war profiteers back in England. Wilfred Owen showed what it was like to be down in the mud with the troops.

> Our brains ache, in the merciless iced east winds that
>   knive us . . .
> Wearied we keep awake because the night is silent . . .
> Low, drooping flares confuse our memory of the salient . . .
> Worried by silence, sentries whisper, curious, nervous,
>   But nothing happens.[26]

Wilfred Owen was one of the authors in D. J. Thomas's study, on the ground floor, behind a stained-glass door. There Dylan would read whatever struck his fancy. He read old ballads, and Henry Newbolt, and William Blake—not necessarily in that order. He read Keats and Shakespeare and D. H. Lawrence. He read Sir Thomas Browne and Thomas De Quincey. He read Traherne and other Metaphysical poets. And he read the Bible. Outside his father's study he read *Chums*, Baroness Orczy, and dozens of a schoolboy's favorite authors.

In the course of his reading he came upon poets who were not taught in the classroom. When he was fifteen he wrote an essay on "Modern Poetry" for the school magazine that started, as such essays usually do, with the claim that "Poetry has never been so wide and varied as it is today," and proceeded to describe "the modern artistic spirit."

The most important element of "poetical modernity" was freedom, "freedom of form, of structure, of imagery and idea." The roots of this freedom were to be found in Hopkins's compressed imagery and the "violation" of language this entailed. Then came the metrical experiments of Robert Bridges, "who introduced free rhythm into the confines of orthodox metre." Da La Mare continued Bridges's mixture of innovation and convention, and "at the present time Sacheverell Sitwell presents a great deal of his strange confusion of thought and beauty in the heroic couplet."

He mentions "neo-Romanticists" such as Eliot and James Joyce, who assume that no subject is unpoetical and write of sordid details, a damp despondent atmosphere, their attraction for the gutter. And W. B. Yeats, "At the head of the twilight poets," who writes of "a fragile, unsubstantial world, covered with mysticism and mythological shadows" . . . Yeats's entire poetic creation is "brittle." He praises the simple beauty and charm of W. H. Davies's lyrics.

He speaks of the Imagists, "founded by John Gould Fletcher." Richard Aldington is the best known of the group; he accentuates the image, but "has modified it and made it more intelligible." Then there are the Sitwells, who are said to be obscure but whose writings, examined closely, reveal images and thoughts "of a new and astonishing clarity."

There has been a revolution in English poetry as a result of the Great War. The war caused some of the bitterest and loveliest poetry in the language to be written, by Siegfried Sassoon, Rupert Brooke, Robert Nichols, Wilfred Owen, Robert Graves, Julian Grenfell, "and the other heroes who built towers of beauty upon the ashes of their lives."

But it is the poetry of today that shows the clearest influence of the war. "The incoherence caused by anguish and animal horror, and the shrill crudity which is inevitable in poetry produced by such war, are discarded. Instead, we have a more contemplative confusion, a spiritual riot. No poet can find sure ground; he is hunting for it . . . Today is a transitional period."

He concludes with thumbnail definitions of some contemporaries: "D. H. Lawrence, the body-worshipper who fears the soul; Edmund Blunden, who has immersed himself in the English countryside; Richard Church, the poet of detached contemplation; Ezra Pound, the experimental mystic . . . ." These men are only laying the foundations of a new art. The poetry that will be built on these foundations promises to be "a high and novel achievement."[27]

No need to show how mistaken Dylan was about the state of contemporary verse, how ridiculous it was to call Eliot and Joyce "neo-Romantic," to think of Yeats as a writer of merely "fragile" verse, to list Richard Church with Lawrence and Pound, "the experimental mystic." However, the essay shows that he has been reading and educating himself at a furious rate within the narrow area of his special interest.

He started writing early. The poem from which the following lines are taken is said to have been written before his tenth birthday.

> She stooped to grief's remembered tears,
> Yearned to undawned delight.
> Ah, beauty—passionate from the years!
> Oh, body—wise and white![28]

Sound is everything, meaning practically nil. A hand, presumably his father's, has made corrections in the margin.[29] It is possible that D. J. did more than correct, that he also made suggestions—though Dylan was precocious this seems too good for a nine-year-old.

At the end of the first term at the Grammar School he published a humorous poem in the school magazine. It was titled, "The Song of the mischievous Dog."

> There are many who say that a dog has its day,
> And a cat has a number of lives;
> There are others who think that a lobster is pink,
> And that bees never work in their hives . . .

The anapests go trotting along so that the absence of logic is hardly felt. At the end there is a surprise:

> But my greatest delight is to take a good bite
> At a calf that is plump and delicious;
> And if I indulge in a bite at a bulge,
> Let's hope you won't think me too vicious.[30]

This is sex, but as the author is supposed to be a dog the lines were able to get by the eagle eye of his father, who was in charge of the magazine. That Dylan liked to think of himself as a young dog, we know—it is the title of one of his books. On other occasions he would use other disguises. In the poems of his late adolescence there are references to masturbation and copulation, but the meaning is concealed in a welter of images. In this way he avoids being understood by his father, always on the *qui vive* for pornography.

A year later "D. M. Thomas" had a poem, "His Requiem," published in the Cardiff *Western Mail*. Many years later it was discovered that this was plagiarism: he had taken a poem by Lillian Gard in the *Boy's Own Paper* and submitted it as his own. Ferris remarks that he must have felt a great need to prove that he was a poet—to his friends, to his father, to himself. The incident brings Dylan's motives into question: he may have wanted the name of a poet more than he loved poetry. And Ferris adds that his poems were "thick with the affectations of poetry." But this is true of most beginners: they want to succeed long before they know how to go about it.

He became one of the editors of the school magazine. P. E. Smart, a coeditor, admired his light verse—it was delightful, "sparkling, bright and clear." But he was aware that Dylan was also writing verse of the kind that people could not understand. When he asked him what was the use of writing "privately" in this way, Dylan couldn't really understand the question—"he wrote," he said, "what was in him, and it was really quite irrelevant whether anyone else ever read it."[31]

By the time he wrote the essay on modern poetry he had become modern. "The Elm," written in 1929, is an imitation of Imagist poems, especially Aldington's. He was becoming ethereal.

> They are all goddesses;
> Nodding like flowers,
> They are further and more delicate
> Than the years that dwindle;
> They are deeper in darkness
> Than the hours.
>
> Celestial,
> Slenderly lethal things,
> Beautifully little like clouds:
> Leaf driftwood that has blown.[32]

A year later he was entering his poems in an exercise book under the heading "Mainly Free Verse Poems." The first poem in the 1930 notebook, "Osiris, Come to Isis," is a serious imitation of Yeats—at the same time that, in the school magazine, he is parodying Yeats with "In Borrowed Plumes." There are two Thomases, one for his private notebook, the other for school—but this is not unusual, as any writer who has been to school will testify. "Cast not your pearls before swine, lest they turn and rend you."

The notebooks show his discovery of a style. It appears as early as 1930:

> Now I may watch
> The wings of the bird snap
> Under the air which raises flowers
> Over the walls of the brass town . . .[33]

Four years later it has been perfected:

> The force that drives the water through the rocks
> Drives my red blood; that dries the mouthing streams
> Turns mine to wax.
> And I am dumb to mouth unto my veins
> How at the mountain spring the same mouth sucks.[34]

The essential quality of this writing is its concreteness. Sound first of all, a linking of vowel and consonantal sounds from line to line.

Then images—objects in nature being compared to parts of the human body. "All thoughts and actions," Thomas wrote Pamela Hansford Johnson, "emanate from the body. Therefore the description of a thought or action—however abstruse it may be—can be beaten home by bringing it on to a physical level. Every idea, intuitive or intellectual, can be imaged and translated in terms of the body, its flesh, skin, blood, sinews, veins, glands, organs, cells, or senses."[35]

A man once asked Thomas to explain his "theory of poetry." "Really," he said, "I haven't got one. I like things that are difficult to write and difficult to understand; I like 'redeeming the contraries' with secretive images; I like contradicting my images, saying two things at once in one word, four in two and one in six."

Then he made the point that is essential for an understanding of his work: "Poetry should work from words, from the substance of words and the rhythm of substantial words set together, not towards words."[36]

He began with words, not ideas. Some critics have ignored this, perhaps not being able to accept it. Elder Olson explains that Thomas's "Altarwise by owl-light" sonnets refer to six levels of meaning "which the poet intricately interrelates."

(1) a level based on the analogy of human life to the span of a year, which permits the use of phenomena of the seasons to represent events of human life, and vice versa;

(2) a level based on an analogy between sun and man, permitting the attributes of each to stand for those of the other;

(3) a level of Thomas' "private" symbolism;

(4) a level based on ancient myth, principally Greek, representing the fortunes of the sun in terms of the adventures of the sun-hero Hercules;

(5) a level based on relations of the *constellation* Hercules to other constellations and astronomical phenomena; and

(6) a level derived from the Christian interpretation of levels 4 and 5.[37]

This is God's plenty! But how are we to reconcile Olson's explanation with Thomas's view of his work? In answer to a man who asked what one of his poems was "about," he said, "I can give you a very rough idea of the 'plot.' But of course it's bound to be a most superficial, and perhaps misleading, idea because the 'plot' is told in images, and the images *are* what they say, not what they stand for."[38]

Moreover, images were not as important as sounds. To someone who asked whether he wrote for the eye or the ear, he said, for the ear.[39]

However, words do mean something, and while one may not want to go as far as Olson it is not possible to read a poem by Dylan Thomas without perceiving that an argument of some sort is going on—though it may be hard to disentangle and no two critics are likely to agree what it is.

But sound came first. From the time he was a child, being read to by his father, it was the *sound* of poetry he was after.

Young Mr. Thomas was at the moment without employment, but it was understood that he would soon be leaving for London to make a career in Chelsea as a free-lance journalist; he was penniless, and hoped, in a vague way, to live on women.

—*Portrait of the Artist as a Young Dog*[40]

Dylan was dropping out of school long before he quit. Outside the classroom he was busy: he had an interest in theatricals and took the part of Cromwell in the school play. Together with Daniel Jones he composed poetry and plays, giving comical concerts, and projected or actually carried out elaborate practical jokes. Jones was clever—in later life a composer and doctor of music—and he appears to have filled the role of Dylan's intellectual friend and mentor. Dylan would listen to his opinion as to no one else's. In later years he would read his poems

to Jones at whatever stage they happened to be and whenever opportunity arose—in Swansea, Laugharne, London, and Oxford.[41]

Jones lived at Warmley, and Dylan was a regular guest in the house.
The Joneses were everything that Dylan's own family was not—"uncon-
ventional and easy-going in the extreme, and unselfconsciously so....
Our games," says Daniel Jones, "literary or musical, were approved,
and sometimes even the older members of the family took part."
Jones's father composed vocal church music and was a great storyteller
in the bargain. Jones's brother also composed a little, and his mother
played Beethoven energetically, but her specialty was needlework—her
tapestries had been exhibited in London. And there was an Aunt Alice
who was a gifted teacher of music. They were, as Pound says of another
artistic family, "a darn'd clever bunch."

Daniel and Dylan tried their hand at various arts. They tried sculpting
heads out of rocks, but after a week Dylan put down the chisel and
said, "I'm fed up with sculpture." They tried composing music, and as
Dylan had no knowledge of music or musical skill the result was never
conventional. They invented a mythology of composers, singers, and
instrumentalists, "above all, the Rev. Percy, who dominated the musical
scene with his innumerable piano pieces for four hands." They wrote
the libretto for an opera; it consisted of a repetition of the word
"Heinrich," "sung with every possible shade of emotion." And they
collaborated in writing poetry, Daniel writing the odd lines, Dylan the
even. These were attributed to one Walter Bram. Here is a specimen:

> They followed for seven days
> The youngest shepherd with exotic praise,
> Seeking grass unshepherded,
> Worship-laden where the magic led.
> They followed the shepherd through diverting ways,
> Watching his satyr footsteps as he fled.

Though most of this, Jones says, was insignificant, they were playing
seriously with words. "We had word obsessions: everything at one time
was 'little' or 'white'; and sometimes an adjective became irresistibly
funny in almost any connection: 'innumerable bananas,' 'wilful mocca-
sin,' 'a certain Mrs. Prothero.' ... these word games, and even the most
facetious of our collaborations, had a serious experimental purpose."[42]

Dylan failed his examination for the school-leaving certificate, and
spent his last year in the Lower Sixth marking time. One of the stories
in *Portrait* evokes this in-between period of adolescence. He is "a lonely
night-walker and a steady stander-at-corners." He walks through the

wet town after midnight, "when the streets were deserted and the window lights out, alone and alive on the glistening tram-lines in dead and empty High Street under the moon. . . ."[43]

In his solitary walks he feels that the world is "remote and over-pressing," but that he is very much a part of it. He is full of love and arrogance and pity and humility, "not for myself alone, but for the living earth I suffered on and for the unfeeling systems in the upper air. . . ." Full of cosmic yearning, he stands under a railway arch with two young men named Tom and Walter. They stand there for a long time, while trains pass overhead and the citizens of Swansea are sitting down to their evening meal in warm, comfortable surroundings. Tom and Walter tell the narrator—we may as well call him Dylan—the story of their relations with two young women named Doris and Norma. The upshot was that the women brought paternity suits against them, whereupon Walter married Norma and Tom married Doris. But Tom doesn't love Doris—Norma was the one he loved—and Walter doesn't love either Norma or Doris. "We've two nice little boys," Tom tells Dylan. "I call mine Norman." The young men, it turns out, are brothers.

The story takes its title, "Just Like Little Dogs," from the remark made by the magistrate who heard the paternity suit. Thomas seems to feel that marriage is a miserable business—at least, as he has seen it. His own parents in their way were just as mismated as Tom and Doris. From standing on street corners he has a depressed view of Swansea—"scorning girls and ready girls, soldiers and bullies and policemen and sharp, suspicious buyers of second-hand books, bad, ragged women who'd pretend against the museum wall for a cup of tea. . . ." It is sordid, but he prefers to stand in the street rather than go home—as much of an outcast as Tom and Walter, though for a different reason. It is better standing under the railway arch, or leaning against the wall of a derelict house, or wandering in the empty rooms, "gazing through the smashed windows at the sea or at nothing. . . ."[44]

Dylan left school at seventeen and his father got him a job on the *South Wales Daily*, later *Evening, Post*. He worked there for eighteen months, beginning in the "reader's room" where he read copy aloud while someone else checked the proof for mistakes. Then he moved on to the reporters' room and did the usual rounds of hospitals, police stations, concerts, and bazaars. Ferris tells us that an older newspaper-man who sub-edited Dylan's copy said that it was "appalling, with many lacunae," and that there are a lot of funny stories about his reporting events that never took place, or not reporting events that did.

These stories, Ferris observes, "are unlikely to have been funny at the time, assuming they ever happened." Dylan did not take pleasure in the stories—"My selfish carelessness and unpunctuality," he wrote to Henry Treece in 1938, "I do not try to excuse as poet's properties. They are a bugbear and a humbug."[45] Nevertheless, he was beginning to have a reputation for irresponsible behavior—it would soar after he became famous.

In December of 1932 he was fired from his job on the *Evening Post*. This brought no real hardship for he was living at home where his mother saw to it that he was properly fed. He had no income, however, so he cadged money from acquaintances and sometimes he would steal. He stole shillings from his sister Nancy's handbag, and when one of her friends came to tea robbed her of a pound note.

In letters to her fiancé, Haydn Taylor, Nancy describes life on Cwmdonkin Drive. Her father has been using foul language and accusing her of being a parasite—"All you and your beautiful brother do is to take my money from me." To be classed with Dylan, she says, is ghastly. She wishes she were dead. "Last night Dylan said one day he'd strangle me."

Dylan is very difficult to live with.

Dylan has just risen (11.30) & is in the most foul temper—rushing and raving like a tormented thing. He stays in bed most mornings & then gets up and writes. In the evening he visits Danny. *Unless* he gets any sum of money— then he goes and drinks. What will become of him Heaven knows. . . .[46]

Nancy escaped through marriage. Dylan stayed home and wrote. "Poets live and walk with their poems; a man with visions needs no other company. . . . I must go home and sit in my bedroom by the boiler."[47]

It was the most prolific period of his life. He wrote drafts of many poems . . . for years he would turn to the notebooks and rework these early drafts. An early version of "The hunchback in the park" is dated May 9, 1932. "After the funeral" first saw light on February 10, 1933, though the draft is rudimentary. It was written on the occasion of the death of Ann Jones, his aunt at Fernhill. The draft trails off with a remark about the uselessness of things—"one more joke has lost its point." The finished version, published five years later, is different—it speaks of the quality of the individual life.[48] The difference is that Thomas now has a point of view, a way of organizing the material so that it appears to say something.

He had another interest, the theater. While still a reporter he had joined the Little Theatre (so did Nancy—it is said that she out-acted Dylan and there was talk of her going on the stage professionally). He appeared in Noël Coward's *Hay Fever*, taking the part of Simon, and in the next two or three years he appeared regularly in Little Theatre plays. Ferris tells us that Dylan's idea of acting was to overact, and that "His voice was already strong; soon it would thicken and begin to acquire the boom that made him as famous as his poetry." It is curious that in later years when he reminisced about his life in Swansea he would never refer to his acting. "An actor in so many things he did, he preferred not to remember himself as one."[49]

He became interested in politics through Bert Trick, an older man who was a grocer and had been an income-tax clerk. Bert was a Communist; he undertook to educate Dylan, explaining the coming demise of Capitalism and the triumph of Communism. For a while Dylan mouthed the platitudes of the Left though it is doubtful that he understood them. His political sophistication may be measured by a statement he made to Daniel Jones: ". . . the only politics for a conscientious artist . . . must be left-wing under a right-wing government, communist *under* capitalism."[50]

He was for revolution—without bloodshed: "All that we ask for is that the present Disorder . . . shall be broken in two, and that all there is in us of godliness and strength, of happiness and genius, shall be allowed to exult in the sun." Everything was wrong that forbade the freedom of the individual.[51]

This was in a letter to Pamela Hansford Johnson. She lived with her mother in London, and when a poem by Dylan, "That sanity be kept I sit at open windows," was published in Victor Neuberg's "The Poets' Corner" in the *Sunday Referee*, she wrote him saying how much she liked it. Dylan wrote back, thanking her for her praise and for letting him see her own poetry. "It shows a tremendous passion for words," he told her. "Your grasp of form and your handling of metre is among the best I know today. And—the main thing—your thoughts are worth expressing. Have you written a great deal? . . ."[52]

He knew how to lay it on thick—with a shovel if need be. Their correspondence, begun with mutual compliments, continued full spate. He preened himself before her as an intellectual and beautiful soul. At times he played the devil-may-care bohemian who smoked too much and drank more than was good for him and was subject to temptations of the flesh—but he hastened to assure her that his ideas about sex were serious. He believed that boys and girls in puberty should be allowed to know their bodies and that their sexual expression should be encouraged. ". . . both would grow up physically and mentally uncontaminated and refreshed."[53]

He was repelled by the sordidness around him, "hideously pretty young girls with cheap berets on their heads and paint smudged over their cheeks; thin youths with caps and stained fingers holding their cigarettes; women, all breast and bottom, hugging their purses to them and staring in at the shop windows; little colliers, diseased in mind and body as only the Welsh can be, standing in groups outside the Welfare Hall."[54]

His opinions were less original than his poems. He thought that marriage was a "dead institution"—no doubt the thought of women "all breast and bottom," staring in shop windows, inclined him to think so. He had an aversion for homosexuals, denouncing them as "willing-buttocked, celluloid-trousered degenerates."

His opinions bring with them the atmosphere of a pub shortly before closing time when talk is loud and the foaming tankards pass swiftly across the counter. Dylan talked with the best and emptied his glass.

He had a romantic view of himself and gave it out that he had consumption. The *poète maudit*—like Chatterton and Keats.

He worked in his bedroom. It smelled of tobacco, for he was a chain smoker. To save money he had bought a machine with which he could roll his own. He would write a line of words, change a word or two, and write the line again. When the sheet was covered he would start on another. Absorbed like a child at play, he scarcely noticed the passing of hours, the changing light outside.

He told Pamela Johnson that the labor of writing was becoming more and more difficult, and that he was becoming more obscure: "It gives me now a physical pain to write poetry." He would work all day on a few lines, but when he had picked them over and cleaned them nothing remained but their "barbaric sounds." The words he used did not mean what he wanted them to, they only came near to expressing the half.[55]

In August 1933, D. J. Thomas's dentist discovered an ulcer on the floor of his mouth, below the tongue. A specialist was called in; he diagnosed the growth as cancer and D. J. was given five years to live. He was taken up to London and admitted to University College where, for a week, he was treated with radium needles. In the following months he made several journeys to London. In October he was again treated with radium, this time for two weeks. For a while his voice was affected.

The treatment, however, was a success; by early in 1934 the ulcer had begun to heal, and the adjoining glands were not affected. D. J. was to live for another twenty years.

As Ferris shows, D. J. Thomas's cancer of the mouth had an important effect on Dylan Thomas's poetry. There are direct references to it in the notebook: "Take the needles and the knives" (September 12, 1933) and "The root of tongues ends in a spentout cancer" (October 17). But, "More significant is that the fact that the first complete, full-blooded 'anatomical' poem is also the first poem to follow the news of his father's cancer...." This is the poem beginning "Before I knocked," in which Thomas sees himself as an unborn child:

> Before I knocked and flesh let enter,
> With liquid hands tapped on the womb ...

There is a reference to D. J.'s ulcer (in a letter Dylan would call it "cancer of the throat"):

> My throat knew thirst before the structure
> Of skin and vein around the well
> Where words and water make a mixture
> Unfailing till the blood runs foul ...[56]

"The stage is set for Thomas' distinctive organic imagery,"[57] and, indeed, it appears that we can date the beginning of his "real" poetry from this incident.[58]

He identified himself with his father, especially his father's voice. The ulcer was located in the mouth, at the base of the tongue—it was poetry, his identity, that was threatened. Therefore he began to write in earnest, drawing images from the physical body.

Ever since he was a child he had lived in his body almost to the exclusion of thought. At Fernhill when he went to sleep the world went away, and it came back the next morning with a cock on its shoulder. The self, the ear that hears, the eye that sees, is the center of everything. Impelled by the dread of not hearing and not seeing he began to write, making poems that were solid, made of bone, flesh, sinew, blood.

The imagery of these poems is "almost totally anatomical."

"But," he says, "I defend the diction, the perhaps wearisome succession of blood and bones, the never-ending similes of the streams in the veins and the lights in the eyes, by saying that, for the time at least, I realise that it is impossible for me to raise myself to the altitude of the stars, and that I am forced, therefore, to bring down the stars to my own level and to incorporate them in my own physical universe."[59]

As Maud says, Thomas uses the word "stars" to mean beliefs. He is presenting himself as a mystical poet, "in the path of Blake." His poems echo the language and imagery of the Bible, and the central Christian mystery of Incarnation figures in his thinking.[60]

How seriously are we to take him as a religious poet? The answer is, not at all, unless we are to expand the word "religion" to mean any writing that uses the properties of religion. The error of readers who take Thomas to be religious comes of their not understanding that in Britain, and especially Wales, chapel-going is part of people's ordinary lives, and that it is possible for a man to be familiar with the Bible—as Dylan's father was—without real conviction. In America, as Church and State are separate, if a man chooses to use the trappings of religion there must be a reason. But this is not the case in Britain; for hundreds of years people have been going to church as they go to the club—it is something to do on Sunday.

The poems of Dylan Thomas are romantic and "cosmic," exactly the kind of thing T. E. Hulme and Ezra Pound had warned poets against twenty years earlier.

He would pack images together without explanatory links so that the poem had the sound and appearance of a concrete thing. At times his poetry appears surrealistic, especially in this early period—that is, it appears to make no sense, to be pure invention of sounds and images. However, it does not fit André Breton's definition of surrealism: "the actual functioning of thought . . . in the absence of any control exercised by reason, exempt from any aesthetic or moral concern."[61]

There is plenty of aesthetic concern in Thomas's arrangement of sounds and images, and even morality of a kind, in order to make an argument and bring the poem to a conclusion. A poem by Dylan Thomas is like the country visited by Alice: once you accept being there, everything that happens is perfectly logical.

Breton's definition, however, is not final, and if we can extend the label of surrealism to cover works with some control by reason and some aesthetic or moral concern—as the Surrealists themselves did, when they honored Lautréamont's *Maldoror* and Walpole's *Castle of Otranto*, and narratives in prose by Aragon and Breton—then some of Thomas's poems are surrealistic. The poetry is a new thing with its own internal organization and does not take its meaning from reference to the world. It can be explained, but we are aware that to explain is to miss the point, the experience of the thing itself.

There has been very little surrealist writing in English. The English-

trained over the centuries to think of literature
ipendage to "life." It resists the idea of imagina-
valid kind of life—of works of art making their
·eason the poems of Dylan Thomas have been
· make them conform to a "meaning." The enter-
mdary importance, and may do more harm than
aning," paraphrasable content, for the experience

poem by Dylan Thomas is to allow oneself to
the poem as they are described.

Light breaks where no sun shines;
Where no sea runs, the waters of the heart
Push in their tides;
And, broken ghosts with gloworms in their heads,
The things of light
File through the flesh where no flesh decks the bones.

A candle in the thighs
Warms youth and seed and burns the seeds of age;
Where no seed stirs
The fruit of man unwrinkles in the stars,
Bright as a fig;
Where no wax is the candle shows its hairs.

Candles are candles, thighs are thighs, and figs are figs. As Thomas
said, ". . . images *are* what they say, not what they stand for."

Dawn breaks behind the eyes;
From pole of skull and toe the windy blood
Slides like a sea;
Nor fenced, nor staked, the gushers of the sky
Spout to the rod
Divining in a smile the oil of tears.

In this writing Thomas is like Rimbaud, especially Rimbaud's "Bateau
Ivre," and, in fact, Thomas would poke fun at himself as "the Rimbaud
of Cwmdonkin Drive." In "Bateau Ivre" Rimbaud undertakes to make
visible a world of waterspouts, sea-monsters, and tropical jungle. He is
a visionary, not a symbolist. The same is true of Thomas: in "Light
breaks where no sun shines" he is envisioning a world that appears to be
an extension of the human body. It begins inside the body, with our
consciousness.

Night in the sockets rounds,
Like some pitch moon, the limit of the globes:

[Day lights the bone;]
Where no cold is the skinning gales unpin
The winter's robes;
The film of spring is hanging from the lids.[62]

What is the purpose of this "anatomical" imagery? Does Thomas believe in the Microcosm and the Macrocosm? Are we, when we read him, deep in Gnostic lore? Or is there a Christian interpretation?

Others have asked another question: is it a hoax?[63]

The way to read these lines is to visualize what they say. We are inside the body, and from this viewpoint we see night, "like some pitch moon," traveling across the sockets. I visualize these as eye sockets, but I could be wrong. The seasons are changing within the body, and Spring hangs on the eyelids.

Light breaks on secret lots,
On tips of thought where thoughts smell in the rain;
When logics die
The secret of the soil grows through the eye,
And blood jumps in the sun;
Above the waste ɛllotments the dawn halts.[64]

We spin the world out from our consciousness of it. We are the Creators of the universe—just as, in fact, we are poets.

Thomas says, "It is my aim as an artist . . . to prove beyond doubt to myself that the flesh that covers me is the flesh that covers the sun, that the blood in my lungs is the blood that goes up and down in a tree. It is the simplicity of religion."[65]

Reading "Light breaks where no sun shines" I find myself falling into the error of interpreting I have warned against. But this is unavoidable to some extent; words have a meaning, and though the poet may want his poem to be a pure invention, there is always a statement of some kind. It is not wrong to interpret the meaning of a poem—it is only wrong to interpret too much. This is where critics go wrong, and the end of it is that the critic sets himself up in the place of the poet.

We must not let the possible meanings of the poem overwhelm the experience of listening and seeing. To read poetry is to be aware of the impression the poem makes, not to try to have the lines fit an argument in every particular. I would go so far as to say that a meaning that does not contribute to the effect a poem makes does not exist.

Before he was twenty Thomas had published poems in the *Adelphi*, the *New English Weekly*, the *Listener*, and other journals. *The Criterion* and *New Verse* had accepted poems for publication, and one of his poems had been read over the BBC. Stephen Spender wrote asking if he would like to do reviews and suggesting that they dine together when Dylan came up to London. Best of all, T. S. Eliot, having read "Light breaks where no sun shines," wrote from Faber and Faber where he was an editor, inviting Dylan to call on him. It would be like having an audience with the Pope.

In June 1934, he was in London. One evening he and Pamela Hansford Johnson decided to get married, but the next day she changed her mind, and at the end of the month he went back to Swansea. He returned to London in August and lived in the house of his fiancée's mother. "The strain of such propinquity in platonic circumstances," says Constantine Fitzgibbon, editor of the *Letters,* "began to tell on the two young people." Thomas took to drinking and staying out late and they quarreled. In mid-September they all went to stay with Thomas's parents in Wales; Mrs. Johnson found Mrs. Thomas boring and it rained for two weeks. Then, says Fitzgibbon, "Pamela discovered Dylan's true age, nineteen, and realized that marriage was out of the question."[66] Why marrying a man younger than herself—she was the older by two years—should have appeared like a breach of nature, is not evident. It was probably an excuse for not marrying, and served as well as any.

In November Thomas came to London with the painter Alfred Janes, and they roomed together off the Fulham Road, near Chelsea, an area of writers, artists, and bohemians. Thomas was in full spate of publishing: his first book, *18 Poems,* was to be published by a small press around Christmas, and he hoped to find a publisher for his stories. He was meeting "notabilities," among them the sculptor Henry Moore, the poet Edwin Muir and his wife Willa, and the painter and novelist Wyndham Lewis.

Dylan was now a professional literary man, his opinions of people determined by what they thought of his work. He disliked Geoffrey Grigson, editor of *New Verse,* until Grigson wrote asking him to submit poems—then he found him tolerable. When Grigson accepted two poems, he wrote to him: "New Verse is awfully good this month, and I was pleased to see William Carlos Williams given one in the eye."[67] When Edith Sitwell included a parody of Thomas's poems in her new book, he called it her "latest piece of virgin dung."[68] Two years later she wrote an enthusiastic review of his *Twenty-five Poems,* whereupon he wrote her: "I hope you aren't cross with me really [He had failed to keep an appointment] . . . Will you meet me again, in spite of things? You're still a great encouragement to me—and always will be."[69]

18 Poems caused a sensation—among poets, that is. It was something new, radically different from the poetry of Auden, Spender, MacNeice, and C. Day Lewis, the currently fashionable poets of the left. They were nothing if not rational; their poems began with ideas, not words. Spender had romantic attitudes, but these played second fiddle to his leftish views, and, like Auden, Lewis, and MacNeice, he wrote the language taught in public schools.

Thomas's poems were also very different from the poems of Eliot. There was nothing diffident about the voice coming out of Wales. People were not sure what Thomas's poetry meant, but they got a definite impression that sex was involved, and some kind of prophecy. On the whole they welcomed the poet who spoke of sensual life in riddling terms.

His second book, Twenty-five Poems (1936), was not so well received —in fact, an air of disappointment hangs about the reviews. Many of the poems had actually been written before 18 Poems; they were less startling in their imagery and easier to understand—with an exception, the "Altarwise by owl-light" sonnet sequence. If readers found some of the poems disappointingly simple, the sonnet sequence was altogether too obscure. The Times Literary Supplement complained about the obscurity, and the New Statesman said that it preferred 18 Poems, "the record of a volcanic adolescence." The new book showed a split between fairly simple poetry and "eerie bombast." The reviewer gave his opinion that Thomas was a really original poet who for the time being seemed to have lost his way.[70]

Whatever the reason, after Twenty-five Poems Thomas wrote hardly any poetry for two years. The spate that began at the Swansea Grammar School had come to a stop. The years from sixteen to twenty were the most productive of his life; in this short time he developed his own original style. He never again was so visited. And though his writing would pick up again, and poems he wrote in later years would be acclaimed, there are readers who prefer the inchoate gropings in the notebooks to the finished poems, and would rather have "Light breaks where no sun shines," with all its obscurities, than the clear sentences and argument of a poem such as "Fern Hill," written long after the time it describes. Or the descriptiveness of "Over Sir John's Hill":

> Over Sir John's hill
> The hawk on fire hangs still;
> In a hoisted cloud, at drop of dusk, he pulls to
>   his claws

> And gallows, up the rays of his eyes the small birds
>   of the bay
> And the shrill child's play
> Wars
> Of the sparrows and such who swansing, dusk, in
>   wrangling hedges . . .[71]

This can be easily understood, but it lacks the excitement of creation that we feel in the early poems; it is reporting the world rather than creating a world of its own. In the later poetry when there is some complexity it appears to have been put in; the difficulty is only skin deep, a matter of style, and if this is stripped away the underlying ideas are trite. But in the early poems it is impossible to separate the surface from the thought: sound, image, and idea are fused together in one solid mass.

In a sense, the rest of Thomas's life was an anticlimax. And he was aware of it—feeling that the best was past contributed to his drinking and self-destructive behavior.

In July 1937, Dylan Thomas married Caitlin Macnamara in a registry office in Penzance, "with no money, no prospect of money, no attendant friends or relatives, and," Thomas said, "in complete happiness." He thought that she looked like the princess on the top of a Christmas tree, or Wendy in *Peter Pan*—but, he cautioned Vernon Watkins, "for God's sake, don't tell her that."[72] The caution was necessary because Caitlin was not sentimental—anything but.

She came of a Protestant Irish family in County Clare, people of property with a mansion that looked down on the surrounding countryside. Her father, Francis, was a great talker who expected that one day he would come into a fortune or write a great book. Shortly after the birth of Caitlin, his third daughter and fourth child, he went away with a married woman and never came back.

Mrs. Macnamara moved from place to place with the children. She had very little money but maintained the standards of a gentlewoman, holding that it was vulgar to pay bills or to worry about paying them at all. Caitlin grew up doing much as she pleased. She had good looks, her father's blue eyes and curly, golden hair, and she is said to have been witty.

She had a passion for dancing and when she was seventeen or eighteen worked as a chorus girl at the Palladium. A talent scout offered her a job in Paris, but her mother would not let her take it. Then she took up "eurhythmic" dancing and, together with an older woman, gave performances in Dublin and Paris, "striking dramatic poses to Bach and Mozart." At one of these performances T. S. Eliot was seen in the audience, looking at his shoes. No wonder, his wife had had a passion for dancing before she became a mental case.

Caitlin sat for the painter Augustus John and went to bed with him, but not, she says, with any enthusiasm: "It was merely a question of a brief dutiful performance for him to keep up his reputation as a Casanova ogre."[73] She may have met Dylan in the Spring of 1936 in a London pub. One account has John introducing her to Dylan. We do know that in July she went with John to the home of the novelist Richard Hughes in Laugharne. Thomas arrived with Fred Janes. They all drove over to Pembrokeshire to see an exhibition of paintings; on the way back there was a scene—John punched Dylan and drove off with Caitlin. "Painter and poet," Ferris remarks, "had fought for her." This was probably the beginning of Dylan and Caitlin's affair.

From the letters he wrote it appears that Dylan was very much in love with her. As he saw it, they were two innocents—"our discreditable secret is that we don't know anything at all, and our horrid *inner* secret is that we don't care that we don't."[74]

So they were married, and began that life together which has become legendary. They would fight and make up. In the view of John Malcolm Brinnin "their marriage was essentially a state of rivalry."[75] The quarrelling was worse after Dylan began his American tours. Caitlin thought that the adulation turned his head.

In the book she wrote after her husband's death she has many acerb things to say. She describes Dylan's father as a small-minded man obsessed with keeping up appearances, and she accuses Dylan of being as puritanical as his Welsh forebears. In spite of his own outrageous behavior he expected her to be turned out prim and proper, "black from head to foot, relieved with a touch of white, as a concession."[76] He had other shortcomings: "He read interminable Dickens novels, to which he was loyally devoted . . . he categorically refused to look at Proust, Jane Austen, Tolstoy, Dostoievsky, and a lot of the obvious classics."[77]

There is no doubt that she had a great deal to put up with. In her book she says that children kill the "holy fire" of marriage—and they had three. While her husband was off meeting editors and doing the rounds of the pubs, she was banging pots and pans or changing nappies. The tasks of parenthood can be hard under the best of circumstances, and their circumstances, always short of cash, were not the best—though, as Brinnin points out, Dylan made enough money for them to have lived comfortably, if they had not been wildly extravagant. It comes down, then, to the people in the case: neither Dylan nor Caitlin Thomas was temperamentally suited for domesticity.

He labored like a man bailing water with a sieve—and the sea kept rushing in. "I must have some money, and have it immediately," he wrote to James Laughlin in America, editor of New Directions. "I am forced to do away with dignity and formality.... Can you, at once, give me money for which, in return, I promise you all the work I have done and will do?"[78]

His wish was to sit at his table in Laugharne covering sheets of paper with lines of poetry. Yet for weeks, sometimes months on end, he couldn't find the time to write poetry at all, but had to write prose instead. For prose has a market, poetry none.

When war threatened—"What are you doing for your country?" he wrote Henry Treece. "I'm letting mine rot." He had the feelings of a liberal who had grown up in the shadow of the Great War. He knew the poems of Wilfred Owen and the preface to the poems: "This book is not about heroes ... My subject is War, and the pity of War. The Poetry is in the pity."[79] Owen's poems and his death spoke to a generation of younger brothers: they could imagine the horrors of trench warfare. Moreover, they were wise, they knew that all wars were a swindle brought about by a conspiracy of the rich.

When England declared war on Germany, Dylan busied himself collecting "statements of objection to war" from young writers. He was not banging a drum, he said, for a Right, "right, left or wrong." He was opposed to the evil of war, "the evil of which is the war itself and not the things it is supposed, wrongly, to be attempting to exterminate." He appears to have thought that the worst possible fate would be to kill or to be killed.[80]

He found his antiwar views supported by the pacifism of the left. Since Nazi Germany and Communist Russia had come to terms, dividing Poland between them, the Communists in Britain had taken the line that it was a "phoney war." "You are right," Dylan told Henry Treece, "when you suggest that I think a squirrel stumbling at least of equal importance as Hitler's invasions."[81]

He went to the Ministry of Information—along with the half-poets, boiled newspapermen, dismissed advertisers, and other Grub Street scroungers. A job with the Ministry might keep him out of the war; he was determined to stay out, and he foresaw being hailed as an objector before a military tribunal and assigned to stretcher-bearing or jail or potato peeling or the Boys' Fire League. Whereas all he wanted was the time to write poems. He humbled himself and wrote to Sir Edward Marsh who, a war ago, had been a friend of Rupert Brooke, and had put out the anthologies of Georgian Poets. Thomas addressed Sir Edward in his best groveling manner: "I am writing to you, a patron of letters, to ask for any help that you may be able to give me. You may have read some of my work, or heard it spoken of. If not, I can refer you to Miss Edith Sitwell and Mr. T. S. Eliot, who will tell you that I am a poet of some worth and deserving help. I have a wife and child and am without private means. . . ." Sir Edward sent him a small sum of money, ten or twenty pounds.[82]

Dylan did not have to be tried as a conscientious objector—the doctors found him asthmatic and unfit for military service. He and Caitlin went on living in Laugharne on some money that had been raised through the magazine *Horizon* on their behalf. When this came to an end they went to stay with a friend in Gloucestershire. In the autumn of 1940 he went to London and found work with a film documentary company, and then he began doing programs on the BBC. He would travel between jobs in London and his family in Wales. A second son, Aeron, was born in 1943.

After the war he conceived the idea of emigrating to the United States. His books were being published there by James Laughlin at New Directions, and he had other friends. An American poet and anthologist, Oscar Williams, was most eager to be of service; he sent Dylan a copy of his poems and a few of his anthologies, "all of them," Dylan remarked, "so heavy and in large lovely type, so dear, and with such lovely ladies and gentlemen to be seen out at the back: all portentously smoking (the pipes of bedpan), prinking, profiling, horizon-eyeing, open-collared and wild-haired in the photographers' wind, facing America and posterity and the music. . . ." How Dylan could run on, especially in prose and especially when he was biting a hand that had fed or was about to feed him! A nip such as might be delivered by a large, playful dog. It left you eyeing your hand, nevertheless.

He would salve the wound, however, on this occasion by praising Oscar's poems. He told him that they were pieces that flew "hot and violent and exuberantly unhappy, off a poem in the making." He told him, "The rules, the form, spring up urgently as the temper of making needs them." He avoided saying anything in particular, and the recipient, bathed in the flood of this gab, may have felt that he was a great poet after all.[83]

Then Dylan got down to business: "I have been trying to find out what legal etc. complications I will have to go through before leaving this country for America." He asked Oscar what his first step should be. If he got the forms from the American Embassy that had to be filled out by a prospective employer in the States, could Oscar "do anything about them?" Meaning, in plain Welsh, could Oscar get him a job? Could he approach *Time* "and get some definite promise, however small from them?"[84]

Dylan had the artist-and-actor's gift of being able to get people to put aside their own petty concerns and devote themselves to his. This requires an unswerving conviction that one's needs are more urgent than anyone else's, one's work more important. In such cases it helps a great deal if the artist-actor has charm. Dylan had it in abundance—very few could resist his gift of the gab.

Some did, however. In 1956 when Robert Conquest put together an anthology, *New Lines*, he said that a "sort of corruption" had affected the general attitude to poetry, "the debilitating theory that poetry *must* be metaphorical."[85] Obviously the chief offender was Dylan Thomas. Among the contributors, and presumably in agreement, were Elizabeth Jennings, John Holloway, Philip Larkin, Kingsley Amis, John Wain, and Conquest himself, sober, rational workmen all.

Amis appears to have had an extraordinary dislike of Thomas. He wrote an insulting "epitaph" for him.

> They call you "drunk with words"; but when we drink
> And fetch it up, we sluice it down the sink.
> You should have stuck to spewing beer, not ink.[86]

In his novel, *That Uncertain Feeling*, he would portray Thomas as a drunkard, a lecher, and a professional Welshman.

It took more than a quarrel over metaphor to produce so much aversion. Kingsley Amis and other postwar English writers were called the Angry Young Men, but they were not angry about the social order, only their place in it. With hard work and a sense of the fitness of things, in time they were sure to arrive. English writers, even poets, were learning to be modest, to write with irony about their marriages and their jobs. It was as though Shakespeare and Milton, Blake and Shelley and Lawrence, had never existed—in any case they were not applicable to postwar Britain. Life was drab and austere, and English writers were withdrawing from Modernism, the kinds of experimental writing that had been imported into Britain in the early decades of the century. The opinion was heard, among novelists and poets, that the whole Modernist enterprise had been a mistake, un-English. Once more Englishmen were putting on their bicycle clips. Truth was to be found in small things and mean streets.

Some people regarded Thomas as a charlatan, and John Wain spoke for others who conceded that he was a poet but were not sure how much. "It is perfectly possible," said Wain, "to furnish even his wildest pieces with a 'meaning' (*i.e.* a paraphrasable content or set of alternative paraphrasable contents), but the gnawing doubt remains as to whether the writer really *cared* whether it meant anything precise or not."[87]

As he approached middle age, Thomas himself was unsure of his meaning. Most of his hard thinking about poetry had been done before he was twenty; then he had produced a stock of images and a distinctive voice. Since that time he had been practicing his craft assiduously and publishing books, but he had not developed intellectually—he still hoped that words, and the passion with which they were uttered, would make a poem. The obscurities that Wain speaks of must have appeared obscure to him too, and no doubt he frequently asked himself if there were really anything there, or only a noise. Poets are very liable to doubt, especially in the modern world when few people care about poetry; all poets have is their own feelings to go on, and suppose these are merely personal, with no support in an objective reality? The poet may attempt to create some sort of reality outside his feelings by writing about ideas, as Pound did in his *Cantos;* or he may choose a material object, as Hart Crane did in *The Bridge,* in the hope that by sheer ingenuity he will elevate it into a myth. But the ideas may be rejected by others, or they may seem inadequate, the object carefully constructed may collapse. It may have no significance really, and then he will think that all his work is rubbish, as Pound did at the end of his life, or he may kill himself, like Crane. Feeling is the only reality poets have, but as they usually live, the world being what it is, outside a community, they have no way to be sure of the value of their feelings or to sustain them over a long period.

As Brinnin remarks, Thomas suspected that his creative powers were failing. He could no longer be the "roaring boy, the daemonic poet"; on the other hand he would never be able to undergo intellectual and moral discipline. "It was my sense," says Brinnin, "that the term of the roaring boy was over, and that the means by which Dylan might continue to grow were no longer in his possession. I was convinced that Dylan knew this and, whether or not he comprehended the meaning of his actions, that the violence of his life was a way of forgetting or avoiding the self-judgment that spelled his doom."[88]

At the point where Crane jumped overboard, Thomas traveled to the States. Brinnin, then director of the Poetry Center in New York, made the arrangements for a poetry-reading tour and, with growing excitement, like a boy about to be let out of school, Dylan interested himself in the business. He would like very much to go to California. He would prefer to fly, "not liking the big dull sea to look at." He presumed that the five hundred dollars to be paid by the Poetry Center included his traveling expenses—hoping, of course, that it didn't. He had ideas about poetry readings: he hoped he would not have to read only his own poems—"An hour of me aloud is hell, & produces large burning spots in front of the mind. "—but he would like to mix in poems by some British contemporaries.[89]

Caitlin would not be coming with him. Their third child, Colm, had been born in the summer of 1949 and she had not been well since. New York in February would not be suitable—he was thinking of her going to Italy instead for three months. Money, as usual, was the difficulty. "I'm having a tough time here at the moment," he wrote James Laughlin. "I want to write only poems, but that can't be. Never have I wanted to more. But debts are battering at me. I cannot sleep for them." He wanted to know if Laughlin would advance money on half a novel he had written—"Well, nearly half."[90]

He arrived at Idlewild Airport on February 21, 1950, and was met by Brinnin, who drove him through Queens in the direction of Manhattan. Thomas stared out at the dismal streets with their junkyards and lots full of weeds and debris. "I *knew* America would be just like this," he said.

He was installed at the Beekman Tower Hotel. Then Brinnin showed him Third Avenue, and he took to it immediately. In the following days he spent much of his time in the bars of Third Avenue and Greenwich Village. People sought him out and he held court behind a table, filling himself with beer. He was not a prepossessing sight: "His hair a matted aureole, his crooked teeth brown with tobacco stains, his paunchy flesh bunched into fuzzy tweeds, he was not even a memory of the seraphic young artist Augustus John had painted some fifteen years before." Among those who descended upon him was a woman who had not seen him for ten years. "Oh, Dylan," she said, "the last time I saw you you were an *angel*." Brinnin remarks that Dylan winced—he would be wincing often in the days to come.[91]

He enjoyed himself, however, being interviewed and asked his opinions of this and that. And he conducted imaginary interviews. "Mr. Thomas, why have you come to America?" "To continue my lifelong search for naked women in wet mackintoshes."

He was extremely nervous before his performances at the Poetry Center. But they went splendidly. As much could not be said for his behavior at parties. Brinnin had been forewarned: a few weeks before, he had met Auden on the subway, and Auden said that he doubted it was wise to invite Thomas to the United States "in view of his London reputation for roaring behavior." Brinnin soon had an opportunity to see for himself. He took Dylan to a literary gathering in New York. The very best people were there.

"We went up into a room buzzing with writers and editors, some of whom were old friends of mine. Wystan Auden was there, James Agee, Louis Kronenberger and the Trillings, Lionel and Diana, and James and Tania Stern and Charles Rolo, Katherine Anne Porter and many others. As Dylan, by a loud and awkward entrance, seemed to demand considerably more attention than the party was disposed to grant him, becoming again the very figure of the wine-soaked poet, I looked at Auden and winced inwardly. I could not help feeling that his eyes showed more than a hint of accusation, that before the evening was out he would somehow say, 'I told you so.' "

At the end of the party Dylan lifted Katherine Anne Porter up to the ceiling and held her there. She was a lady, says Brinnin, and did not seem distressed, but other of the guests were "half amused, half appalled."[92]

Auden's dislike of Thomas had complex roots. Auden was an Englishman of the professional middle class, Anglican in religion, educated at public schools and Oxford or Cambridge. Thomas's people were Welsh dissenters, and anyone who does not know the suspicion with which most Englishmen regard the Welsh, Scots, and Irish, knows little of England. Celts are dreamers—they even believe in magic. They are music hall turns, entertaining there perhaps, but nowhere else. Moreover, not only was Thomas a Welshman, he came of a lower class—his father had raised himself by his bootstraps. Finally he was in bad taste: he cadged money, he drank too much, his behavior was a disgrace.

When it came to poetry, Auden and Thomas stood at opposite poles.

Auden was rational, Thomas "demonic." "Insofar as poetry," said Auden, "can be said to have an ulterior purpose, it is, by telling the truth, to disenchant and disintoxicate."[93] Thomas's whole purpose, on the other hand, was to enchant. Auden wrote with irony and in many voices—Thomas had a distinctive voice; he seemed to be standing personally behind every line he uttered. "He can create worlds," said a critic, "but he creates worlds in his own image, and remains the centre of his own thought and feeling."[94]

Auden was a reasoner, harking back to a time when poets explained their ideas—a theory of psychology, their belief in Marxism or Existentialism. Thomas was a poet of "the most exalted emotions, the most exalted grief or joy."[95] At times he spoke like a prophet, another Blake:

> Hear the voice of the Bard!
> Who present, past, and future, sees;
> Whose ears have heard
> The Holy Word
> That walk'd among the ancient trees.[96]

Thomas looked forward to a new generation of poets who would express their emotions and adopt a prophetic stance. It was the voice of Dylan, speaking with an authority that was entirely personal, that woke the sleeping poets of America. Before Dylan, poetry readings had been tame, academic gatherings—one has only to listen to a recording by Auden or Elizabeth Bishop to get the tone—dry, impersonal discourse. Dylan's readings changed all that: he showed that a poetry reading could be a highly dramatic performance. For better or worse he brought back personality, and the audience loved it. Offstage he was gregarious, a hard drinker, and a bedder of women—at least he gave that impression. He appeared to be enjoying life passionately and on a large scale.

Kenneth Rexroth testifies to the transformation wrought in San Francisco by Thomas's public readings. Ginsberg, however, disclaims the influence—"I like 'Fern Hill,'" said Ginsberg, speaking to students at Berkeley in the sixties, "it's something like 'Intimations of Immortality'—but on the whole I don't really dig Thomas. He's too romantic. With his kind of gift, the way to groove was to begin with bricks and build a starry tower, but Thomas *began* in a starry tower." Ginsberg went on to speculate about the psychology of Thomas and Hart Crane. They had tried to recreate the unconscious through rational, conscious means, "so maybe they had.to drink to get at it. They didn't follow what Stein said—that like the mind is goofy enough itself if you only listen to it." He said that Thomas and Crane were too influenced by people like Keats and Yeats and Bridges—whereat, says Ginsberg's biographer, his audience groaned. Ginsberg said that he himself, in contrast to Thomas, had been influenced by Stein, Pound, Whitman, and Williams.[97]

Ginsberg had a point: Thomas's obscure writings were very different from the direct expression of thought that would be the Beats' stock in trade. Thomas began as a young man by imitating the Imagist poets, and he still wrote in images, making his thoughts as concrete as possible:

> Especially when the October wind
> With frosty fingers punishes my hair,
> Caught by the crabbing sun I walk on fire
> And cast a shadow crab upon the land . . .[98]

The Beats, on the other hand, would express their thoughts in plain words. They had no time for imagining—they were in a hurry to live, and writing was merely one means to this end. For the Beat poets, words were not realities as they were for Thomas, they were an extension of life.

His influence, however, was considerable, and though Ginsberg would write in a different way, he found the way a great deal easier because Thomas had been before him. Thomas was the icebreaker—he ended the Age of Auden.

The change can be seen if we look, for example, at the poems of Theodore Roethke. Roethke was always very conscious of what was in and what was out, and trimmed his sails accordingly. His early poems contain Audenesque passages.

> Though the devouring mother cry, " 'Escape me? Never—' "
> And the honeymoon be spoiled by a father's ghost,
> Chill depths of the spirit are flushed to a fever,
> The nightmare silence is spoken. We are not lost.[99]

When Thomas appeared, Roethke forgot about Auden and learned to write like Thomas.

> And I acknowledge my foolishness with God,
> My desire for the peaks, the black ravines, the rolling
>   mists
> Changing with every twist of wind,
> The unsinging fields where no lungs breathe,
> Where light is stone.
> I return where fire has been,
> To the charred edge of the sea . . .[100]

Thomas made a second visit to America in 1952, this time bringing Caitlin. According to John Malcolm Brinnin, she was thoroughly suspicious, and with reason: Dylan had become seriously involved with two American women on his first tour and had been quite willing to go to bed with others. Caitlin hated these women: they "hunted singly, in pairs, and more often in packs . . . they were candidly, if not prepossessingly, spreadeagled, from the first tomtomed rumour of a famous name."[101] She found American charm cloying, especially when it met Dylan's "professional" charm. She disliked the intelligence of Americans, who had all been to college and received such a thorough grounding in so many subjects.

Standing in the wings at the Poetry Center as Dylan was about to go on, she told him, "Just remember, they're all dirt!"

A whispered, high-pitched argument ensued, but then he was on stage, being greeted by an ovation that lasted two minutes. He read a selection of his own new poems, and poems by other British poets, including a hilarious imitation of T. S. Eliot's voice in a parody by Henry Reed.[102]

The Thomases departed on a cross-country tour, quarreling as they went. When they returned to New York things had reached the breaking point. Dylan had neglected to pay his son Llewelyn's school fees back in England—he did not get around to mailing the check, so that Llewelyn had been dismissed from school. When Caitlin was informed of this she announced that she was leaving America and leaving Dylan —he could make his own plans for the future. Dylan went out to a bar with Brinnin. "Nothing," Brinnin says, "would help Dylan now, neither liquor nor my words of comfort that attempted to convince him that Caitlin was but justifiably upset, and that I at least did not take seriously her threat of leaving him. 'She knows just how to hurt me most,' was all he said."

This passed, however. Caitlin did not leave, Llewelyn was readmitted to school, and "the air was cleared and the way opened for the next still nameless but inevitable crisis."[103]

Thomas made a third trip to America between April and July of 1953. When in New York he would frequent the White Horse Tavern on Hudson Street. Business there doubled, the customers standing two deep to catch a glimpse of him.

A winter sun gleamed outside and the oil stove shone. On the facing wall hung his own drawing of the Two Brothers of Death, one a Christ that looked syphilitic, the other Moses with a green beard. Their skins were the color of figs, their feet were set on a ladder of moons. He could hear the hot water hissing in the pipes, but his hands were frozen.

He used to sit for hours covering sheets of paper with lines, crossing out words, rocking his head for a better word, smoking the while, filling the room with a reek of tobacco. In those days the only relief he had had was acting—the part of a madman or one of the nasty "modern" young men, or low comedy. He had been a roaring boy, a foursquare stander-up for life, taking no guff from the arty types, the amateur hobos and homos of Bloomsbury.

Over a pint he had been willing and able to give anyone the hard facts of communism and a reasoned program for Revolution.

He caught the eye of the stewardess as she came down the aisle, a pretty woman with ash-blonde hair and marble-bright eyes. "Another, if you please," holding up his glass. "Sir, there is a limit of two to a customer," she said. "Ah, but I'm Welsh," he answered, quick as a flash. "Your rule doesn't apply to us." He gave her his cupid smile. "Well," she said, "I'll see what I can do."

So that when he arrived at the airport he was walking six inches above the tarmac, and bubbly when the welcoming committee met him at the gate: two young men who looked like overgrown puppies, and herself, the rich woman who gathers visiting artists to her talcumed breast and hurries them into a limousine, and through the outskirts of the city, the crowd of dead souls going home at twilight from their dreary jobs, up a driveway to her mullion-windowed house, Tudor.

You enter, preceded by the puppy-men, one carrying your bag, the other your coat, a big room where people sit in chairs and sofas pretending not to have been kept waiting. How well you know them: the rich woman's husband, smirking and offering the hand that decides men's fate down at the office, but here lies dead as wax. And Grandmother, blue hair and white cheeks, a hectic spot the size of a sixpence in each. And, may Heaven preserve a poet, their daughter who has come all the way home from Wellesley College in the East, just for the occasion. "We have just been studying your *Portrait of the Artist as a Young Dog*," she whimpers, shoving her tits in your face. She has auburn hair and legs made for long hours afield and abed. This is temptation, and a man needs a drink or two to deal with it.

And a drink or two at dinner, the faces now growing steamy above the white cloth and shining crystal. They are cracking the claws of lobsters and lifting salad on forks. They are slicing thick, black-crusted steaks and stuffing their mouths with floury baked potatoes. The wine glasses are filled again and again.

At some point in the evening's proceedings he found himself telling the story about Oscar Wilde and the jockey. This was after someone asked if he had ever met Mr. Warwick Deeping the novelist, and he realized that authors were all alike to them, the living and the dead. That there was no difference between a Deeping and a Dickens, a Thomas and a Tambimuttu. So then he told the story about Wilde and the jockey—to make a definite impression.

An hour later he was in a hall big enough to house a dirigible and he played the part, stumbling over chairs on his way to the platform. He sat slumped forward during the introduction, trying not to slide off sideways like a ton of coal. The introduction was delivered by one of the professors at the university—which university, for Christ's sake? Minnesota? Michigan? He had lost track. The professor made some references to the bardic schools of Wales and Ireland. But at last he had finished.

Whereupon drunken Thomas, rude Thomas, Thomas the unspeakable, rose straight up and advanced to the lectern and, seizing it with both hands, spoke to the people gathered there in a voice that sounded like deep music, a voice from the beginning of creation, when hills and valleys were new and the beasts came forth to be named.

He said that he would first read a handful of poems by other men, beginning with a quiet poem by Thomas Hardy of which he was fond, perhaps because it was not like his own. He read the poem, "Lizbie Brown," and indeed it was very quiet and still in the room—when he finished you could have heard a pin drop. He read a poem by Yeats and one by Ransom. Then he began to read his own poetry, his voice booming out, a sound to melt the marrow in men's bones, and women's too.

> Do not go gentle into that good night,
> Old age should burn and rave at close of day;
> Rage, rage against the dying of the light . . .[104]

He then read aloud the poem "Fern Hill," about his childhood:

> . . . honored among wagons I was prince of the apple towns
> And once below a time I lordly had the trees and leaves
> Trail with daisies and barley
> Down the rivers of the windfall light . . .[105]

There was a poem, he said, about the life and death of one particular human being he had known—and not about the very many lives and deaths whether seen, as in his first poems, in the "tumultuous world of his own being," or, in his later poems, in war, grief, and the "great holes and corners of universal love."[106] The ending of the poem was strange—perhaps all original images in poetry are strange, and it still appears so now that I have the book in front of me. It speaks of something I have seen for myself, the concentration of feeling that certain lives collect about them.

> ... this monumental
> Argument of the hewn voice, gesture and palm,
> Storm me forever over her grave until
> The stuffed lung of the fox twitch and cry Love
> And the strutting fern lay seeds on the black sill.[107]

Within three years of his coming to America, Thomas would be dead. He killed himself with drink. At the end he had *delirium tremens*, and the doctors spoke of "insult to the brain." The curious phrase was repeated—it stuck in people's minds.

While he lasted he put on a terrific show. The writing of verse had been becoming an exercise in reason—he reminded people of what they had forgotten: that poetry can be passionate speech, and that this proceeds from the life of an individual.

"The Eye Altering Alters All"

A GRAY, WET AFTERNOON at Columbia, yellow windows shining through the rain. . . . Seven or eight students wend their way to a room in the library, each of them carrying the *Collected Poems* of William Butler Yeats.

How naïve we were in those days! We did not read "secondary sources," just the poems. The only authority we appealed to was the man sitting at the head of the table, fairly tall, with no flesh to spare, a plain face like an Illinois farmer's, nose and mouth cut in brown clay with a few straight lines, eyes set in fine wrinkles, alive with curiosity and amusement. When you spoke he listened. He expected you to say something worth listening to. And sometimes you did.

Mark believed that the way to think was to be inspired. An idea passionately held draws you forward—and the little details fall into place. This was not the way English was being taught in graduate schools: there students were told to write on a limited topic that they would be able to research, one that no one had dealt with before, so that they could make an "original contribution." More than likely, the reason no one had written about it before was that it had not been worth doing, that it was not worth the trouble.

> Pretty! in Amber to observe the forms
> Of hairs, or straws, or dirt, or grubs, or worms . . .[1]

On the other hand, Mark's enthusiasm could be accused of being mere impressionism, and when they had left Columbia some of his students, finding themselves in a dull part of the world doing a dull job, would wonder where it had all vanished. How could they make a connection between Thomas Hardy's Wessex and the brick walls they saw when they looked out the window? Between Yeats' Ireland and the used-car lot? Had they, for four years of their lives, been under an enchantment?

For Mark himself, as a poet, the love of literature held disadvantages: it removed him from the people you have to deal with every day. Not to mention fools and villains. But writing has to take these into account —the best writing seems to hover on the edge of an abyss. To write well is to tell the whole truth as far as you see it, it is a matter of nerves, and is sometimes done in a state bordering on dread. There is no precedent for it and no comfort—you know that you are risking failure. But when he wrote his poems Mark did not take risks; he wrote in the manner of a tradition, in literary English and regular lines. Mark was a cause of originality in other men, of confusion in some cases, but when he himself sat down to write he expunged from his mind those thoughts and rhythms that make one pause, like the sound of a bell from far away.

Perhaps he liked teaching too well. It is possible to teach with creative energy, the same kind that goes into writing. For a poet this is to be dreaded.

He believed in spontaneity. When he wrote a poem he finished it that day—unlike Robert Frost, the poet he was sometimes compared to. Frost had been known to carry an image thirty years.

> The clouds were low and hairy in the skies,
> Like locks blown forward in the gleam of eyes.[2]

When Frost conceived this, Pre-Raphaelitism was the fashion: artists and writers were in love with hair. But the poem was not finished until years later when plainness was the style, and the transported image peers out freakishly from a waste of cold, gray water. This was not Mark's way—he would have an idea and set it down in words that came to mind. As he had read much, especially in English literature, they were literary words.

> My only need—you ask me, and I tell you—
> Is that henceforth forever you exist.
> You are not mine; I may not ever bell you
> Like an owned animal for night and mist.[3]

He would write "Time's tooth devours," and not worry about a new way to say it, or not saying it at all. This was strange, for he had read Ezra Pound on making it new, and he had read William Carlos Williams on "No ideas but in things." Mark had read everything! Yet he did not apply their experiments to his own case.

He was satisfied to be spontaneous—he did not trouble to be innovative as well. And this was an age when men prized innovation above all—it was the *sine qua non* of Modernist writing. As a consequence, Mark was "out of it," not one of the poets critics wrote about. In return he stated that he was not interested in contemporary criticism. Some thought that he meant he would no longer write book reviews —he had been a critic for *The Nation*, among other things—but he really meant that the thoughts he prized and the way he wrote were not fashionable. He wanted nothing to do with the New Criticism, excruciating the text for every drop of irony that could be got out of it.

Spontaneity was his gift to the next generation. Only a few in the generation realized this—most would talk about Pound and Williams, but out of Mark's classroom came—Kerouac, for example: "... on gray November afternoons ... sittin ... room ... cutting ... Contemporary Civilization. I had nothing but disrespect for my perfessor, I did. Later on, when Mark Van Doren made me realize professors could be real interesting, I nevertheless spent most of my time dreaming on what he must be like in real reality instead of listening to what he was saying. The one big thing, though, I do remember him saying, is, 'A perfect friend you always meet every two or three years, accidentally, and you can't stop talking with him; and when he leaves for another two, three years, you don't feel sad at all; when you meet him again, it happens again. He is your perfect friend.' This must have been Van Doren himself. They give that man banquets, his alumni students do, and cry, all sarcastic professional men, too. He looked up from a paper I had written and said, 'Giggling Lings?' to make sure I did say 'Giggling' before the Chinese name 'Lings' and that was the only question he asked. Can you wonder that men love him? I don't know who this guy is, I just came across him—while this man tended his farm in spare hours, or that is, did a few chores among the flowers, and dreamed, my father sat at a linotype machine puffing a cigar and spitting into a spittoon into which occasionally also pieces of hot lead would fall, smoking. The difference in their class ... styles of accomplishment."[4]

Kerouac saw what Mark's view of things left out: the pieces of hot, smoking lead, the spittoon, the cigar. Mark doing light chores in Connecticut or sitting at his writing desk seemed to be removed from the pressures of the age. He did not seem to know what it was like to be unemployed like Kerouac's father, a life on the edge of poverty and sometimes falling into it, the mean and sordid side of things.

When Mark came to write his autobiography, some who had known him were puzzled, so much had been left out. It was nice to hear of the teachers and friends, the books Mark had loved—it was good to have wisdom—but what of the individuals and ideas he disliked? Mark in person was very capable of expressing a dislike. He thought very little of Auden, and he was not fond of Lionel Trilling, his colleague at Columbia who was the antithesis of everything Mark stood for— Trilling was interested in educating students for careers, turning them into copies of himself; he was not interested in education for its own sake. But of these antipathies there was no hint in Mark's autobiography. It is all well and good to maintain the decencies, but when one is a writer it is more important to speak one's mind. As Rémy de Gourmont says, "Speaking one's mind frankly is a writer's only pleasure."

Where was the Mark who was capable of sending a student out of his house visibly shaken? The student was Ginsberg. He had been talking to Mark about the Hiss case—he said that he guessed Hiss was guilty because the jury said so, and Mark told him to get out. What he said exactly was, "I don't want to hear any more of that shit."

"He was really angry," Ginsberg said. He seemed surprised—he would always be surprised by the world's refusal to conform to his vision of it. According to the generation rules, Van Doren was to be a sounding board—he was not supposed to react. The remark about Hiss was stupid, Ginsberg now admits.

But getting back to Kerouac. He came of a French-Canadian family in Lowell, Massachusetts. His father owned his own printing business and was a well-known figure in Lowell, and well-liked, as Arthur Miller might have said. But he lost his money during the Depression and an overflow of the Merrimac River swamped the plant. He was forced to sell his business and seek work as a journeyman printer, leaving his family for periods of time. The mother then became all-powerful. In his account of Kerouac's life Tytell says that his mother "tended to shun the world, especially its newness, and looked to the past for guidance. She dominated her son, and much of his need for privacy and his suspicion of institutions can be traced to her influence."[5]

Kerouac's father died after a long illness, tended by his son who, says Tytell, was "morbidly fascinated by the process of disintegration and death." On his deathbed Kerouac's father made him swear to take care of his mother for the rest of his life, "a burden that the son accepted faithfully."[6]

Kerouac was a track and football star in high school. He drove himself to train; he was "entirely self-motivated, self-taught, and extremely

wilful."[7] He went to Columbia on an athletic scholarship after a prepara-
tory year at Horace Mann.

In his freshman year at Columbia he broke his leg playing football
and as a consequence immersed himself in reading. Then he walked
out on the team and out of Columbia.

He worked as a gas station attendant in New Haven, then went back
to Lowell where he worked as a sportswriter on the *Sun* and discovered
James Joyce and the stream of consciousness. He quit the newspaper
after two months. "It was difficult," Tytell remarks, "for him to remain
in one place for long."[8]

He enlisted in the Coast Guard and Marines—both on the same day
—and shipped out as a dishwasher on a merchant marine ship making
the run to Greenland. Then he went back to Columbia for a few weeks,
resumed playing football, and walked out on the team again—according
to Tytell, because Coach Lou Little wouldn't let him play in the opening
game. According to Kerouac, on the tape he made with Cassady, it was
because he heard Beethoven's Fifth Symphony.

One afternoon it started to snow. Beethoven came on, it was time for me to
go to scrimmage . . . the snow was falling . . . ta ta ta taaa! (*Beethoven theme*)
ta ta ta taaa (*each time Cody says* Yeah *solemnly listening*) (*as Jack solemnly
sings*) I said to myself "Scrimmage my ass . . . I'm gonna sit here in this room
and dig Beethoven, I'm gonna write noble words," *you* know . . .[9]

At the end of the semester Kerouac enlisted in the Navy. But he
couldn't take the discipline: "He flung his rifle to the ground one morning during drill and walked to the base library where he was apprehended
by men with nets. In June of 1943, just a little past his twenty-
first birthday, he was discharged as a paranoid schizophrenic. His six
months in the Navy had been spent mostly under observation by naval
psychiatrists."[10]

Both Kerouac and Ginsberg spent time in the bughouse, as they called
it, and afterwards they would frequently express the opinion that the
best people were crazy. "The only people for me are the mad ones," says
the narrator of *On the Road*, "the ones who are mad to live, mad to talk,
mad to be saved, desirous of everything at the same time, the ones who
never yawn or say a commonplace thing, but burn, burn, burn like
fabulous yellow roman candles exploding like spiders across the stars
and in the middle you see the blue centerlight pop and everybody goes
'Awww!' "[11]

Allen Ginsberg was born in Paterson, New Jersey. His father was a
poet of an old-fashioned, sentimental, rhyming kind; his mother had

been confined in an insane asylum. Ginsberg appears in Kerouac's first novel as "Leon Levinsky," at nineteen "one of the strangest, most curiously exalted youngsters" the narrator had ever known. Levinsky was "an eager, intense, sharply intelligent boy of Russian-Jewish parentage who rushed around New York in a perpetual sweat of emotional activity, back and forth in the streets from friend to friend, room to room, apartment to apartment. He 'knew everybody' and 'knew everything,' was always bearing tidings and messages from 'the others,' full of catastrophe. He brimmed and flooded over day and night with a thousand different thoughts and conversations and small horrors, delights, perplexities, deities, discoveries, ecstasies, fears. He stared gog-eyes at the world and was full of musings, lip-pursings, subway broodings—all of which rushed forth in torrents of complex conversation whenever he confronted someone."

Kerouac says that Leon Levinsky had read a thousand books, and had dreamed of becoming a great labor leader, but now that was all in the past, his "poor little Jew's past," as he put it.[12]

At Columbia, Ginsberg came under Van Doren's influence, but his feelings about Van Doren would not be as simple as Kerouac's. In a letter to William Carlos Williams in which he speaks of his education at Columbia, Ginsberg says, "I liked Van Doren most there."[13] On the other hand he has said that no one at Columbia knew anything about the writing of poetry. "That was the whole horror of Columbia, there was just nobody there (maybe except Weaver) who had a serious involvement with advanced work in poetry. Just a bunch of Dilletantes [sic]."[14]

But Van Doren did have an effect on Ginsberg, by way of Kerouac. Van Doren was Kerouac's idea of the perfect friend, and Ginsberg loved Kerouac and, he says, learned more about poetry from Kerouac than anyone else. What he learned was to write spontaneously, so Mark's gift arrived, after all, in the most unlikely hands, washed up on the shore of the Beat Generation.

It is necessary in reconstructing Ginsberg's early years to remember that many things were going on at the same time. Like Leon Levinsky he went rushing from room to room, from one person to another, receiving and delivering messages.

Lucien Carr taught him something. "The father of the Beat Generation," says Aaron Latham, "was not Jack Kerouac or Allen Ginsberg or William Burroughs. It was Lucien Carr."[15] That is as it may be, but Carr did have a powerful effect on Kerouac and Ginsberg. In recent years Ginsberg, looking back, has spoken of "paranoia criticism," borrowing a phrase from Salvador Dali. "I define the paranoia-critical method," says Dali, "as a great art of playing upon all one's own inner contradictions with lucidity by causing others to experience the anxieties and ecstasies of one's life in such a way that it becomes gradually as essential to them as one's own. But I very early realized, instinctively, my life formula: to get others to accept as natural the excesses of one's personality and thus to relieve oneself of his own anxieties by creating a sort of collective participation."[16]

Carr, Kerouac, Ginsberg, and Burroughs had the kind of collective participation that Dali describes. They saw themselves as extraordinary. They had mystical experiences which they discussed, like characters in a novel by Dostoievsky. Carr had developed a "life formula" that he called the New Vision.

In 1944 Carr was a sophomore in Columbia College. He had a friend named David Kammerer who had followed him to Columbia and taken a job as janitor to be near him. Kammerer kept following Carr around. One night they went down to Riverside Drive, and there Carr killed Kammerer with a knife.

This was Dostoievsky with a vengeance! The *Daily News* called it an "honor slaying"—Carr had been defending himself against the advances of a homosexual. The *Journal-American* reported that he passed the time in his cell reading Rimbaud's *A Season in Hell* and Yeats' *A Vision*.

In order to raise Carr's bail Kerouac married his girl friend, whose parents had money. They put up the bail, and the lovers moved to Detroit. Burroughs went home to St. Louis. Carr pleaded guilty to first-degree manslaughter, was sentenced to an indefinite term, and entered Elmira reformatory in October 1944.[17] Ginsberg moved out of the hotel on 115th Street where he had met Carr, and into Livingston Hall on the Columbia Campus. He wrote in his journal, "The libertine circle is destroyed with the death of Kammerer."

The murder had been frightening and exciting. Ginsberg came from a middle-class family. His mother, Naomi, was mad, but still she was respectable—there is some insanity in the best of families. His father, Louis, was a schoolteacher with conventional ideas. The murder of David Kammerer was like an abyss opening between the life Ginsberg had led so far and experiences he would have in the future. If Lucien, with whom he had often talked, arguing about the meaning of life, was able to kill, then words and ideas were real! Visions could put on flesh and blood, be seen arriving at police stations, stand in the light of flashbulbs and have their fingerprints taken. Interviewed by newspapermen at the precinct station, Ginsberg told them about the New Vision.

Carr had accomplished what Dali recommends: caused Kerouac and

Ginsberg and Burroughs to experience the anxieties and ecstasies of his life in such a way that it became as essential to them as their own. When Ginsberg thought about the scene on Riverside Drive he could see it vividly, Carr driving the knife—his Boy Scout knife, as the newspapers pointed out—into David Kammerer's chest.

From this time on Carr's friends felt that they had special insight into the criminal mind. It was more than understanding, it was admiration. Kerouac in all his writing, and Ginsberg in "Howl," would argue for the superiority of those whom the law condemned. They were the ones who dared to live their ideas, to experiment, though they were punished for it —in contrast to the people who only knew about life through books.

In the spring of 1945 Ginsberg's windows in Livingston were very dirty. In order to encourage the chambermaid to wash them he drew obscene pictures in the dirt and wrote "Nicholas Murray Butler has no balls" and "Fuck the Jews." The maid reported this to her superiors, and an investigation revealed something more . . . Kerouac asleep in Ginsberg's room, in spite of his having been warned to stay off the campus.

Ginsberg was summoned to appear before the Dean of Students. "Ginsberg," he said, "I hope you realize the enormity of what you have done."

"Oh, I do, sir, I do," said Ginsberg, but the Dean had a look in his eye that meant, "Ginsberg, I've got you this time." Ginsberg felt as if he were trapped with a bunch of maniacs. "You can't imagine what colleges were like in those days. The whole syndrome of shutdown and provincialism extended to the academy. Like, at Columbia, Whitman was hardly taught and was considered a creep."[18]

The Dean wanted him expelled, but Professors Trilling and Van Doren interceded and he was merely suspended with a promise of readmission when he could show a letter from a psychiatrist stating that he was fit to resume his studies. So Ginsberg took his leave and went to work at a variety of jobs, spot welder, night porter, dishwasher in Bickford's cafeteria. He became familiar with Times Square and the hustlers and deadbeats who infested the area, and learned the hip talk of jazz musicians.[19]

For four months he was enrolled as a trainee in the Merchant Marine Academy at Sheepshead Bay in Brooklyn, and tried to act the part of a regular guy, but his classmates found him out—reading Hart Crane's poems. He graduated at the end of 1945, was ill for a while with pneumonia, then shipped out on a tanker that made ports along the Atlantic and Gulf coasts. The voyage, says Tytell, "became the psychological equivalent of a monastic retreat," bringing Ginsberg in close contact with ordinary seamen and helping to "violate the protective sheath of academic life that had separated him from the world."[20]

During this year Burroughs was back in New York and Ginsberg used his apartment on Morningside Heights as a *pied à terre*. Other members of the household were Burroughs' girl, Joan Adams, Kerouac, and Herbert Huncke, a drug addict who supported his habit by stealing. Burroughs took over Ginsberg's education, "giving him copies of Mayan codices to study, and drilling him on works of the writers they admired —Kafka, Spengler, Blake, Yeats, Céline, Korzybski, Vico, and Rimbaud." Ginsberg submitted to psychoanalysis by Burroughs, lying down for an hour each day to free-associate. When Ginsberg was finished, Kerouac would lie down for an hour and Burroughs would analyze him.

These arrangements lasted until the time that Ginsberg was readmitted to Columbia. Then the household broke up: "Huncke was in and out of jail, Burroughs, who had developed a morphine habit, had been arrested for a false script and had fled to Texas, where he married Mrs. Adams (she had been married before), settled down on a little swamp farm in the bayous west of Houston, and began raising fine-grade marijuana, Kerouac went off with Neal Cassady, on the cross-country drive that he later wrote about in *On the Road....*"[21]

Toward the end of 1946 Hal Chase introduced Kerouac and Ginsberg to Cassady. Cassady was impressed with Ginsberg's ideas and so let Ginsberg make love to him. Upon returning to Denver where he lived, Cassady felt a need of Ginsberg, comparing himself to a "woman about to lose her man." Cassady was bisexual, though he preferred women. In any case, from Denver he wrote to Ginsberg proposing that they might "assume a responsibility toward each other and entertain a certain erotic attraction (lover idea)." So in the spring of 1947 Ginsberg set off for Denver, hoping to form a bond with Cassady, the kind of thing Whitman had meant when he spoke of "adhesiveness" and "the manly love of comrades." But when Ginsberg got there he found Cassady busy with his wife, his new girl friend, and his job, working for the May Company, driving commuters from parking lot to department store in a shuttle taxi. Ginsberg reproached him with not taking advantage of the opportunity to improve his mind: "The point," he wrote in a letter, "is that I am the only one capable of mastering you right now and moving you by will and intelligence and insight and presumption out of the sterile round of self-destructive love and work and activities and emotions, the whole impasse of your existence."[22]

Ginsberg stayed a month in Denver. Then they all left town, hitch-hiking. Kerouac went back to New York and Ginsberg went with Cassady to Texas where Burroughs and Joan Adams had just raised their first crop of marijuana. They were preparing to bring it East and sell it. Cassady stayed with Burroughs, and Ginsberg was given the assignment of making some money for the Fall. It was decided that he would ship out from Galveston and meet them in New York. So Ginsberg signed on an old tanker that was sailing to North Africa.[23]

While at sea he wrote a poem, "Dakar Doldrums," in the manner of *Childe Harold's Pilgrimage.*

> Cursed be this month of Fall! I fail
> My full and fair and near and dear and kind.
> I but endure my role, my own seas sail,
> Far from the sunny shores within thy mind.
> So this departure shadoweth mine end:
> Ah! what poor human cometh unto me,
> Since now the snowy spectre doth descend,
> Henceforth I shall in fear and anger flee.[24]

The poem was a passionate leavetaking of Cassady. He kept falling in love and writing about people he was in love with, and he was in love with Neal for years.[25] Besides the "Doldrums" he wrote "A Western Ballad" about it.

> When I died, love, when I died
> there was a war in the upper air:
> all that happens, happens there . . .[26]

At Columbia College he had never mastered poetics "as analyzed by New Critical prose"; instead he tried to write sincere, though elegant quatrains. The ballad to Cassady registered both renunciation of what he held most dear in terms of the human body and a "breaking-open of consciousness." It gave him "a sort of eternal bliss contact of sumpin' beyond my body, or something that appeared beyond my body. Poetry, really."[27]

1948 was the watershed of generations. Before 1948 it had been possible to think of God and Country and the war against Hitler. But history came to an end in 1948, and from then on everyday life was a vision, opening up into some "eternal planet place," where the magic was created by individuals.[28]

This was Ginsberg's idea of history. And indeed there was a gulf between people like Ginsberg who had been too young to take part in the Second World War and those who had defended their country. To Ginsberg and his friends America was

> Moloch! Solitude! Filth! Ugliness! Ashcans and
> unobtainable dollars! Children screaming under
> the stairways! Boys sobbing in armies! Old men
> weeping in the parks![29]

America was the System. America was in an awful state, complete anarchy, violent chaos, "sado-masochistic barroom confusion, and clinical hysteria." All this hysterical irresponsibility had found its consummation in the atom bomb. Meanwhile, the pure in heart were being driven underground. "All our healthiest citizens are at this very moment turning into hipsters, hopheads, and poets."[30]

One day when he opened his book of Blake's poems he heard Blake's voice commanding and prophesying to him from eternity. It was, he says, a "hallucinatory-mystical experience . . . I . . . felt my soul open completely wide all its doors & windows and the cosmos flowed thru me, and *experienced* a state of altered apparently total consciousness so fantastic & science-fictional I even got scared later, at having stumbled on a secret door in the universe all alone."

He made a vow to be faithful to the "Absolute Eternal X" he had seen face to face. There was a danger, however, that others might think him mad, so he cooled it and continued to live his normal life. Then there was a fall, for once when he summoned the Great Spirit and it appeared, it brought with it "a sense of Doom & Death so universal, vast & living" that he felt that the universe had come alive and was a hostile entity in which he was trapped and by which he would be eaten consciously alive.[31]

This was in the summer of 1948. He was living in a rented apartment in Harlem, living on vegetables and giving shelter to Huncke, who was too beat to look after himself. It was Huncke who introduced the word "beat" to Ginsberg, Kerouac, and Burroughs—meaning exhausted, out of it, and therefore blessed.[32] Ginsberg was fond of Huncke, who was harmless, yet always going to jail. Huncke was a martyr, living testimony to America's repression of the instincts, driving the weak into criminal activities.

Ginsberg talked to Huncke about his own troubles and Huncke listened. Over the next few weeks Huncke removed the books in the apartment—it had been rented from a theologian—and sold them. He removed the record collection, the clothing, the plates and silverware. At last Ginsberg began to notice that the apartment was becoming empty, whereupon Huncke left.

Ginsberg moved to an apartment on York Avenue and settled down to typing his thesis on "The absolute inside, inner, beyond language meaning of mythology." As he had finished his course work at Columbia, he went to work for the Associated Press, taking teletype off the machines and delivering it to the right desks. This glimpse of the world of affairs gave him a poem, "Stanzas: Written at Night in Radio City."

> If money made the mind more sane,
> Or money mellowed in the bowel
> The hunger beyond hunger's pain,
> Or money choked the mortal growl
> And made the groaner grin again,
> Or did the laughing lamb embolden
> To loll where has the lion lain,
> I'd go make money and be golden.[33]

Toward the end of the year Huncke tracked Ginsberg to his new apartment. Huncke had been in and out of jail again; the cops had chased him away from Times Square; it was snowing outside and his feet were bleeding; he was in an almost suicidal state. Ginsberg let him have the couch and he stayed on it, catching up on his sleep, for three weeks. Then he went out and stole some money from a car. "I was overjoyed!" says Ginsberg. "He'd come back to life."

Ginsberg considered Huncke. At Columbia they talked about right and wrong, ethics and morality and social good. But the people who talked this way were scrambling to get ahead and making atom bombs. Huncke was a victim of "a monstrosity of laws and attitudes." He was an addict with a twenty-year habit; under any decent system he would have been given a pension and supplied with the drugs he had to have, but instead he was sent to jail. Thinking about the way society treated Huncke reinforced Ginsberg in his alienated view of society.

Huncke went about his old business of stealing. Ginsberg didn't approve or disapprove, he was content to let it happen—besides, he was busy with his own work, writing poems and psalms. Then Huncke began bringing people to the apartment. There was a tall redheaded girl, Priscilla Arminger, who had been a prostitute at a hundred dollars a shot. Ginsberg knew her: she had taught him and Kerouac to use Benzedrine inhalers, and she was a great user of pot—"Really a remarkable, beautiful, good-hearted, tender girl." She had a boyfriend, Little Jack Melody, "a sort of subdivision cousin of the Mafia," and she was going to have Little Jack's child. "So it was," Ginsberg says, "like a whole *Beggar's Opera* scene at my house."

Huncke, Little Jack, and Priscilla stole chests of silver, silver sets, radios, phonographs, and stored them at the apartment. They stole some clothes from the house of a detective in Harlem. Ginsberg became uneasy, but he didn't feel that he could kick them out; so he decided he would leave himself, travel down to New Orleans and visit Burroughs. He packed his manuscripts and correspondence in cartons. Little Jack had a car, and the plan was for them to drive out on Long Island—Little Jack had some things he wished to drop off at his mother's—then they would leave Ginsberg's stuff with his brother, a law student at NYU. Huncke stayed home.

They drove out on the Island, Little Jack, Ginsberg, and Priscilla. Little Jack took the wrong turn down a one-way street at the end of which a police car was standing. Little Jack panicked—the car he was driving was stolen, and the things, men's suits he was taking to his mother's house, had been stolen. He stepped on the gas. The police tried to wave down the car and Little Jack almost ran over one of them. The police gave chase with drawn guns. Little Jack went tearing down Utopia Parkway. He tried to swerve into a side street and hit a telephone pole, and the car went rolling over. Ginsberg's life flashed before his eyes, all his errors coming to this place. He remembers singing "Lord God of Israel, Isaac, and Abraham" from the *Messiah*. "Which," he remarks, "was a very weird thing."[34]

The car settled down and Ginsberg crawled out, in a welter of paper—manuscripts, love letters, incriminating letters about pot in Texas. He had lost his glasses. He thought that he would have to get back to the apartment at once. The police would soon be there, and it was full of stolen goods. It had to be cleaned out immediately. He had to phone Huncke.

The police car had gone by, so they had some time. They ran off in different directions. Priscilla got to a friend's house. Little Jack was caught and beaten up by the police. Ginsberg wandered into a candy store and asked the way to New York. Are you in a car, they asked him. No, he said, he was a naturalist, taking a walk with nature. He borrowed twelve cents which, together with the few cents he had on him, was enough for a phone call to Huncke. Then he got back to New York somehow, hitchhiking and borrowing ten cents for the subway. When he came into the apartment Huncke was slowly sweeping the floor. Ginsberg said, "What are you doing, Herbert? The police will be here any minute."

"Oh, it's hopeless now," said Huncke. "I've been through this so many times. There's nothing you can do." Then the police arrived.

It made the *Daily News,* with a picture of Ginsberg on the front page. What had been a Dostoievskyan experience, "with like *real* people," was presented as the "total stereotype of a giant robbery operation—six-foot, marijuana-smoking redhead, three-time-loser pariah criminal, boy-wonder mastermind."

At Columbia they thought that this time Ginsberg had really surpassed himself. Van Doren could not understand. How could Ginsberg have consorted with common criminals? A lot of people around Columbia, he told Ginsberg, thought it was time for him to hear the clank of iron. Ginsberg did not understand when Van Doren explained that if you really felt that people like Huncke were saintly, then "you should be prepared to suffer for them and go to jail, or *something.*"

Professor Meyer Schapiro was more sympathetic: it reminded him of the time he had been jailed for vagrancy in Europe. Lionel Trilling was horrified but friendly and helpful: he took Ginsberg to see Professor Herbert Wechsler at the Law School, for advice. The advice he gave was for Ginsberg to plead insanity.

So Ginsberg's father found a lawyer, and Ginsberg was admitted to the Columbia Psychiatric Institute.

There he had leisure to brood on many things—the effect on his family: "Why does it have to be *our* son? Why does he *do* these things?" On reality—"What *is* reality? Is it my visions, or Huncke's void, or what's actually going on?" He felt guilty thinking about his friends who were going to jail whereas he hadn't even had to go to court, merely to tell some psychiatrist that he heard voices and had visions. Then he felt angry with Huncke, who had known what he was getting into when he stole, and should have protected him. He brooded about Huncke's robbing people's cars and inconveniencing people, and, on the other side, the ignorance and cruelty of the law. How the police had confiscated his copy of the *Bhagavad Gita,* saying, "We don't allow anything but religious books in the can," and all the way down to the station he had tried to tell them about the *Bhagavad Gita.*

Then, says Ginsberg, a fat man in a bathrobe—fat from shock treatment with insulin and metrosol—came over and spoke to him. It was Carl Solomon. "Who are *you?*" he said to Ginsberg. "I'm Myshkin," Ginsberg said. "I'm Kirilov," said Carl Solomon.[35]

Solomon had been a Marxist and a member of the Tom Paine Club. After the war he shipped out on merchant marine vessels. He had an interest in existentialism and surrealism; in 1947 he jumped ship in France and attended a reading by Artaud in Saint-Germain-des-Prés. On his return to New York, he was in a depressed condition, thinking about suicide and lobotomy. Having read Gide's *Lafcadio's Adventures* he decided to commit a gratuitous crime: he stole a sandwich and showed it to a policeman. This was how he came to be in the Psychiatric Institute.[36]

Ginsberg and Solomon talked and argued. Solomon called Ginsberg a "dopey daffodil" because he seemed sensitive and Wordsworthian—not Artaud's idea of the poet as brute. Ginsberg saw Whitman as a sexual revolutionary, whereas Solomon thought his political ideas more significant. They argued over the merits of their analysts: Solomon was being treated by a disciple of Harry Stack Sullivan, Ginsberg by a Freudian.

Ginsberg remained in the hospital for eight months. Upon his release he introduced Carl Solomon to his friends. Solomon became known as the "lunatic saint"—he was given to practical joking—throwing potato salad at a lecturer, pretending to be W. H. Auden at an exhibition and signing autographs in Auden's name. He had a job selling ice cream in front of the United Nations. " 'Every man lives by a set of rules to which he is the only exception,' Solomon once wrote. To Ginsberg, Solomon was an instance of the artist as outrage, a man capable of an intuitively quick surrealistic buffoonery that exposed the pretentious stuffiness of the world. Like Huncke, he was an outcast artist, an exile within the culture."[37]

1948 was the beginning of the Golden Age. "I remember these sleepless epiphanies of 1948," Ginsberg would say years later, "everywhere in America transcendental brain consciousness was waking up from Times Square to the Banks of Willamette River to Berkeley's Groves of Academe."[38]

There had been his own "Blake epiphany experiences"; Robert Duncan's "Venice Poem"; the "Berkeley Renaissance community," including Jack Spicer and Timothy Leary; Olson's *Call Me Ishmael*, and Gary Snyder in Portland "finished his Amerindian anthropology unified field theory honors thesis to graduate."

One morning before dawn Snyder finished writing the thesis and went down to the Willamette River, where he sat down exhausted, musing over the silence of nature. Then, just as the sun rose, he heard a rushing of wings and thousands of birds came out of the trees, and he looked around, and his head turned inside out, and he suddenly realized, "Everything is alive—the entire universe is alive. Every sentient being is alive, like myself."

Snyder had a very definite opening of consciousness. It was from there, that single experience, that he went on to do his sitting (zazen).[39]

After his release from the mental hospital Ginsberg moved back to Paterson, "home for the first time in seven years."[40] He lived with his father Louis and new stepmother Edith—his own mother had been insane for years—and took part in the life of the family. "And finally," he noted in his journal, "the family bared its bones at the luncheon table—Louis complaining abstractly (hypothetical situations) about Sheila (stepdaughter)—seeming to have a meaning, a lurking resentment undertoning his words, and Edith his wife sat by & interpolated arguments. And I took him head on, 'You're like a comic strip Poppa.' . . . "[41]

Allen took over an upstairs bedroom of the house and had it papered with a Chinese calligraphic print. There he experimented with peyote, noting the bitter, metallic aftertaste and feeling of stomach sickness and heaviness of body, followed by a feeling of transparency: ". . . eyes closed toward light leaves in eye a golden glow hue—which darkens when you pass hand over lidded eye." Sitting in the backyard he looked into the sky and watched the clouds floating away to the end of the world, and thought about matter and infinity and the origin of Creation.[42]

One night he went to hear William Carlos Williams read his poems at the Museum of Modern Art in New York. It was the turning point. Ginsberg was still the Columbia student, imitating Marvell or the English Romantic poets, and he kept listening for a meter, some hidden iambic pentameter or quatrain that wasn't there. Then Williams read his poem, "The Clouds," which ends ". . . lunging upon / a pismire, a conflagration, a . . ." Ginsberg had never heard a poem end in mid-sentence, though he had heard people talk that way all the time. Now he suddenly realized, *"Oh, he's just writing the way he talks."*

The meaning of the poem was identical with its form, the rhythm was identical with the arrangement of the words on the page, and the words on the page were what the poet wanted to say and how he wanted to say it. This, Ginsberg says, "was like a revelation of absolute common sense in my entire universe of complete bullshit! Aesthetically a totally hallucinated universe where like every possible poetic form made absolute sense. And also made absolutely pretty rhythm, too."[43]

A few days after the reading at the Museum, Ginsberg wrote a letter to Williams. It is included in Book Four of Williams' *Paterson*, and from it we learn that Ginsberg had visited Williams two years before to interview him for a local newspaper, and that Williams invited him to come back, but Ginsberg did not, "as I had nothing to talk about except images of cloudy light, and was not able to speak to you in your own or my own concrete terms."[44]

The letter gives a resumé of Ginsberg's life up to this point. He has spent most of the last year in a mental hospital, and is now back in Paterson, at loose ends. "My literary liking is Melville in Pierre and the Confidence Man, and in my own generation, one Jack Kerouac whose first book came out this year."

He speaks of his own poems with diffidence. He has been trying to renew and transfigure "an old style of lyric machinery" which he uses to record "the struggle with imagination of the clouds," and he is enclosing a few samples. "All that I have done has a program, consciously or not, running on from phrase to phrase, from the beginnings of emotional breakdown, to momentary raindrops from the clouds become corporeal, to a renewal of human objectivity which I take to be ultimately identical with no ideas but in things."

With this sentence Ginsberg puts himself in the Doctor's hands for help and direction. He disclaims any intention of following in Williams' traces out of ambition to be poetic, but it may be pleasing to Williams to realize that his experience has been inherited by one actual citizen of his community.

He may need a new measure himself, Ginsberg says, "but though I have a flair for your style I seldom dig exactly what you are doing with cadences, line length, sometimes syntax, etc., and cannot handle your work as a solid object—which properties I assume you rightly claim. I don't understand the measure. I haven't worked with it much either, though, which must make the difference. But I would like to talk with you concretely on this."[45]

With the letter Ginsberg enclosed some of his poems: the Radio City poem, "a mad song (to be sung by Groucho Marx to a Bop background)," an "Ode to the Setting Sun," and an "Ode to Judgment." The poems were traditional, echoing his studies of Tudor lyrics, the Metaphysical poets, Marvell, Blake, and the Romantics. Williams sent them back with the comment, "In this mode, perfection is basic, and these are not perfect."

For some time Ginsberg had been keeping a prose journal of things he had seen or heard, "whatever completely photographic, instamatic sensory detail that could be seen through a window, or heard in the wind." He now rearranged some of these prose paragraphs to make lines of verse:

> Two bricklayers are setting the walls
> of a cellar in a new dug out patch
> of dirt behind an old house of wood
> with brown gables grown over with ivy
> on a shady street in Denver. It is noon
> and one of them wanders off. The young
> subordinate bricklayer sits idly for
> a few minutes after eating a sandwich
> and throwing away the paper bag . . .[46]

When Williams saw these new poems he wrote back, "Ah, this is it." One so impressed him with its local images that he wanted Ginsberg to take him to the place so that he could describe it in *Paterson*.

Ginsberg went to see Williams. They went for walks around Paterson and, says Ginsberg, "He'd show me his Paterson, and I'd show him mine—I'd show him what my epiphanous places were. Places like by the river, under the bridge, where I masturbated for the first time. Where I saw that girl who moved away. Where I saw a gang fight. Where I always felt ashamed for some reason. The hedge where I was lonely. And I showed him the library, where I first read Dostoievsky."[47]

They discussed meter and rhythm. Williams was taking the rhythms of his poems directly from his own speech or from speech overheard. He showed Ginsberg a phrase he had heard some workmen use, "I'll kick yuh eye," and pointed out that there was a little syncopation in "yuh eye" that would be very difficult to reproduce in regular meter. He was arriving at "little refrains, little rhythmic squiggles" unheard in poetry until now, taking them from the life around him, "right into his own ear from the streets."[48]

He gave Ginsberg advice: to cut out lines that were vague, leave a poem unfinished rather than try to fill it out with unnecessary words. Only what was "active," that is, presented "an active piece of information," was worth keeping.

After one visit to Williams, Ginsberg jotted down notes of their talk. They had discussed Williams' autobiography, written with difficulty while he was recovering from a stroke. He had written it in order to tell the truth: "I've lived all now, my life is through now, why shouldn't I tell the truth?" That was the purpose of writing, "to tell truthfully why people act as they do." Williams told of having paid a visit to Auden: "Clutter and dirt, boy cooking food at other end of table." He and Auden had found that they had nothing to say to each other except formalities.

He spoke of meter and measure: "It's a matter of time. Get local speech accents and rhythm, write in that idiom. I don't even know," he told Ginsberg, "if Paterson is poetry. I have no form, I just try to squeeze the lines up into pictures." He said that the next generation would have to make some standard for the line.[49]

In 1952 Williams wrote an introduction for Ginsberg's unrhymed poems, the collection later published under the title, *Empty Mirror*. Williams praised the monotony of the writing, "like the monotony of our lives," and said that Ginsberg, "This young Jewish boy," was the Dante of a new, industrial Inferno. Ginsberg had invented a new sort of line "measured by the passage of time without accent, monotonous, useless." It moved not to a dancing but a shuffling beat, the rhythm of human beings in an industrial civilization on their way to the bathroom, the subway, the office. In order for the poet to attract the attention of the crowd he must speak to them in language they would understand, the language of the daily press. At the same time, out of his love for the crowd the poet must use his art to please. "He must measure, he must so disguise his lines that his style appears prosaic (so that it shall not offend) to go in a cloud." This poetry must not set out "to sneak over a poetic way of laying down phrases." It must be prose, "but prose among whose words the terror of their truth has been discovered." He concluded by saying that Ginsberg's craft was flawless.[50]

Some of the poems in *Empty Mirror* are close imitations of Williams:

> When I sit before a paper
>   writing my mind turns
> in a kind of feminine
>   madness of chatter . . .[51]

This might have been written by the old man himself. So might the poem on a painting by Cézanne and the poem about trees:

>   . . . I saw
> the scarlet-and-pink shoot-tips
> of budding leaves wave
>
> delicately in the sunlight,
> blown by the breeze,
> all the arms of the trees
> bending and straining downward
> at once when the wind
> pushed them.[52]

Ginsberg's poem about ". . . the girl / who proposed love to me in the neon / light of the Park Avenue Drugstore," and who died a few months later of "an unforeseen / brain malignancy," might have come from the typewriter Doc Williams kept in his office, on which he wrote poetry between appointments.[53]

Monotonous, Williams called these early poems by Ginsberg, and they are. *Empty Mirror* is an in-between book: Ginsberg has got rid of English conventions, is trying to be "objective" in the manner of Williams— "no ideas but in things." On the whole the effect is a drab, depressing realism.

Two poems, however, go beyond this. From his reading of Artaud and other Surrealists, Ginsberg saw that you could admit anything into the poem, however crazy it seemed. There was even a precedent for this in English literature, the psalms of Christopher Smart. Smart had included everything he knew in his locality together with the City of God; there was no dividing line of here and there, life and vision—everything that lives is holy.

Ginsberg tried writing like Smart. The poem, titled "Hymn," stands out from the drabness of *Empty Mirror*:

> No hyacinthine imagination can express this clock of
>   meat bleakly pining for its sweet immaterial
>   paradise which I have celebrated in one gone
>   dithyramb after another and have elevated to
>   that highest place in the mind's angelical empyrean
>   which shall in the course of hot centuries to
>   come come to be known as the clock of light . . .[54]

It is only a step from this to a poem that is absolutely Ginsberg's—the title, "Paterson"; the date, 1949:

> What do I want in these rooms papered with visions of money?
> How much can I make by cutting my hair? If I put new heels on
>   my shoes
> bathe my body reeking of masturbation and sweat, layer upon
>   layer of excrement
> dried in employment bureaus, magazine hallways, statistical
>   cubicles, factory stairways,
> cloakrooms of the smiling gods of psychiatry;
> if in antechambers I face the presumption of department store
>   supervisory employees,
> old clerks in their asylums of fat, the slobs and dumbbells
>   of the ego with money and power
> to hire and fire and make and break and fart and justify their
>   reality of wrath
> and rumor of wrath to wrath-weary man,

what war I enter and for what a prize! the dead prick of
   commonplace obsession,
harridan vision of electricity at night and daylight misery of
   thumb-sucking rage . . .[55]

With "Paterson" Ginsberg discovered his own voice. Though he would
go on to write more impressive poems, "Paterson" signaled his emer-
gence. Though he would play many variations, "Paterson" remains the
touchstone of his style.

He has gone beyond Williams, the short line that Williams preferred,
being a cautious man. The rhythms of Ginsberg's poem are a chant; the
long, rushing lines overwhelm the listener and make him share the poet's
emotion. Unlike Williams, too, is the language, ranging from mention of
factory stairways to Golgotha. Williams was a pragmatist and nowhere
in his writing admits any visionary or hallucinated speech.

In June 1966, Ginsberg testified before a Senate subcommittee on his
experience with drugs. He said that drugs had helped him to break out of
stereotypes of feeling, to release his feelings for other human beings,
especially women, and for nature—feelings that had been atrophied by
the mechanization of modern culture. The psychedelics had helped to end
the Cold War atmosphere of fear and repression. "Now so many people," he told his audience, "have experienced some new sense of openness, and lessening of prejudice and hostility to new experience through
LSD, that I think we may expect the new generation to push for an environment less rigid, mechanical, less dominated by cold-war habits."

Generally, Tytell remarks, Ginsberg used drugs as an aid to "releasing
blocked aspects of his consciousness which are expressed in his poetry,
like the Moloch vision in 'Howl' which was induced by peyote, or 'Kaddish,' written while using amphetamines."[56]

Ginsberg once listed the drugs and hallucinogens he had used: 'Peyote,
Mescaline, Ayahuasca, Lysergic Acid, Hashish concentrates, & Psylocy-
bin Mushrooms & Strobiscopic lights."[57]

One day when he was living on the Lower East Side in New York,
Timothy Leary paid him a visit. Leary had heard of Ginsberg's use of
drugs, and he was concerned how to handle "this new LSD thing, concerned that it be done with sincerity and openness rather than as some
sort of manipulative scientific game." Ginsberg thought Leary a bit naïve
—"he had no idea that every poet in San Francisco had lived with Indians and taken peyote and mescaline long ago. Or that everybody was
smoking pot. He'd never smoked pot." Ginsberg undertook to enlighten

him. They had some pot and a long talk. Then Ginsberg went with Leary up to Harvard where he saw Leary's big professor's house, and everybody wandering around stoned, "like it was some happy cocktail party" —which, Ginsberg says, shocked him at first, because he thought of himself as a "serious, religious meditator."

Leary couldn't imagine that there would be any "academic opposition" to his proselytizing the use of LSD. He was thinking, "We'll turn on Schlesinger and then we'll turn on Kennedy." To calm him down Ginsberg suggested turning on artists first, people like Robert Lowell and Dizzy Gillespie. So one week Leary came down to New York with some acid, and he and Ginsberg made a list of names and went around turning people on.[58]

Ginsberg claims to have gained superior or unusual insight, on occasion, through the use of drugs; consequently he has not been bound by the law or by what people think. Kramer has an anecdote that shows this: Ginsberg has a friend, Maretta, who is following the precepts of the religion she adopted in India. Her friend the Swami is known to have "a rather uncharitable opinion" of meat, spirits, marijuana, and psychedelics. Maretta speaks of this as follows: "There's the vow to avoid intoxicants as beclouding the mind . . . which you might say I break all the time with hashish. That bothered me for a bit in India, but I thought about it and figured that since I didn't *think* about hash as an intoxicant, and I didn't use it to get beclouded precisely, then, man, I wasn't breaking any vows."

When she has said this she looks inquiringly at Ginsberg, who says "*Om*" and bursts out laughing.

Any discussion of Ginsberg's poetry must take his use of drugs into account. The excited tone of some of his writing is like that of a man in a state of hallucination. The poem called "Wales Visitation," he tells us, was written on LSD.[59] Drugs made it easier for him to express his personality and confirmed him in the belief that the self is the center of everything.

Turning to the poems he wrote between 1948 and 1952 we can see the difference these experiments made. The following passage is typical of the drab realism that pervades the 1948 poems:

> I sat on my bunk, three tiers up
> next to the ceiling,
> looking down the grey aisles.
> Old, crippled, dumb people were
>
> bent over sewing . . .[60]

Compare this with the second half of "Paterson," dated 1949. This is a different kind of writing altogether. Three drugs are mentioned: heroin, marijuana, and peyote, and the writing appears to be an attempt to recapture a "high." It speaks of being crucified and coming back to the world:

> screaming and dancing in praise of Eternity annihilating
> the sidewalk, annihilating reality,
> screaming and dancing against the orchestra in the
> destructible ballroom of the world,
> blood streaming from my belly and shoulders
> flooding the city with its hideous ecstasy, rolling over
> the pavements and highways
> by the bayoux and forests and derricks leaving my flesh
> and my bones hanging on the trees.[61]

Drugs remove the boundary between what is real and what is not.

Drug users describe a state of "pure awareness" in which the user is "completely and vividly aware of his experience, but there are no processes of thinking, manipulating, or interpreting going on. The sensations fill the person's attention, which is passive but absorbed in what is occurring, which is usually experienced as intense and immediate. Pure awareness is experienced without associations to what is there . . . objects are experienced as sensory qualities, without the intrusion of interpretation."[62]

Ginsberg experimented with one drug and another, and sought to convey his perceptions directly, without interpretation. A poet must use words, but his words would be as close to vision as possible; he would write with sounds and images. If need be, with cries and howls.

Kerouac helped: in 1952 or 1953 he developed a theory of instantaneous composition, "that the gesture he made in language was his mortal gesture, and therefore unchangeable." Robert Duncan told Ginsberg the same thing: "Well, look, I've taken a step across the room, how can I go back and revise my step? I've already done it." This, Ginsberg says, made complete sense. "Obviously if you've written a sentence it's there in eternity."[63]

Commenting on a taped conversation between Kerouac and Neal Cassady, in *Visions of Cody,* Ginsberg says, ". . . at that point in progress of Jack's art he began transcribing *first* thoughts of true mind in American speech. . . ." Kerouac placed "the taped actual teahead-high speech of his model-hero . . . in the center of his book as an actual sample of the Reality he was otherwise Rhapsodizing." At that time "Neal was smoking experimentally excessively, that is *all* the time, & experiencing such

aphasia or language disconnection & emotional alienation as that experiment might cause, as well as awe at the emptiness of mind which simul-
taneous is both mystical Virtue, & psychological pathology. 'Man I'm
thinking. I've just spent the last minute thinking and I had a complete
block.' "

Ginsberg is aware that the tape can be "hung up and boring," but he
thinks it is art anyway. It is "as 'twere breakthru & historic first inci-
dence of the later universal American style of 'Anything we *do* is art.'

"The art lies in the consciousness of doing the thing, in the attention
to the happening, in the sacramentalization of everyday reality, the God-
worship in the present conversation, no matter what."[64]

He states that he has learned a great deal from Kerouac. "Jack always
accused me of stealing from him, & rereading 20 years later I see now
how much it was true, my Greyhound poem taken from his description of
dock-loading *President Adams* for instance, the very syntax & phrasing
is similar, 'cept his is half decade earlier: 'There's ammo in the hold and
a special locker full of some priceless cargo bound for Penang, probably
champagne . . . Valentine's Meat Juice from richmond . . .—barrels for
L.A.' Later see 'whole families eating in Clifton's' similar to my Supermarket's 'whole families shopping at night.' His phrasing was archetypal
for this moment of consciousness enlarging in wonderment to notice
Americanist minute particulars aside from the centers of Attention-
Power. . . ."

Further down the page: "Then I discover that I influenced him back.
The 'monkey image' was a robot fortuneteller in monkey plaster brown
face that selected your fate cards on Times' Square Pokerino chance-
game arcade."[65]

In 1952 Ginsberg tried without success to get *Empty Mirror* published,
but even the introduction by Williams did not help. *New Directions* accepted some of his prose poems for their annual issue, but he was dissatisfied. "I must stop *playing* with my life in a disappointed gray world,"
he wrote Cassady.[66]

He had to figure "How to get out of fantasy world—stop all phantasy!
live in the physical & real sensation situation, moment to moment, seize
opportunities, take offers you want.

"I must put down every recurrent thought."[67]

At fourteen, he wrote in his journal, he had been an introvert, an
atheist, a Communist and a Jew, and still wanted to be President of the
United States. At nineteen he had been a practicing homosexual and believed in a "supreme reality." He was an anarchist and hipster, totally

apolitical—he had wanted to be a great poet instead. At twenty-two he was a hallucinating mystic—he believed in the City of God and wanted to be a saint. A year later he was a criminal, a despairing sinner, a dope fiend—"I wanted to get to reality." Then, after being a jailbird, he was a schizoid screwball in the bughouse. "I got layed, girls, I was being psychoanalyzed." Now, at twenty-six, he was shy, he was going out with girls, he was writing poetry, he was a freelance literary agent and a registered Democrat. He wanted to find a job. "Who," he wrote in his journal, "cares?"[68]

It seemed that nothing could be done in New York for the present. In 1950 he had seen something of Mexico on a trip with Lucien Carr, and he would like to visit Neal who was living in California. So in December, 1953, he set out, hitchhiking down to Florida. He spent Christmas there with Burroughs and his family. Then, by way of Cuba, he arrived in Yucatan.

One day when he was looking at the Mayan ruins near Palenque he met a woman named Karena Shields who claimed to have played Jane in Tarzan movies, and she invited him to stay on her plantation in Chiapas.

He stayed six months in Mexico. The journal of this period shows him making an attempt to observe the outer world in keeping with his resolution to "live in the physical & real sensation situation." At moments his notes verge on what will be most original in his later writing, a sense of everything being perceived physically and, at the same time, as a metaphysical presence.

Because town on slope & possible to view it from uphill or bridge above on either side get impression of curious smallness and intimacy to the terrain— and vasty armadas of white fragmentary clouds in bright sky are real blue transparency—a few pink trees in flower—recurring crow of cocks from this side and that challenging and responding in various cockly hoarse tones as if they existed in a world of pure intuitive sound communicating to anonymous hidden familiar chickensouls from hill to hill.[69]

He also made notes of his dreams, analyzing himself. He had had some experience of psychoanalysis in New York. His first analyst, a Reichian, had dismissed him for smoking marijuana. After some time had gone by, the day he heard Blake's voice reciting "Ah! Sun-Flower" he telephoned this doctor and told him that he had to see him, for William Blake was in the room. The doctor shouted, "You must be crazy!" and hung up. His second experience was with a psychiatrist at Columbia Presbyterian who also thought he was crazy. The third time he had better luck: there was a young Freudian at the same hospital with whom he got along. This doctor changed Ginsberg's diagnosis from psychotic or schizophrenic to "extreme but socially average neurosis," which gave him a lot of confidence—he now had formal proof that he wasn't crazy. But the young doctor married and moved to Park Avenue, and raised his rates. He advised Ginsberg to get a better job.[70]

Ginsberg's interest in dreams was poetic rather than Freudian. The most important thing about dreams was the existence in them of "magical emotion, to which waking Consciousness is not ordinarily sentient. Awe of vast constructions; familiar eternal halls of buildings; sexual intensity in rapport; deathly music; grief awakenings, perfected lodgings."[71]

He returned to the United States, crossing the border at Mexicali, "alone naked with knapsack, watch, camera, poem, beard." As he thought of Cassady he noted that there was less of a quickening at heart than before.

He found Neal in San Jose preoccupied with his own concerns as a husband and father, and apparently not happy. "Neal who has money & love is desperate at the gate of heaven...."

He doubted that Neal even wanted him to be there. Neal's wife did, perhaps, as long as he was not too intimate with Neal. He felt himself sacrificing part of his being to Neal, but no real return on his part—just money and some time and attention, given offhand and in patronizing ways. But no sacrifice of his real being or self. "I feel," Ginsberg wrote, "like a strange idiot, standing there among wife & children all to whom he gives needs of affection and attention, aching for some special side extra sacrifice of attention to me."[72]

He gave it up finally and went to San Francisco. There, as he tells it, he worked for a year in market research, and had two secretaries, "and strode down Wall St. (Montgomery here) whistling in the morning."[73]

He had arrived at the furthest distance from his true self—whereupon he did an about-face. One day he was telling his psychiatrist, a man named Hicks, how dissatisfied he was with his life, and Hicks said, "What would you like to do? What is your desire, really?" Ginsberg said that he didn't think the doctor would find it very healthy, but he would like to stop working forever, never do anything like the work he was doing now, and do nothing but write poetry and spend the day outdoors and go to museums and see friends. He would like to live with someone, maybe even a man, and "explore relationships that way." And he would like to cultivate his perceptions, "the visionary thing in me."

"Well," said Hicks, "why don't you?"

That night Ginsberg wrote a report to his company pointing out how much they would save by having a small IBM machine to replace him and the two secretaries. The report served its purpose—he was fired.[74]

He lived on unemployment insurance for half a year. He planned on taking an M.A. at Berkeley, but quit after a month. Meanwhile he was reading: Christopher Smart, Apollinaire, Lorca, Hart Crane, Catullus, Dylan Thomas. The *Journals* list forty authors he read between January and July of 1954, including Lawrence, W. H. Auden, Kant, Bertrand Russell, Céline, Gertrude Stein, Karen Horney, T. S. Eliot, the *Bhagavad Gita*, Plato, Pound, Dante, and Rimbaud. It seems likely that he read like Doctor Johnson, the parts that interested him, forgoing the rest.

At the urging of Kerouac he had tried to understand Zen Buddhism, and he had looked at Japanese and Chinese art. The *Journals* show him trying his hand at writing haiku. This was important—the ellipsis in the haiku would be a model for the ellipses in *Howl*.[75]

> Drinking my tea
> Without sugar—
> No difference.[76]

> My mother's ghost:
> the first thing I found
> in the living room.[77]

He made another, equally important discovery: Walt Whitman, "a vast mountain so big I never saw him before."

He came to know the San Francisco poets who were writing "a kind of buddhist influenced post Pound post Williams classicism full of independence and humor AND gift of gab, native wordslinging."[78]

And he found a partner, Peter Orlovsky. "We made a vow to each other," Ginsberg says, "that he could own me, my mind and everything I knew, and my body, and I could own him and all he knew and all his body; and that we would give each other ourselves, so that we possessed each other as property, to do everything we wanted to, sexually or intellectually, and in a sense explore each other until we reached the mystical 'X' together, emerging two merged souls."

In the fall of 1955 Ginsberg organized a poetry reading at the Six Gallery in San Francisco. Kenneth Rexroth read his own poetry and introduced the other poets: Allen Ginsberg, Philip Lamantia, Michael McClure, Gary Snyder, and Philip Whalen. On that night Ginsberg read "Howl" for the first time. The reading caused a sensation. "Except for the response to Dylan Thomas' readings in America, never before had a modern audience reacted so passionately, or identified so completely with a poet's message."[79]

In a letter to John Hollander, who had called *Howl* a "dreadful little volume," Ginsberg explained his aesthetics.[80] He adjured Hollander not to harden his heart, not to retire into the ignorance of his Columbia education, talking about "tradition," not to be like Norman Podhoretz, who had written against "bop prosody" in *Partisan Review*: "unmitigated stupid ignorant ill-willed inept vanity . . . stuck in his own hideous world." He wasn't trying to persuade Hollander that free verse was the only path of prosodaic experiment, or that Williams was a saint, or that he had some horrible magic secret; he just wanted Hollander to understand what others beside himself were trying to do, and not to get in the way—even encourage where he could see some value. "You're in a position to encourage, you teach, you shouldn't hand down limited ideas to younger minds."

The whole poem ("Howl"), the whole book, was an experiment in what could be done with the long line. He had become sick and tired of short-line free verse as not expressionistic enough, not swinging enough, unable to develop a powerful enough rhythm. He had started writing Part I "accidentally," in solitude, diddling around with the form, "thinking it couldn't be published anyway (queer content my parents shouldn't see, etc.)." In the writing he changed his mind about "measure." "Part one uses repeated base . . . as a sort of kithera BLANG, homeric (in my imagination) to mark off each statement, with rhythmic unit." The experiment consisted of writing longer and shorter variations on the fixed base, the principle being that each line had to be contained "within the elastic of one breath."

He used "suitable punctuatory expressions" when he had to build a longer line, let off steam with a jazzy ride.[81]

HOWL
for Carl Solomon

I saw the best minds of my generation destroyed by madness, starving
    hysterical naked,
dragging themselves through the negro streets at dawn looking for an angry
    fix,
angelheaded hipsters burning for the ancient heavenly connection to the
    starry dynamo in the machinery of night,
who poverty and tatters and hollow-eyed and high sat up smoking in the
    supernatural darkness of cold-water flats floating across the tops of cities
    contemplating jazz,

who bared their brains to Heaven under the El and saw Mohammedan
  angels staggering on tenement roofs illuminated,
who passed through universities with radiant cool eyes hallucinating Ar-
  kansas and Blake-light tragedy among the scholars of war . . .[82]

In Part II the basic repeated word is "Moloch," and it is repeated
within the line—the rhythm depends on this. The long lines are broken
into short phrases with rhythmical punctuation: "!" The lines are longer
than in Part I: "a sort of free verse prose poetry STANZA form invented
or used here." This builds to a climax ("Visions! omens!") and falls off
in a coda.

Part III may be an original invention: "I thought so then but this type
of thinking is vain & shallow anyway." As in a litany there is a basic
phrase, "I'm with you in Rockland," followed by a response, "where
you're madder than I am." The responses get longer, building to the climax of a long long long line, the penultimate line, too long for one
breath. Then the poem opens out and gives the answer, "O starry-
spangled shock of mercy the eternal war is here. . . ."

All this is rather like a jazz mass: "I mean the conception of rhythm
not derived from jazz directly, but if you listen to jazz you get the idea
(in fact specifically old trumpet solo on a JATP Can't Get Started
side). . . ."

The "Footnote" is "too lovely & serious a joke to try to explain." The
rhythmic pattern is similar to that in the Moloch section. The section is
dedicated to his mother who died in the madhouse and, says Ginsberg,
"it says I loved her anyway & that even in worst conditions life is holy."

Such is the structure of "Howl," and in his letter to Hollander Ginsberg expresses his resentment of those who have refused to see it, who
come up to him with a silly look in their eye and begin bullshitting about
morals and sociology and tradition and technique. "Nobody's interested
in literature," he exclaims, "in technique, all they think about is their
goddam lousy ideas of what they preconceive writing to be about and
IM SICK OF LISTENING TO THAT AND READING ABOUT THAT
AND UNLESS THERE IS MORE COOPERATION FROM THE SUP-
POSEDLY RESPONSIBLE PARTIES IN UNIVERSITIES & MAGA-
ZINES I ABSOLUTELY CUT OUT AND REFUSE TO GIVE MY
HEART WRUNG POEMS TO THE DIRTY HANDS AND MINDS OF
THESE BASTARDS AND THEY CAN TAKE THEIR FUCKING literary
tradition AND SHOVE IT UP THEIR ASS—I don't need them and they
don't need me and I'm sick of putting myself out and being put down
and hit on the head by jerks who have not interest but their ridiculous

devilish social careers and MONEY MONEY MONEY which is the root of the EVIL here in America and I'M MAD."[83]

"315,000 copies in print" reads the copyright page of *Howl and Other Poems*. And this does not say it all, for thousands have heard the poems who never bought the book. Ginsberg has surely triumphed over his critics, if popularity means anything.

But there are those who still do not like the poem. In the first place they do not like what it says. "Howl" expresses an alienated view of society and elects, as a band of saints, the rejected, the deviant, the criminal, and the insane. It is a paranoid view of life in the United States.

This is to treat the statements as though they really meant something. As we have seen, Ginsberg objected to people who spoke to him about "morals and sociology"—he wanted the poem read for its technique. But how is one to avoid reading "Howl" as morals and sociology? Every page is an expression of morals and sociology. The poem is as full of moral attitudes as a sermon by a Baptist preacher, only in this case morals have been stood on their head.

The trouble with "Howl" is that it is so little a work of imagination and so much an expression of Ginsberg's opinions.

This is not true of other poems in the book: "A Supermarket in California," "Sunflower Sutra," and "America." In the first Ginsberg manages to get outside himself and use his imagination; his affinity with Whitman enables him to put himself in the old man's shoes:

> I saw you, Walt Whitman, childless, lonely old
> grubber, poking among the meats in the refrigerator
> and eyeing the grocery boys.[84]

Here there is detachment from self and contact with humanity, and the sign of it is humor.

"Sunflower Sutra" contains some of Ginsberg's best descriptive writing, perhaps owing to the example of Kerouac who appears in the poem.

> . . . the gray Sunflower poised against the sunset, crackly
> bleak and dusty with the smut and smog and smoke of
> olden locomotives in its eye—
> corolla of bleary spikes pushed down and broken like a
> battered crown, seeds fallen out of its face, soon-
> to-be-toothless mouth of sunny air, sunrays obliterated
> on its hairy head like a dried wire spiderweb,
> leaves stuck out like arms out of the stem, gestures from
> the sawdust root, broken pieces of plaster fallen out
> of the black twigs, a dead fly in its ear,

Unholy battered old thing you were, my sunflower O my soul,
   I loved you then![85]

The care with which these things are described gives an impression of spiritual insight. Mere expressions of feeling would not have done so. Attention to what is actually present is the only way that states of "altered consciousness" can be suggested in writing.

"America" like "Howl" deals with the human condition, but it is very different. The poet of "Howl" speaks directly to the reader, asserting his view of things; in "America" the poet is part of the world he describes, a character in the drama, ineffectual and bewildered. The view is expressed through this character, and is taken as part of the character. It has the reality of fiction.

The character is not defeated. He is willing to try. He still believes in America. This gives him a Chaplinesque pathos. "America" is one of the truly humorous poems, the verse equivalent of a story by Gogol. In order to write it Ginsberg had to understand himself and admit the middle-class man who owned a gray flannel suit and had two secretaries and walked on Montgomery Street. He had to admit to being the son of Louis and Naomi Ginsberg. Then he could write the final lines of "America."

> America you don't really want to go to war.
> America it's them bad Russians.
> The Russia wants to eat us alive. The Russia's power mad.
>   She wants to take our cars from out our garages.
> Her wants to grab Chicago. Her needs a Red Readers' Digest.
>   Her wants our auto plants in Siberia. Him big bureau-
>   cracy running our fillingstations.
> That no good. Ugh. Him make Indians learn read. Him need
>   big black niggers. Hah. Her make us all work sixteen
>   hours a day. Help.
> America this is quite serious.
> America this is the impression I get from looking in the
>   television set.
> America is this correct?
> I'd better get right down to the job.
> It's true I don't want to join the Army or turn lathes
>   in precision parts factories, I'm nearsighted and
>   psychopathic anyway.
> America I'm putting my queer shoulder to the wheel.[86]

In "Kaddish" (1959) Ginsberg had a subject that engaged all his creative powers. A lament for his mother, Naomi, the poem also depicts his background, a Jewish family with a history of intellectual striving, Communism, playing the violin, et cetera. The subject is very rich, and Ginsberg puts aside his preoccupation with self in order to do it justice. "Kaddish" is written in the long lines and "prose poetry STANZA form" he claims to have invented, with ellipses that suggest the jumps of a mind actually thinking.

Tytell speaks of Ginsberg's use of ellipsis as though it were new: "the sacrifice of what Ginsberg called "syntactical sawdust,' articles, prepositions, and connectives that impeded the flow and did not actually occur in the mind." And he goes on to say that the result is "a richer texture and greater density of language."[87]

But this way of writing had been practiced by French poets since the beginning of the century; Futurists, Dadaists, and Surrealists were less "syntactical" than Ginsberg. As for "a richer texture and greater density," the impression of density in writing is created by penetration into the subject, not by leaving out articles, prepositions, and connectives.

Tytell says, "As the mind does not perceive in the orderly arrangement of expository prose, it becomes almost a pretentious fiction to write a poem or a story as if it did." This expresses a view of art that was common in the 1960s; it assumes that the aim of writing is to represent the working of the writer's mind, and the phrase "pretentious fiction" suggests that only a literal account of the writer's life is admissible.

Thus Puritanism, the spirit that suspects that any kind of imagining is evil, that banned plays and made it wicked to read anything but the Bible, comes full circle in America as the voice of the avant-garde.[88]

There is a narrative line in "Kaddish" not found in Ginsberg's other writing, and there is also the portrayal of a person not himself, Naomi Ginsberg, shown in her insanity but also evoked as a young bride:

> O Russian faced, woman on the grass, your long black
> hair is crowned with flowers, the mandolin is on your knees—
> Communist beauty, sit here married in the summer among
> daisies, promised happiness at hand—[89]

The poem relates how Ginsberg took his mother out to the country, at the onset of one of her spells of madness, and left her in a rest home, and returned by himself to Paterson. Then Naomi became violent and her husband had to go and get her.

> Louis in pyjamas listening to phone, frightened—do now?—Who could know?—my fault, delivering her to solitude?—sitting in the dark room on the sofa, trembling, to figure out—[90]

The episode culminates with Naomi having an attack of paranoia in a drugstore in Lakewood—the people in the drugstore astounded, Louis humiliated, and Naomi rising to heights of madness, terrible to see:

Naomi, Naomi—sweating, bulge-eyed, fat, the dress unbuttoned at one side— hair over brow, her stocking hanging evilly on her legs—screaming for a blood transfusion—one righteous hand upraised—a shoe in it—barefoot in the Pharmacy—[91]

"Kaddish" gives the impression of lives being revealed for the first time— not only the lives of Naomi, Louis, Allen, and Eugene, but many others who have never spoken of their shame and grief and humiliation. Before "Kaddish" no one would have thought that these things could be said in a poem.[92]

In the nineteenth century, Romantic authors praised nature and celebrated the individual. The artist with his unusual powers of feeling was regarded as a hero. But by the middle of the century disillusionment had set in: that is, artists were disillusioned. Science and industry were making great advances, and people seemed to think little of art, only of making money.

Zola and the naturalists felt that the claims of art might be revived by adopting the methods of scientific enquiry; the novelist, by showing the principles of human behavior, could serve a moral purpose. There was a catch, however: when the day came that human passions were understood and regulated, there would no longer be any need of art.

There was another point of view: art should not cleave to life but suggest a higher reality. Flaubert said: "What seems beautiful to me, what I should like to write, is a book about nothing, a book dependent on nothing external, which would be held together by the strength of its style, just as the earth, suspended in the void, depends on nothing external for its support; a book which would have almost no subject, or at least in which the subject is almost invisible, if such a thing is possible. . . ."[93]

Writers such as Flaubert concentrated on the internal organization of their poems and stories. This could not be maintained absolutely—their works have discernible points of connection with life—nevertheless, this way of working made a difference. Writers who believed in the impersonality and independent reality of the work of art produced a number of masterpieces, among them James Joyce's *Ulysses* and T. S. Eliot's *The Waste Land*.

There was a reaction: Henry Miller, for example, describes his impatience: "There were plenty of writers who could drag a thing out to the end without letting go the reins; what we needed was a man, like myself for instance, who didn't give a fuck what happened. Dostoievsky hadn't gone quite far enough. I was for straight gibberish. One should go cuckoo! People have had enough of plot and character. Life isn't in the upper story: life is here and now, any time you say the word, any time you let rip."[94]

The assumption here is that life determines art, and other writers after World War II would agree. The war may have helped, making them impatient with the laborious construction of art objects that might vanish overnight. In the world of concentration camps and atom bombs it had become impossible to believe in the permanence of art. There was a shift to a different way of thinking: the self was the only thing you could be sure of. You could know your own feelings—for the moment.

Talk of art was beside the point. "I'm not concerned," Ginsberg said, "with creating a work of art . . . And I don't want to predefine it . . . what I do is try to forget entirely about the whole world of art, and just get directly to the . . . fastest and most direct expression of what it is I got in heart-mind. Trusting that if my heart-mind is shapely, the objects or words, the word sequences, the sentences, the lines, the song, will also be shapely."[95]

This was the opposite of T. S. Eliot's idea of poetry. Eliot once remarked: "Poetry is not a turning loose of emotion, but an escape from emotion; it is not the expression of personality, but an escape from personality."[96] For thirty years Eliot's ideas had dominated the writing and teaching of poetry, but now, in a new generation, personality came back with a vengeance.

"Kaddish" is a work of art in the Modernist sense, with characters and a plot; "Howl" is post-Modernist, a direct expression of the writer's personality. Moreover, Ginsberg sees himself as a bard and prophet. "All you have to know is what you actually think & feel & every sentence will be a revelation."[97] So that besides expressing Ginsberg's personality, "Howl" reveals eternal truth.

Dickstein is probably right: it would be a mistake to regard Ginsberg as a merely "confessional" writer like Anne Sexton. Through his poems Ginsberg aimed to render an account of his spiritual development and to be speaking for the multitudes.[98]

In the 1960s he appeared to be doing so. Of the many poets who took part in poetry readings Ginsberg was far the best known. No gathering or march to protest against the war in Vietnam was complete without the familiar figure of Allen Ginsberg. He was known to newspaper readers and watchers of television—the first American poet ever to be a celebrity.

We heard that he had been made to leave Havana. That the police had put him on a plane out of Czechoslovakia. It was true: 100,000 people in Prague had crowned him Kral Majales, King of the May, and he had been ordered to leave and driven to the airport by detectives wearing business suits. Neither in Havana nor Prague were his views on total liberation welcome; he represented total liberty, to use drugs, for example, and free speech, and neither of these were permitted under Communist regimes. Kral Majales had to leave; he went rejoicing and celebrating himself. He said that he was neither Communist nor Capitalist, but himself, a man of superior spiritual insight.

> And the Communists have nothing to offer but fat cheeks
>   and eyeglasses and lying policemen
> and the Capitalists proffer Napalm and money in green
>   suitcases to the Naked . . .
> . . . .
> And I am the King of May, which is the power of sexual
>   youth,
> and I am the King of May, which is industry in eloquence and
>   action in amour,
> and I am the King of May, which is long hair of Adam and
>   the Beard of my own body
> and I am the King of May, which is Kral Majales in the
>   Czechoslovakian tongue,
> and I am the King of May, which is old Human poesy . . .[99]

Ginsberg was one of the older generation who were elected by youth to lead them through the sixties. He smoked pot with them and talked about being queer, and said that he was learning to make it with chicks too, with the help of LSD. "It's like apple pie and the American flag."[100]

He told them about poetry, who to read: Blake and Whitman, Pound and Williams. Not T. S. Eliot (they groaned) or cats like Wyatt and Donne.

Truth to tell, they didn't read much. They hadn't ever read Eliot, and Blake's prophetic books or Pound's *Cantos* would have been much too demanding. They were of the first generation that had grown up with television, accustomed to gaze at the bright screen with its flitting shadows and sounds. Middle-class white boys and girls from apartment buildings in Manhattan, houses with lawns and trees in Grand Rapids, from California redwood villas with picture windows.

They were thinking, Marshall McLuhan told them, in a new way.

Reading was "linear"; when you read, one thought came after another, but they were thinking in patterns induced by electronics. McLuhan seemed to think this was fine. In any case, it was what was happening.

Listening to Ginsberg they felt they were into the new age. Young kids, he told them, were beginning to break through the shell of consciousness that had grown up in America in the last half century, and find themselves born into a new space-age universe. It was a little scary to discover they weren't the people they thought they were and their teachers and parents weren't the people they grew up with and that maybe "the whole universe *doesn't exist even*." But there were ways of handling it: some kinds of stable rituals were useful, whether they were American Indian or Jewish or Christian or Tibetan or Zen Buddhist or Islamic.

He spoke of the different *saddhanas* or disciplines or rituals, of what the *Yorubas* were up to, and what the *Balubas* were up to, and what the South American herb doctors were up to, and the Hindus, and what the Zen Buddhists were doing sitting around on their behinds.[101]

Ginsberg told them about the Crazy Wisdom of the Whispering Tradition of Kargupta (or other) school of Red Hat Sect Tibetan Vajrayana Path Mahayana Buddhist Doctrine.[102]

He told them how in Cuba the remnants of the Yoruba tribe of Nigeria had a thing called Santería, which was the worship of various gods: Chango, a phallic god, and Yemaya, the Blue-Bodied Goddess of the Ocean, female. They worshiped their gods through the drum; the priests made ritual patterns on the drum, and the worshipers danced before the drum. What he saw there had been very similar to what he noticed in the caves of Liverpool where electric rock groups were dancing. The drums and the electronic instruments set up vibrations which penetrated the lower abdomen. The dancing patterns of the Liverpool rock dancers were like the dancing patterns of the Yorubas, communal rather than individual. Also, the Yorubas would flip out and go into trance states, just as the kids flipped out and went into trance states for George Harrison or John Lennon. It all made sense, for the Africans brought music to America when they were brought over as slaves. This evolved into other forms with other instruments, but the rhythms remained the same.

Jazz went upriver from New Orleans, to Chicago, to New York, and over the sea to Liverpool, and emerged as *the children's sacramental assembly of worship*, because rock's the one thing the flower children do take seriously. In America and England it's the one major social form that has qualities of Invocation of the Divine, as in Dylan or Donovan or the Beatles . . . they're all preaching messages about tolerance, transcendency, and ecstasy. What has happened is that the basic religion of the slaves, because it was genuine, because it was real "soul," is finally being accepted by the white children and is waking them up spiritually.[103]

He ended in the Hindu way, hands pressed together, head bowed to the god within.

"Ideally," Ginsberg told an interviewer, "the ambition, my childhood desire to write during a prophetic illuminative seizure. That's the idea: to be in a state of such complete blissful consciousness that any language emanating from that state will strike a responsive chord of blissful consciousness from any other body into which the words enter and vibrate."[104]

And if it didn't come at all, then that was the illumination. These days he wasn't writing enough. Writing was like prayer, a yoga that evoked Lord mind. It took walking all day to get deep into the state of consciousness in which "Howl" and "Kaddish" and other poems were written. But now he was spending all his time and energy on other things. On music. He spent more time composing music—he spent more time composing music and putting Blake's songs to music than composing his own poetry. He also had to answer letters—there were maybe twenty a day—and this diverted him from what he ought to be doing. He was going to withdraw from it: "hereby as a signal I'm making an appeal for people to stop writing me letters."

He was involved in a project for the P.E.N. Club; he was a member of the Executive Board and Freedom to Read Committee, in which he was surveying the government's attack on sixty percent of the underground newspapers; he was involved in a research project investigating dope peddling by the Narcotics Bureau and the CIA involvement with traffic of opium in Indochina.

Everybody's busy. "A total proliferation of signals in every direction, and photographs. Nobody can read or keep track of everything any more."

What difference does it make, one little problem about little magazines or the CIA peddling dope, or the poisoning of the oceans and the atmosphere, or the population overleaping itself, when every newspaper that reports it is a further drain on the tree life, and using batteries to discuss it is a drain on electric power, and every time you switch on a recording machine the flowers burn. Maybe every time I open my mouth, he said, it's polluting the environment. It's hard to know what to do.

The only way out was to grow your own food and compose in an art form that didn't require material consumption. In other words, poetry that could be memorized, bypassing print and television and radio. The oral tradition, right back to Neolithic, an art just requiring our bodies.[105]

Jack Kerouac died and was buried in Lowell, Massachusetts.

> Jack no more'll step off at Penn Station
> anonymous erranded, eat sandwich
>   & drink beer near New Yorker Hotel or walk
> under the shadow of Empire State.
>
> Didn't we stare at each other length of the car
>   & read headlines in faces thru Newspaper Holes?
> Sexual cocked & horny bodied young, look
>   at beauteous Rimbaud & Sweet Jenny
>   riding to class from Columbus Circle . . .[106]

Neal Cassady, the great experiencer and Midwest driver and talker, ingested a mixture of alcohol and barbiturates and was found dead on a railroad track outside San Miguel de Allende, Mexico.

Allen was said to be living on a farm that he owned in Cherry Valley. He also had an apartment on the Lower East Side in New York. Then we heard that he was associated with some Tibetan monks who had started an institute in Colorado. I saw him a few years ago at the annual meeting of the American Academy and Institute of Arts and Letters where they give out prizes. Ginsberg is a member of the Academy. With his beard, bald head and intent brown eyes he is definitely a personality, as American as apple pie and the flag.

Black,
Banded
with
Yellow

*O*TTO EMIL PLATH was born in Grabow, in the territory separated from Germany by the Treaty of Versailles to form the Polish Corridor. He used to say that his parents were German but that he had a Polish grandmother.

His nationality was uncertain. Yet, more than most men, he would have liked everything to be straightforward. *Recht ... link ... recht!*

His father was a skilled mechanic who earned a living as a blacksmith. When Otto was sixteen his grandparents, who had emigrated to the United States, paid the passage for him to come over. He lived in New York for a year, working for an uncle who owned a food and liquor store and, by special permission, sitting in on English classes in a grade school. He applied himself so well that by the end of the year he had completed all eight grades.[1]

Otto's grandparents were farmers in Wisconsin. They agreed to put him through Northwestern University on the understanding that he would enter the Lutheran ministry. Otto did well in college, majoring in classical languages. But he was not fitted to be a minister. He much preferred science.

When he was a boy in Grabow he had a craving for sweet things. So he devised a way of getting wild honey by tracking bees to their hives underground. He would lie on the earth and suck up the honey through a straw. Then he moved some bees into cigar boxes that he kept in the garden so as to have a constant supply. People called him the Bee King. From that time on he had a special interest in bees and entomology.

At the seminary, however, he found that the reading of Darwin was forbidden. Moreover, his fellow students were not sincere. They had not had a calling or been given a sign from God. After six months he decided not to go into the ministry, whereupon his grandparents struck his name from the family Bible.

Later on Otto's parents came to America, with his three brothers and two sisters, but he would have very little to do with them.

There were setbacks, an unfortunate marriage. But he persevered and rose to be a professor, teaching biology at Boston University.

In the autumn of 1929 he also gave a course in Middle High German. One of the students was a young woman named Aurelia Schober. Her parents were Austrian immigrants; in the home only German was spoken, but they were citizens and voted the Republican ticket. At the end of the semester Otto asked her to marry him. But first he would have to obtain a divorce from his wife, from whom he had been separated for thirteen years. In the meantime they went hiking and planned on working together. He introduced her to the pleasures of ornithology and entomology. "The Evolution of Parental Care in the Animal Kingdom," says Aurelia Plath, "was our most ambitious project, planned to be embarked upon after we had achieved some lesser goals and had established our family of at least two children."

Aurelia was employed as a teacher of German and English in Brookline High School until January 1932 when she and Otto were married. "Then," she says, "I yielded to my husband's wish that I become a full-time home-maker."

As a girl she had been a devoted reader of novels—by Louisa May Alcott, Harold Bell Wright and Gene Stratton Porter. In high school she was fond of Emily Dickinson's poetry and read the works of Scott, Dickens, Thackeray, and other English novelists. But her father decided that she should be a "business woman," so she entered a two-year course in the Boston University College of Practical Arts and Letters. In the summer she worked at part-time jobs. Then she persuaded her father to let her take two more years of college to prepare herself for teaching English and German, along with vocational subjects, on the high school level.

In college she worked with a professor at M.I.T. who gave her lists of books to read: Greek drama, Russian literature, the works of Hermann Hesse, the poems of Rilke, and books of philosophy. It was the beginning, says Aurelia, of her "dream for her children," the ideal education of children she hoped some day to have.

The man she had married was twenty-one years older than she; he was a professor and she had been his student; and he was accustomed to living by himself or in college dormitories. All this led to an attitude of "rightful dominance" on his part. "At the end of my first year of marriage," says Aurelia, "I realized that if I wanted a peaceful home—

and I did—I would simply have to become more submissive, although it was not my nature to be so."

Two years after they were married Otto Plath published his doctor's thesis on *Bumblebees and Their Ways.* Then, with his wife's help, he wrote a treatise on "Insect Societies" for inclusion in a textbook. "Social life," says Aurelia, "was almost nil for us as a married couple. My dreams of 'open house' for students and the frequent entertaining of good friends among the faculty were not realized. During the first year of our married life, all had to be given up for THE BOOK. After Sylvia was born, it was THE CHAPTER."

They were living in an apartment in Boston. Aurelia Plath's parents, the Schobers, lived nearby at Point Shirley, with a view of the bay on one side, the sea on the other, and Deer Island prison in the distance. There Sylvia had her first experience of the sea. "My childhood land-scape," she writes, "was not land but the end of the land—the cold, salt, running hills of the Atlantic." One day when she was learning to creep her mother set her down on the beach; she crawled straight for the coming wave and "was just through the wall of green" when her mother caught her by the heels.[2]

She explored the beach, picking up lucky stones, the ones with a white ring around them, and blue mussels with rainbow colors on the inside. For a time she believed "not in God nor Santa Claus, but in mermaids."

Sylvia was born on October 27, 1932. Two and a half years later, just as Otto Plath wanted, his wife gave birth to a son. They named him Warren. Years later Sylvia Plath would write that the event caused her suddenly to feel cast out: "I hated babies. I who for two and a half years had been the centre of a tender universe felt the axis wrench and a polar chill immobilize my bones. I would be a bystander, a museum mammoth. Babies!" This, however, was written for the BBC; it is clearly intended as a key to "Morning Song," the first poem in *Ariel,* and altogether too neat in its analysis. "As from a star," she says, "I saw, coldly and soberly, the *separateness* of everything. I felt the wall of my skin: I am I. That stone is a stone. My beautiful fusion with the things of this world was over." She goes on in this vein. Not that it is untrue, but she is dramatizing considerably.[3]

While her mother was in the hospital Sylvia stayed with her grand-parents. She was very attached to them; in later years when writing about her childhood she would describe experiences with her father that had actually taken place with her grandfather: he would play games with her and take her swimming. Her father did neither; according to his wife he did not take an active part in tending to or playing with the children. Nevertheless, "he loved them dearly and took great pride in their attractiveness and progress."

In 1936 they moved to Winthrop, close to the beach and Aurelia's parents. Sylvia would recall a hurricane that swept the New England coast as a contest between the elements and her grandmother. It buried the furnace in sand, stained the upholstered sofa, and left a dead shark among the geraniums. ". . . But my grandmother had her broom out, it would soon be right."[4]

When they were living in Winthrop, and Sylvia was interested in mermaids, her mother read Arnold's "The Forsaken Merman" aloud. Sylvia was fascinated, she tells us, by the description of

> Sand-strewn caverns, cool and deep,
> Where the winds are all asleep;
> Where the spent lights quiver and gleam . . .

of sea beasts feeding in the ooze, mailed sea snakes, and whales that

> Sail and sail with unshut eye,
> Round the world forever and aye.

She says, "I saw the gooseflesh on my skin. I did not know what made it. I was not cold. Had a ghost passed over? No, it was the poetry. A spark flew off Arnold and shook me, like a chill. I wanted to cry; I felt very odd. I had fallen into a new way of being happy."[5]

However, there is more to it—knowing what we do about the life of Sylvia Plath, "The Forsaken Merman" reads like a dream she might have had.

The merman is speaking to his children. Their mother, Margaret, has forsaken them.

> Once she sate with you and me,
> On a red gold throne in the heart of the sea . . .

But she wanted to return to the land in order to pray for her kinfolk.

> " 'Twill be Easter-time in the world—ah me!
> And I will lose my poor soul, Merman, here with thee . . ."

She has gone and has not returned. The merman, telling the children what they must already know, relates how once they went in search of their mother. They went to the town and the church, and stood on gravestones in order to see inside. They could see Margaret sitting there, but though they called she did not hear them. So they came back to their caverns under the sea.

The merman tells them that from time to time Margaret will think of the past, and then she will sigh

> For the cold strange eyes of a little Mermaiden,
> And the gleam of her golden hair.

Sometimes they will go by moonlight to gaze on the sleeping town, and come back down, singing

> "There dwells a lov'd one,
> But cruel is she,
> She left lonely for ever
> The kings of the sea."

This is better than a dream, it is prophecy. The merman and his children have been abandoned, and Aurelia and her children will be abandoned by Otto when he dies. But the "little Mermaiden" with golden hair has a special relationship with the absent one. It is for her that Margaret sighs—and Sylvia will have a special relationship with her dead father. He will still be thinking of her, in death.

Apart from the story there are images that may have made an indelible impression—of a world beneath the sea:

> In the caverns where we lay,
> Through the surf and through the swell,
> The far-off sound of a silver bell . . .

and a moonlit world where

> We will gaze, from the sand-hills,
> At the white, sleeping town . . .

In 1936, Otto Plath's health began to deteriorate; he lost weight and "had a chronic cough and sinusitis"; he wearied easily and was upset by trifles. After a time he withdrew from the life of the household; it was as much as he could do to teach his classes; then he would come home and collapse on a couch in the study. But he refused to see a doctor, saying that he had diagnosed his illness himself and that he would never submit to surgery. Apparently he was afraid he had lung cancer. It fell upon his wife to take care of him, and when the baby, Warren, too, was ill, with bronchial pneumonia and asthmatic attacks, she could hardly get an unbroken night's sleep.

In August of 1940, following an accident to Otto's foot, a doctor was consulted. Gangrene was setting in; the doctor took blood and urine samples and diagnosed Otto's case as "a far advanced state of diabetes mellitus." The illness could have been controlled had it been detected before, but now it was too late: Otto was dying.

The leg had to be amputated. "How," said the doctor, "could such a brilliant man be so stupid." The amputation was carried out but this did not save Otto's life. He died three weeks later.

When her mother broke the news to Sylvia, she looked "sternly for a moment, then said woodenly, 'I'll never speak to God again!'"

Her mother told her that she need not go to school that day if she would rather stay at home. From under the blanket which she had pulled over her head came her muffled voice, "I *want* to go to school."

That day when Sylvia came home from school she made her mother sign a paper promising never to marry again. Apparently her classmates had been talking about the possibility of having a stepfather. Mrs. Plath says that she signed at once, hugged Sylvia and gave her a glass of milk and some cookies. Sylvia ate and drank with good appetite. "That done, she rose briskly, saying matter-of-factly, 'I'm going to find David and Ruth.'"

The life of Sylvia Plath has been much discussed, so that readers may be tired of it and wish just to read her poems. But her poems bring us back to her life—she wrote about real people and incidents. This does not mean that her writing was "confessional"; the poetry is based on experience but it has been transformed, she is creating a "mythology." Nevertheless, if we wish to know why she felt a need to transform experience and to write the kind of poetry she did, it is necessary to understand her life.[6]

Before her father's death she appears to have been happy. Then she draws darkness over herself. On the surface she is brisk and matter-of-fact, as her mother describes her, but it is clear that an inner world has been overthrown.

The week after their father's death, both children came down with measles, Warren having pneumonia in the bargain and Sylvia developing sinusitis. This wasn't all. Mrs. Plath's father lost his job as a cost accountant and began to have serious difficulty with his eyesight.

Aurelia obtained work as a substitute teacher in Braintree High School, teaching three classes of German and two of Spanish daily, at twenty-five dollars a week. In order to improve her Spanish she took private lessons.

The house in Winthrop was sold and, in October 1942, they moved to a small, six-room, white frame house in Wellesley. There were reasons: the taxes were low, the school system had a fine rating, and Wellesley College would admit outstanding students on a town scholarship. The down payment on the house used up the last of Otto Plath's life insurance, most of which had gone in medical and funeral expenses. "We were operating," says Mrs. Plath, "on a tight margin and had to plan very carefully."

The small white frame house makes one think. It was a strange place for a poet to grow up in—perhaps all places are, but a white frame house is particularly dispiriting, antiseptic and antipoetic. Wallace Stevens has said that the people in such houses are haunted by white nightgowns, not green nightgowns, or purple nightgowns with green rings, or any other exotic combination. Yet, here and there,

> an old sailor
> Drunk and asleep in his boots,
> Catches tigers
> In red weather.[7]

and at the age of twelve Sylvia was writing rhymes. She made sketches to accompany them and slid them under her mother's napkin to surprise her.

She wrote her first poem a few months after her father's death.

> Hear the crickets chirping
> In the dewy grass.
> Bright little fireflies
> Twinkle as they pass.

She would later describe her childhood poems as being about "Nature, I think: birds, bees, spring, fall, all those subjects which are absolute gifts to the person who doesn't have any interior experience to write about. I think the coming of spring, the stars overhead, the first snowfall and so on are gifts for a child, a young poet."[8]

The firefly poem was published in the Boston *Sunday Herald*, with her first drawing, for which she won a prize.

She went to the Marshall Livingston Grammar School and joined the Girl Scouts. Then she attended the Gamaliel Bradford Senior High School. Sylvia was an outstanding student—"Those perfect report cards began coming in, with always an 'A,' a '100,' an 'excellent' after every subject, including deportment." She won awards and prizes, was elected to honor societies and received scholarships, "the goals and lures," George Stade remarks, "for what are now called aggressive achievers." No doubt, this "inexorable academic success" was encouraged by her mother whose own academic ambitions had been sacrificed; she wanted Sylvia to be less restricted, and independent of men.[9]

The heroine of Sylvia Plath's novel, *The Bell Jar,* says: "My mother had taught shorthand and typing to support us ever since my father died and secretly she hated it and hated him for dying and leaving no money because he didn't trust life-insurance salesmen." Esther Greenwood feels that being married, for a woman, is like being brainwashed, "and afterward you went about numb as a slave in some private, totalitarian state."[10]

In her dislike and contempt for her mother's way of life Esther is obviously speaking for Sylvia. But not the whole truth. When she wrote *The Bell Jar,* Sylvia Plath was venting her anger in order to make a break with the past. She also loved and respected her mother—there are the letters to prove it—but the burden of gratitude at times seemed intolerable, a debt she could never repay, however hard she tried. She could never work hard enough and win enough prizes to repay her mother's devotion. And what if she failed?

It is no wonder that at times, and when she wrote *The Bell Jar,* she struck out savagely. It was the only way she could make the break, find a measure of freedom by repudiating the debt.

She was driven. Everyone says so. One of her teachers recalls that she was the kind of student who turns up wanting to know why she has received an "A minus" instead of an "A."[11] Not a likable trait. But, apart from everything else, there was the question of money. Some who have spoken of Sylvia Plath's "inexorable" will to succeed appear not to have considered this: she had very little money, far less than some of the girls she would be going to school with. Her wish to excel was not just a matter of choice—she *had* to!

She thought of being an illustrator, a dress designer, a writer. She wrote a poem when she was fourteen that made her English teacher say, "Incredible that one so young could have experienced anything so devastating." She had done a pastel drawing; her grandmother tossed her apron onto the table and it brushed against the drawing and smudged it. "Don't worry," said Sylvia cheerfully, "I can patch it up." But she wrote a melancholy poem.

> Then, suddenly, my world turned gray,
> and darkness wiped aside my joy.
> A dull and aching void was left
> where careless hands had reached out to
> destroy

my silver web of happiness.
The hands then stopped in wonderment,
for, loving me, they wept to see,
the tattered ruins of my firma-
ment.[12]

The poem ran to seven stanzas; she was like Tom Sawyer looking on at his own funeral and loving every bit of it.

She was aware that everyone did not like poetry or poets. "I am doubt-ful," she wrote in her diary, "about poetry's effect on the little strategy of 'popularity' that I have been slowly building up." But she felt that she had to be a writer:

There is a voice within me
That will not be still.[13]

She submitted her writing to the "It's All Yours" section in the magazine *Seventeen,* and received personal notes of rejection from the editor, ad-vising her to slant her writing to suit the needs of the magazine—she must read back issues and discover the "trend." Sylvia did so, and kept submitting.

Writing was a way out of the small white frame house. "I am afraid," she wrote in her diary, "of getting older. I am afraid of getting married. Spare me from cooking three meals a day—spare me from the relentless cage of routine and rote. I want to be free—free to know people and their backgrounds—free to move to different parts of the world so that I may learn that there are other morals and standards besides my own."[14]

In August 1950, just before she entered college, *Seventeen* published one of her stories, "And Summer Will Not Come Again." In November, they published a poem, "Ode on a Bitten Plum." It was curious, when she wrote in a happy, exuberant mood about happy things, it only brought rejection slips; the story or poem with a touch of pathos was found more acceptable. "More people," says Aurelia Plath, "could iden-tify with the plain heroine beset with doubts and difficulties."[15]

She entered Smith College in the Fall of 1950, on funds provided by the Smith Club of Wellesley, a Nielson scholarship, and Olive Higgins Prouty, a popular novelist and writer of radio serials.

She was one of the "scholarship girls," and went to Smith as to the arena. "We brought to even the most trivial activity," says Nancy Steiner, who also was at Smith as a scholarship girl, "an almost savage industriousness—a clenched-teeth determination that emanated from us like cheap perfume."[16]

Sylvia had more reason than most. In a letter to her brother Warren, speaking of their mother, she writes, "After extracting her life blood and care for 20 years, we should start bringing in big dividends of joy for her."[17] That is, she was deeply in debt and had to get out.

Moreover, her "vanity" desired "luxuries."[18] She wanted the happiness —good clothes, boyfriends, the fun—that other girls had. As no one was going to help her to them she would have to help herself.

But, above all, she had an idea of perfection that might even have surprised the scholarship girls, had they known. "Never, never, never will I reach the perfection I long for with all my soul—my paintings, my poems, my stories—all poor, poor reflections."[19]

What the other girls did see was an "all-around" girl who "not only did well scholastically but was socially acceptable by both sexes," and a "service-oriented person who made a contribution to her peer group and the community."[20] A far cry, indeed, from the young poet who wrote:

(How frail the human heart must be—
a mirrored pool of thought . . .[21]

She tells her mother that the most divine thing has happened. She was standing innocently in the parlor, having coffee after supper, when a senior said, sotto voce, in her ear: "I have a man all picked out for you." The senior had met a young man who had gone to Culver Military Academy and was now a freshman at Amherst, "tall, cute, and—get *this* —HE WRITES POETRY. . . ."

"I love everybody," Sylvia writes. "If only I can unobtrusively do well in all my courses and get enough sleep, I should be tops. I'm so happy. And this anticipation makes everything super. I keep muttering, 'I'M A SMITH GIRL NOW.' "[22]

Her letters are like letters from the front, desperately cheerful. She has to pass certain tests: for instance, the interview with Miss Mensel, who wants to meet all the scholarship girls in the freshman class "and get to know them so she can describe them and their needs to the Board." In other words, "she is the personal medium through which the Board gets to know who we are and what we deserve." In her interview she told Miss Mensel how stimulating her courses were, how French related with History and Art with Botany. And how much she wanted to take creative writing and art courses. She told her how she loved her house and the girls in it—"the older ones, too, who could give us a sort of perspective on college life." And, so as not to give Miss Mensel—"the dearest person . . . with a keen, vital twinkle in her blue eyes"—the impression that she was a greasy grind, she told her how much she liked to dress up and go out on weekends and just go bike riding through the countryside. "I had to keep myself from getting tears in my eyes," says Sylvia, "as I told her how happy I was."[23]

The interview was a success—they didn't take away her scholarship.

It is a "sterile period" emotionally, for she needs to feel physically desirable, and mentally desirable as well if the boy is intelligent, but at present there is none. It is an "interregnum between boys." She has no one to pour herself into except a close girl friend, and that is only too rare.[24]

She tells her mother that she has been up in her room talking to "a lovely girl," one of the people she can really confide in. She had no date for the weekend and was miserable about it. Then a call came from Louise: three boys had dropped over and would she like to go out tonight? So she threw on her clothes, "all the time ranting . . . on how *never* to commit suicide, because something unexpected always happens. . . ."[25]

It is the casualness of the idea that surprises, as though to think of suicide were the most ordinary thing in the world, the first thing one thinks of when one hasn't a date. It is a definite slip; for a moment the mask has been lifted and we see into her mind. People with a secret vice reveal it in this way, by assuming that others share it. To the drinker everyone is thinking about the next drink, and Sylvia thinks that people often think about committing suicide.

She thinks about it often—it is always in reserve, to be imagined when she is weary of working hard and trying to be socially acceptable and a "service-oriented person."

She writes to her mother about a friend who has been unable to do her work, and letting it slide, and who can only reiterate, "I can never do it, never." She has told Sylvia that her parents have either deceived her into thinking she is creative or else do not realize how incapable she is. She has been saving sleeping pills and razor blades and can think of nothing better than to commit suicide. Sylvia writes that she has been talking to the girl all afternoon, and is thinking of writing to her parents —the girl has been talking of suicide at home—and telling them how tired she is and how much she needs a rest. The girl's mother keeps telling her she is foolish and can do it all; she cannot see that the poor girl is unable to think in this state. "If you were her mother," Sylvia ends, "it would be all right."

The letter has a footnote by Mrs. Plath saying that "the girl in question was not suicidal," and that when Sylvia "found herself in a similar state" two years later, razor blades and sleeping pills were "her first thoughts." In writing about the "suicidal" girl Sylvia was describing her own situation.

There is a poem she has learned by heart—her mother used to read it aloud—Edna St. Vincent Millay's "Renascence." It is related by someone in the first person, telling how she lay on the earth and found herself sinking into it.

> Ah, awful weight! Infinity
> Pressed down upon the finite Me!
> My anguished spirit, like a bird,
> Beating against my lips I heard;
> Yet lay the weight so close about
> There was no room for it without.
> And so beneath the weight lay I
> And suffered death, but could not die.
> Long had I lain thus, craving death,
> When quietly the earth beneath
> Gave way, and inch by inch, so great
> At last had grown the crushing weight,
> Into the earth I sank till I
> Full six feet under ground did lie,
> And sank no more,—there is no weight
> Can follow here, however great.
> From off my breast I felt it roll,
> And as it went my tortured soul
> Burst forth and fled in such a gust
> That all about me swirled the dust.

She rests deep inside the earth. Then she hears the "pitying rain" begin to fall. The rain is kind, and she wishes to be alive again. She has a vision of the earth sparkling after a shower and realizes that lying here in the grave she cannot see sunlight, the sky, the beauty of Spring. Then,

> O God, I cried, give me new birth,
> And put me back upon the earth!

The utterance of this wish brings her back to life. The rain "in one black wave" strikes the grave and opens it. She begins to have the use of her senses, to smell and hear and see. She is alive—"I breathed my soul back into me." She springs up from the ground and throws her arms around the trees. She hugs the ground, she has been reborn to a new life, she has seen God and from now on she will see Him everywhere.

> God, I can push the grass apart
> And lay my finger on Thy heart![26]

When Sylvia thought of "Renascence" she forgot where she was. The walls, the table with the typewriter, her shelves of books, her bed—the world of a scholarship student—vanished, and she was lying underground in a cool, dark place. She could hear the rain beginning to fall, pattering on the earth, like a murmur of distant voices. She opened her eyes and moved her arms and legs. The earth seemed to move away and the voices were closer. She found herself standing upright under the stars. There was a sigh, people were standing close by; their faces were hidden in the shadows under the trees, but she could sense their presence and the wonder they must feel to see her standing so. She was filled with great love for them; she had so much to tell, so much to give.

She was writing poems and stories. In the summer when she held various jobs—as picker on a vegetable farm, mother's helper on Cape Cod, waitress in a cooperative house at Smith, she took note of people who could be used as characters. The means of breaking out of her narrow, stifling existence lay in her own hands. She typed neatly— thank God for the typing lessons—and sent stories to *Mademoiselle* and *Seventeen.*

She was scrubbing tables in a hotel on Cape Cod when she heard that she had won the *Mademoiselle* fiction contest with a short story, "Sunday at the Mintons." The prize was five hundred dollars.

This was magical. "I can't wait," she wrote her mother, "till August when I can go casually down to the drug store and pick up a slick copy of *Mlle*, flip to the index, and see ME, one of two college girls in the U.S.!"[27]

Sylvia and the slicks! Why did she want so much to be published in *Mademoiselle* and *Seventeen?* Obviously she needed the money, yet you would think that the education she was receiving would have set up a conflict in her mind. In all the courses she took at Smith—French, Botany, Art, Government, History, Russian literature, English—didn't she come up against ideas that were incompatible with the fiction provided by these magazines according to a formula?

Her idea of fiction agreed with that of the editors: it was a "problem" that was solved at the end in a pleasant, entertaining manner. This was what Smith girls wanted life to be, and when she was invited to Maureen Buckley's coming-out party in Sharon, Connecticut, Sylvia saw that life could be the same as fiction: "Up the stone steps under the white colonial columns of the Buckley home. Girls in beautiful gowns clustered by the stair. Everywhere there were swishes of taffeta, satin, silk. . . ." She danced with a "lovely grinning dark-haired boy" whose father was a Russian general, and with another boy whose father was

the head of Twentieth Century-Fox productions. The dark-haired boy
drove her home.

> When we drove into the drive at last, he made me wait until he opened
> the door on my side of the car and helped me alight with a ceremonial
> "Milady" . . .
> "Milord," I replied, fancying myself a woman from a period novel, entering
> my castle.[28]

When she published a story or a poem, people thought it wonderful!
They came by to look at her. They asked questions and sat listening
when she answered. "Do you type your stories?" one of them asked.
They all turned and looked at the typewriter on a table with a stack of
paper next to it. When she said that she did, they looked at one another.
Things she herself had taken for granted, her most ordinary habits
and thoughts, now seemed important. Her life had meaning, a definite
purpose—she was a writer.

But elation would vanish as suddenly as it came and she again faced
the "black, immovable wall of competition."[29] Having read a newspaper
story about the suicide of one of her brother's classmates at Exeter,
she must telephone her mother to discuss it, and this is followed by a
letter in which she has "practically considered committing suicide" in
order to get out of the science requirement. "My whole life is mastered
by a horrible fear of this course."

"When one feels like leaving college and killing oneself over one
course . . . it is a rather serious thing." And what will the college
authorities think? She has managed to make a pretty good impression
so far, but if she goes insane over what she thinks is a horrible, wasteful
course, it will only make them expel her. She has been wondering if she
should see the college psychiatrist, but how could she explain that
these horrible formulas and dry, useless chunks of memory are driving
her mad? "No rest cure in the infirmary will cure the sickness in me."[30]

It was all up or down with Sylvia: either she was the center of attention or in outer darkness and chaos. When something she wrote was
accepted she was free. But when many things were required of her, and
when her time was taken up with duties and she couldn't get to the typewriter, lose herself in an imagined situation, she wanted to die and
shrink into the earth.

She heard the thunder roll and rain pattering down. She slept through
the storm, and woke refreshed.

In March 1953, W. H. Auden spoke in the chapel at Smith. Sylvia was
in the audience. Auden, she wrote to her brother, was her conception

of the perfect poet, "tall, with a big leonine head and a sandy mane of hair, and a lyrically gigantic stride." He had a wonderfully textured British accent and she adored him with a big Hero Worship. "I would like someday to touch the Hem of his Garment and say in a very small adoring voice: Mr. Auden, I haveapomefor you: I found my God in Auden."

> He is Wonderful and
> Very Brilliant, and
> Very Lyric and Most
> Extremely Witty.[31]

Auden came to her class in Modern Poetry and talked about one of his own poems for two hours. She thought it the privilege of a lifetime to have heard the "brilliant play of minds, epigrams, wit, intelligence and boundless knowledge."[32]

For a while she tried to write like Auden. She had been imitating Emily Dickinson; in a poem titled "Admonition" she caught Emily's off-rhymes and psalm-book rhythm perfectly, and had her imagery down pat. She absorbed Emily's attitude, preening herself on being a poet, whom the world in its bungling incomprehension strives to suppress.

> If you dissect a bird
> To diagram the tongue
> You'll cut the chord
> Articulating song.[33]

Now she tried to be witty in the manner of Auden. It was a low point in her knowledge of herself; months later, looking back on this period, she would recall that she had been reading nothing more meaty than the jokes in *The New Yorker* and writing nothing but glib jingles in an attempt "to commune with W. H. Auden."[34]

These Audenesque jingles have not been published,[35] but there is a sonnet enclosed in a letter dated April 1954, the first poem, she says, she has written in a year, that bears the mark of Auden. The title, "Doom of Exiles," is taken from Auden's early poetry with its echoes of Anglo-Saxon: "Doom is dark and deeper than any sea-dingle. / Upon what man it fall . . ." Plath's manner is grave and discursive, like Auden's in his later, declamatory, "public" poems. She writes:

> Now we, returning from the vaulted domes
> Of our colossal sleep, come home to find
> A tall metropolis of catacombs
> Erected down the gangways of our mind.[36]

The "colossal sleep" is the attempt to kill herself—when she lay unconscious in a cellar for three days. She is treating the incident in an impersonal manner like Auden, turning a private experience into a public statement. Like Auden, too, is the representation of a state of mind through landscape and architecture. Auden wrote, in "The Quest":

> Nor all his weeping ways through weary wastes have found
> The castle where his Greater Hallows are interned;
> For broken bridges halt him, and dark thickets round
> Some ruin where an evil heritage was burned.[37]

In her attempt to write about history and culture in the manner of Auden, Plath diverged from her best subject—experience and what to make of it—as far as she would ever go.

She was not alone: the influence of Auden was strong in these years. Young poets tried to write like Auden about history, with irony and wit, using traditional forms. Writing such as this has been associated with a university education, but surely this is unfair to universities. All sorts of writers have come out of universities. At the present time if one made a list of American poets who teach in universities or read their poems to university audiences, it would be run into the hundreds. The way people write seems to depend on their intelligence rather than on where they live, and the "smelly little orthodoxies," as Orwell called them, grow in bohemia just as well as on Morningside Heights.

Auden continued to influence Plath's style and choice of subjects over a longer period than her remark about having tried to "commune" with him would suggest. Her poem, "Two Views of a Cadaver Room," published in November 1959,[38] presents a scene in Auden's detached manner alongside a vivid bit of reporting. The first half tells of a visit to a dissecting room where there are cadavers and foetuses in bottles: "In their jars the snail-nosed babies moon and glow." This is all her own—the cadavers and foetuses are also in *The Bell Jar* where Esther goes to see "some really interesting hospital sights"[39]—but in the second half she follows Auden closely. The poem she has in mind is his "*Musée des Beaux Arts,*" which describes Breughel's painting of Icarus falling into the sea. Meanwhile, life continues as usual; a ploughman goes about his work, and

> ... the expensive delicate ship that must have seen
> Something amazing, a boy falling out of the sky,
> Had somewhere to get to and sailed calmly on.[40]

Auden says, "In Breughel's *Icarus*, for instance..." Plath says, "In Breughel's *panorama*..." Her poem describes two lovers who are engrossed in each other, the man singing, the woman bending over him holding some pages of music, both of them "deaf to the fiddle in the hands / Of the death's head shadowing their song." It concludes: "Yet desolation, stalled in paint, spares the little country / Foolish, delicate, in the lower right-hand corner." The imitation of Auden is so close that she uses the same adjective, "delicate," for the country untouched by death that he uses for the ship that goes sailing on.[41]

This elegance was very much of the period. New Critics emphasized the qualities in verse that lent themselves to "explication." Irony and ambiguity were especially favored. If the poem didn't fit the tools they kept the tools and threw away the poem. Cleanth Brooks' and Robert Penn Warren's *Understanding Poetry*, from which a generation learned how to read, contained six poems by Donne and not a single poem by Whitman.[42]

Allen Ginsberg has said that in 1948 "everywhere in America transcendental brain consciousness was waking up." In that year he had his "Blake epiphany experiences," Charles Olson had published *Call Me Ishmael*, and Gary Snyder, having finished his thesis, sat by the Willamette River at dawn and saw a thousand birds fly out of the trees. Everything, he realized, was alive, the entire universe was alive.[43]

But these feelings were not general, and it would be another ten years before Ginsberg made an impression and Olson had a following. The admired poets of the period were Robert Lowell, Richard Wilbur, and, most of all, Auden. They stood for poetry written in traditional forms and in a language removed from actual speech. There were a dozen younger poets who agreed with them in principle.

It was in this climate that Sylvia Plath served her apprenticeship— with a difference. Unlike the young poets who wanted to be published in the *Kenyon* or *Hudson* or *Partisan Review*, she wanted to be published in magazines with a large circulation. "Some day," she wrote, "Phyllis McGinley will hear from me. They can't shut me up."[44] For Sylvia, Phyllis McGinley's being a famous, much published author was enough—it made her someone to emulate. She went about her work "professionally"—writing slowly, "plodding through dictionary and thesaurus, searching for the exact word to create the poetic impression she intended."[45]

She was rewarded with a guest editorship at *Mademoiselle* for the month of June. She bought some new clothes and, tremendously elated, set off for New York. What she did there is described in *The Bell Jar*.

She lived at the Barbizon Hotel—in *The Bell Jar* called the Amazon— with other young women who had secretarial jobs, or careers, or were waiting to be married. As Managing Editor she read copy and saw that people met their deadlines. She wrote an article about "Poets on Campus," based on interviews with Alastair Reid, Anthony Hecht, Richard Wilbur, and William Burford. She interviewed the novelist Elizabeth Bowen. It was hard work but fun. She was scheduled to go on fashion tours, tours of the United Nations and the *Herald Tribune*, to attend a movie preview, a ballet at City Center, a television show, and a dance at the St. Regis.

At the end of the month when she came home she was "tired, unsmiling."[46] In retrospect she would speak of the time in New York as having been "a series of frustrations . . . What should have been a stimulating, exciting round of gala festivities produced only a mounting tedium that did not subside even at the chance to meet and interview outstanding figures in the literary world. She found the work artificial and banal."[47]

Passages in *The Bell Jar* evoke a feeling of emptiness and desiccation: "The city hung in my window, flat as a poster, glittering and blinking, but it might just as well not have been there at all, for all the good it did me."[48] The characters in the novel are either foolish or insincere and hypocritical. Esther Greenwood's life has no meaning; it is loveless and as dry as dust.

In a poem, "Mad Girl's Love Song," published in *Mademoiselle* that August, Plath writes:

> I shut my eye and all the world drops dead;
> I lift my eyes and all is born again.
> (I think I made you up inside my head.)[49]

This is her own version of Edna St. Vincent Millay's "Renascence"—the ritual of dying and being reborn. Before she went to New York she had been toying with the idea. Her experiences there took her over the edge.

The job, that had seemed such a prize, turned out to be disillusioning. She had a small-town girl's idea of the big city. She meant to live there one day. It was the culmination to which all her striving would lead. But the reality turned out to be very different—"avocado pear after avocado pear being stuffed with crabmeat and mayonnaise and photographed under brilliant lights."[50]

She had counted so much on being a successful writer. It was going to make up for everything else, the sense of desolation that swept over her at times. She had stopped feeling happy long ago: "My father died, we moved inland. Whereon those nine first years of my life sealed themselves off like a ship in a bottle. . . ."[51] But when she wrote poems and stories she felt that her life had a purpose. And now she found that it was stuffed avocados.

She was repelled and fascinated by the grotesque: deformed men on the subway "with short arms that curled like pink, boneless snakes around a begging cup." At Yankee Stadium she saw "all the stinking people in the world."[52]

One or two incidents made her feel personally soiled—"All that liquor and those sticky kisses."[53]

When Sylvia came home her mother broke the news that she had not been accepted as a student in Frank O'Connor's short-story writing class at Harvard summer school. "I could see Sylvia's face," says Aurelia Plath, "in the rearview mirror; it went white when I told her, and the look of shock and utter despair that passed over it alarmed me."[54] After this Sylvia seemed to have lost all joy in life. She would sunbathe with a book in hand, but never reading it.

One morning her mother noticed some partially healed gashes on Sylvia's legs. When she asked about it, Sylvia said, "I just wanted to see if I had the guts!" She grasped her mother's hand and cried, "Oh, Mother, the world is so rotten! I want to die! Let's die together!"

Within the hour, Mrs. Plath took Sylvia to see the family doctor. She recommended psychiatry, and this was tried. Sylvia didn't like the psychiatrist—he reminded her of a handsome but opinionated date she had outgrown. He recommended shock treatments. "I felt so inadequate," says Aurelia Plath, "so alone." Sylvia underwent the shock treatments. Then she was referred to another psychiatrist who prescribed sleeping tablets.

As the fall term approached, she became more agitated. On August 24, Mrs. Plath went to the movies with a friend; Sylvia urged her to go; she said she wanted to stay home with her grandparents. "She looked particularly well this day; her eyes sparkled, her cheeks were flushed."

In the middle of the movie Mrs. Plath was filled, she says, with terror such as she had never experienced in all her life. She wanted to rush home but forced herself to stay to the end. Then she went straight home. There was a note on the dining table in Sylvia's handwriting: "Have gone for a long walk. Will be home tomorrow."

The police were called and the disappearance of a Smith College co-ed made newspaper headlines.

On the third day, when the family were at lunch, Sylvia's brother heard a moan from the basement. She was discovered in the crawl space beneath the downstairs bedroom, a half-empty bottle of sleeping pills at her side. Her face was lacerated and swollen; in struggling to rise she had scraped it on the wall. They took her to the Newton-Wellesley hospital.

Her first words on regaining consciousness were, "Oh, no." When her mother told her how glad they were that she was alive, she said, "It was *my* last act of love." Later she said, "Oh, if I could only be a freshman again. I so wanted to be a *Smith* woman."[55]

She was treated at the Massachusetts General Hospital, then transferred to McLean Hospital in Belmont where she underwent insulin therapy and shock treatments. In February 1954, she was readmitted at Smith, "welcomed back by her classmates and the faculty."[56]

There were some evident changes; she was trying out, says Mrs. Plath, "a more daring, adventuresome personality," and striving for "competency" in her life and work. Nancy Hunter, who first met Sylvia when she returned from the hospital, has given her impressions. Sylvia was tall, almost statuesque. "Her yellow hair, which had been lightened several shades from its natural brown, was shoulder length and had been carefully trained to dip with a precise and provocative flourish over her left eyebrow." Her eyes were very dark, her cheekbones "high and pronounced," marred by a faint brown scar caused by scraping against the cellar wall.

"She was writing again and she was opening up, sharing her fears and flourishing in the safe, protected, regulated environment of dormitory life." Sylvia and Nancy were roommates; they worked long hours and had a busy social life, pursuing "boys, clothes, and entertainment."[57]

The heroine of *The Bell Jar* took no pleasure in sex; she had an inhibiting notion of purity. "When I was nineteen," says Esther Greenwood, "pureness was the great issue . . . I saw the world divided into people who had slept with somebody and people who hadn't. . . ."[58] Sylvia Plath decided that this had to change. According to Edward Butscher, who got it from Jane Truslow, on her return to Smith, Sylvia took up sex "with enormous enthusiasm and would astound everybody with her frank approach, dragging the boy off into a dark room on the first date."[59]

The final episode of *The Bell Jar* tells how she went about losing her virginity.

In the summer of 1954, Nancy Hunter shared an apartment with Sylvia and two other girls in Cambridge. As she tells it, Sylvia would spend her share of the household money preparing gourmet meals, and then not contribute anything for staples. She was miserly, writing her name on leftover boxes of crackers and bags of potato chips and placing them out of reach. She kept the contents of her drawers neatly arranged, everything in its place. "If anyone disarranged my things," she told Nancy, "I'd feel as though I had been raped intellectually."[60]

Nancy and Sylvia met a tall, balding, myopic young man whom they thought brilliant, the most brilliant man they had ever known. He dated Nancy and chased her around his apartment, and then he dated Sylvia. In spite of what she knew about his attempt to bed Nancy, or perhaps because she knew, Sylvia was willing to be alone with him. And he raped her. "He was," says one who had it on good authority, "a totally other worldly mathematician, with only *one* hobby or attachment that related him to the rest of humanity: he had an insatiable appetite for women, one after the other, and it was an absolutely weird combination—as if some other worldly philosophical mathematical far-eyed wild-haired violinist/physicist turned out to be reading copies of Playboy instead of Wittgenstein. . . . Later, he had cancer of the testicles."[61]

Nancy tells of Sylvia's coming home the next day to hemorrhage and collapse in a pool of blood. She herself took care of everything—Sylvia was hysterical.

The same incident is seen in *The Bell Jar* from a different point of view. Esther Greenwood is the cool one, her friend Joan motivated by prurient curiosity. "For a minute," says Esther, "I thought Joan would refuse to call a doctor until I confessed the whole story of my evening with Irwin. . . ."[62] Joan is portrayed as a lesbian, a "big, horsey girl" with "pebbly eyes." At the end of the novel she kills herself.

In his introduction to Nancy Hunter Steiner's memoir George Stade remarks that she is nothing like Joan and that the character is "a kind of disposal unit for traits the Sylvia Plath came to reject in herself."[63] This appears to be true; when she wrote *The Bell Jar* she was trying to rid herself of the past, and in order to do so she had to be rid of people who had witnessed her humiliation. So she made them out to be contemptible.

"As the book stands by itself," says Aurelia Plath, "it represents the basest ingratitude."[64] The author herself felt very uneasy, and tried to disassociate herself from Esther Greenwood: "I've tried to picture my world and the people in it," she said, "as seen through the distorting lens of a bell jar."[65] But Esther was more than a point of view, she was one of Plath's other selves.

The rape did not change Sylvia's attitude to sex—she was still very much interested. She dated men at Harvard and Yale and invited them up to Smith. She was, says Butscher, "like a collector of specimens, in a way, each boy signifying a different aspect of the perfect male: Lotz the athlete, Lameyer the naval officer, McCurdy the educator, George the scientist, and S—— the decadent European." Sylvia liked to manipulate these men, all but "S—— the decadent European," who "was not above slapping her on occasion."[66]

Sylvia Plath's habit of writing about her life has made it common property, and people who knew her have·hastened to tell all. Peter Davison tells us that during their relationship she was "outwardly at least, voracious about sex . . . It was very athletic. She was quite proud of her hard muscles and sun tan." He surmises that he must have been "a sloppy disappointment to her by comparison."[67]

In her last year at Smith, Sylvia wrote an honors thesis on the other self or "double" in literature, reading novels by Dostoievsky, stories by E. T. A. Hoffman, Wilde's *Dorian Gray*, Stevenson's *Dr. Jekyll and Mr. Hyde*, Poe's "William Wilson," and writings by Otto Rank, Freud, Frazer, and Jung that dealt with the subject—"all fascinating stuff," she wrote her mother, "about the ego as symbolized in reflections (mirror and water), shadows, twins—dividing off and becoming an enemy, or omen of death, or a warning conscience, or a means by which one denies the power of death (e.g., by creating the idea of the soul as the deathless double of the mortal body)."[68]

As Judith Kroll shows, Plath was always trying to "transcend" the life she actually had.[69] She thought of it as "spoiled," and in poem after poem projected an image of her life in order to dispose of it. She was aiming at something better.

But what was this to be? She imagined that she was a daughter of "The Disquieting Muses" rather than her actual parents; she wished to be rid of her "spoiled history" and to be reborn. Yet, her attitude toward different aspects of the self was far from clear. She did not know which aspect was the "true" one. Was it the superior, "absolutely white person" or the "old yellow one" underneath? Was it the self attached to the dead father or the self ruled by the Muse?

She would decide, finally—be rid of the idea of perfection and rid of the dead father once and for all. This is what the poem "Daddy" says, and the title poem "Ariel" attempts to convey the ecstasy, the feeling of transcendence—"suicidal" in the sense that it requires the death of the old life. It is to be a new beginning,

at one with the drive
Into the red

Eye, the cauldron of morning.[70]

The thesis was awarded a prize, and at the end of her senior year she was able to list no fewer than eleven prizes and awards that she had received for her writing during recent months. One of the high points was the Glascock Poetry Contest held at Mt. Holyoke. There she met Marianne Moore, "vital and humorous as someone's fairy godmother incognito." Sylvia read her poems aloud, and the audience was responsive, laughing at the witty places. She thought that she might like being a humorous public speaker; it was very gratifying to make people laugh. She tied for first place with a boy from Wesleyan, and John Ciardi, who was one of the judges, wrote a letter saying that she was a real discovery, and sent a list of quarterlies to which she might submit specific poems, with his recommendation. So it was not a completely indifferent world, after all![71]

In February she was accepted by Cambridge University in a two-year program leading to the B.A.; three months later she received a grant from the Fulbright Foundation that gave her the money she would need to study in England.

The autumn of 1955 saw her installed in Newnham College, Cambridge. Her supervisor was a Miss Burton, for whom she wrote papers on Tragedy, and she had a tutor in practical composition and criticism. She was reading for her exams in June. One exam would be on the English Moralists—philosophy and ethics from Aristotle to D. H. Lawrence. She attended lectures by F. R. Leavis, "a magnificent, acid, malevolently humorous little man ... like a bandy-legged leprechaun," and Basil Willey, and was hoping to hear David Daiches on the Modern Novel. She hoped it would be modern, for at Cambridge modern poets were considered to be Wordsworth, Arnold, and Coleridge.[72]

From looking at magazines in the bookstalls she thought that poetry in Britain was "fast fading from galloping consumption."[73] But she studied the magazines, as usual, with an eye to the market for her own writing.

She tried out for the part of Rosalind in *As You Like It* at the Amateur Dramatic Club, and for a part in a play by Tennessee Williams. One "nice, ugly little boy" told her afterwards what a wonderful voice she had—"such joy!" And she was accepted as a member of the Club.

She explored King's Chapel with its lace ceiling, and "the backs," and watched people punting on the Cam. She walked to Grantchester for tea and saw that "the clock was set at ten of three" as Rupert Brooke said it was.[74]

One day the Queen and the Duke came to Newnham "for sherry and a few presentations," and Sylvia stood right at the foot of the platform where the ceremonies took place. The Queen looked radiant and the Duke was enchanting; he made "many amusing observations" as they walked down the line chatting with the girls. It was all quite lovely, and Sylvia ran out in the rain afterwards to see them off in the royal car.

She told her mother that she could not get accustomed to the idea of men making tea, she shook with silent mirth as she watched. She was dating an Englishman named Mallory; he was extremely handsome in a rugged way, "quite different from the pale, delicately made Englishmen."[75]

Writing to her benefactress, Mrs. Prouty, she assured her that she need have no fears on her behalf: "Instead of working rather frantically, as I once did, to be brilliant, creative and successful all at once, I now have a steadier, more practical approach which admits my various limitations and blind spots and works a little day by day to overcome them slowly without expecting immediate, or even eventual, perfection. Life is rich, full, and I am discovering more about it by living here every challenging day."[76]

In a few months, however, she had misgivings: there were gaps in her education. Chaucer, Shakespeare, Milton, the nineteenth and twentieth centuries, some Russian writers, this was the extent of her knowledge. The English girls knew a great deal about minor figures of the sixteenth, seventeenth and eighteenth centuries, and she would have to grind if she wanted to catch up. She doubted that she was cut out for a scholar. The dons looked ridiculous, like a series of grotesques when they sat at the head table. There was one tall, cadaverous woman with purple hair (really!), and another like "a midget Charles Addams fat creature" who had to stand on a stool to reach the soup tureen. The experience of people like these struck her as secondary, a kind of living death; she wanted to live in the real world where people grew and suffered and the "real books" were people's minds and souls.[77]

Mallory, who was a Jew, introduced her to some of his friends. He was a Rock of Gibraltar, calling for her every night at the theater where she had a small part in *Bartholomew Fair,* and biking home with her. He brought her a ritual apple which they shared by the garden gate at

Whitstead. She met a "lovely, light-skinned Negro" named Nat LaMar who had published a story in the *Atlantic*—he became her best friend at Cambridge.

She was in love with Richard Sassoon, whom she had known back in the States and who was now in France, studying at the Sorbonne.

In the Christmas vacation she went over to France—Paris first, then Venice and Nice: she wrote her mother of "Terraced gardens on steep slopes of rich red earth, orange and lemon trees, olive orchards, tiny pink and peach houses." She visited the Matisse chapel at Venice and found it closed. A peasant told her that rich people came in cars from Italy, Germany, and Sweden, on the wrong days, and were not admitted. She stood behind the nunnery and sketched a corner of the Chapel, then went back to the front and stared through the barred gate. She began to cry. "I knew it was so lovely inside, pure white with the sun through blue, yellow, and green stained windows." Then she heard a voice: "Ne pleurez plus, entrez." It was the Mother Superior, who let her in, after so many rich people had been turned away.[78]

The only sadness of the trip was her realization that Sassoon was not the man for her. Nor was Mallory. "I do need to meet older men. These young ones are so fluid, uncertain, tentative, that I become a mother to them." She missed the humor and "savor" and love of career that older men had. "I feel that I am certainly ready for that."[79]

Sassoon was the only man she had ever really loved, and she defined real love: "accepting the faults and working with them," but she feared for his particular nervous health when she thought of children. But, she told her mother, she was definitely meant to be married and have children and a home, and be a writer like the women she admired: Marianne Moore, Jean Stafford, Hortense Calisher, and Phyllis McGinley.[80]

She was writing at least a few hours every day. She felt compelled to write. Not that she had to publish—that was another matter—but to give aesthetic form to chaotic experience was for her, as it had been for James Joyce, a kind of religion, as necessary as confession and absolution were to a Catholic. But she no longer had illusions about her writing; she thought she could be competent and publish occasionally, but it was being involved in the process that mattered.[81]

She wanted to be "worth fine, intelligent men, like Sassoon, and Nat, and his friends, rather than only an empty hectic fear of being alone." One had to be able to live alone creatively before being ready to live with anyone else. "I *do* hope," she wrote Aurelia, "someday I meet a stimulating, intelligent man with whom I can create a good life, because I am definitely not meant for a single life." It was hard to know that she was not a career woman, only a competent small-time writer—though this would make her happy enough—and to know that she had so much love and strength to give someone, and yet not to have met anyone she could honestly marry.[82]

This was at the end of January 1956. A month later she met Ted Hughes, at a party in Cambridge held to inaugurate the *St. Botolph's Review*. Hughes was an ex-Cambridge man now working for Rank films in London. She wrote a poem about him afterwards, and in a letter to her mother said that he was the only man she had met at Cambridge who would be strong enough to be her equal. But she would probably never see him again. Such is life.[83]

In April she told Aurelia that "the most shattering thing" was that she had fallen in love, "terribly in love," which could only lead to great hurt. He was the strongest man in the world, a brilliant poet whose work she had loved before she met him, "a large, hulking, healthy Adam, half French, half Irish, with a voice like the thunder of God ..."[84]

After meeting Ted Hughes, Sylvia began to change. There would be no more poems in the manner of W. H. Auden or Phyllis McGinley; instead, she would be passionate.

Two of Hughes' poems, in the November 1954 issue of *Chequer*, had caused a stir at Cambridge. One was about a jaguar "hurrying enraged / Through prison darkness after the drills of his eyes ..."[85] Hughes' jaguar bore a distinct resemblance to Rilke's panther in the Paris zoo; nevertheless it struck Cambridge as exotic—foot-beagling was as much as most undergraduates knew about animals. Hughes' other poem, about a downed airman, was violent, bloody, and unpleasant.

On March 9 Sylvia sent her mother a poem she had written about a panther.

> There is a panther stalks me down;
> One day I'll have my death of him.

The author of "Pursuit" is no naturalist: her panther kisses his victims, and

> In the wake of this fierce cat,
> Kindled like torches for his joy,
> Charred and ravened women lie ...

Its appetite compels a "total sacrifice." The speaker attempts to run away from her own "secret" desires.

Appalled by secret want, I rush
From such assault of radiance.

She climbs into the "tower" of her fears, and shuts and bolts the door, but

The panther's tread is on the stairs,
Coming up and up the stairs.[86]

Like D. H. Lawrence and Dylan Thomas, Ted Hughes was an outsider: he was not raised in the Home Counties, nor educated at a public school, and he went to Cambridge by grace of winning an Open Exhibition. From the start he and Sylvia had this in common: they knew what it was to have no money and depend on one's talent.

He was born on August 17, 1930, in Calder Valley of the Yorkshire Pennines. Ted was the youngest of three children. His father was a carpenter; he had fought in the Great War, and as a boy Ted liked to imagine that the farms and moors, with bones of animals scattered about, were battlefields.

He has spoken of "the peculiar and desolate spirit that cries in telegraph wires on moor roads, in the dry and so similar voices of grouse and sheep, and the moist voices of curlews." Everything in West Yorkshire is "slightly unpleasant." The people seem only half-born from the earth, and the graves are too near the surface. "A disaster seems to hang around in the air there for a long time. I can never escape the impression that the whole region is in mourning for the first world war." And yet, in spite of this "the moorland is exultant, and," Hughes says, "this is what I remember of it."[87]

When he was a child he collected toy animals made of lead until they went right around the fireplace; he made drawings of animals and models in Plasticene. Later he would go along with his brother as a retriever when he went shooting magpies, owls, rabbits, weasels, rats, and curlews.[88]

In his book on Ted Hughes' poetry Keith Sagar describes the Calder Valley where Hughes grew up as a "shut-in, in-bred" industrial community inhabited by people who believed in decency, hard work, thrift, and good-neighborliness. They were puritanical and stiflingly respectable, adhering to "an aggressive self-congratulatory materialism and philistinism." They held intellectual and artistic activity in contempt. For a child to use an unfamiliar word in the playground was to risk being mocked for having "swallowed a dictionary." Yet, Sagar says, the language of the region, the West Riding dialect, "has remained

Hughes' staple poetic speech, concrete, emphatic, terse, yet powerfully, economically, eloquent."[89]

When Hughes was eight the family moved to Mexborough in South Yorkshire where his parents kept a newsagent's and tobacconist's shop. They moved back to the Calder Valley in 1952. "In Mexborough, like Lawrence before him in a similar area, Hughes was obliged to lead a double life, one with the town boys, sons of miners and railwaymen, the other in his bolt-hole—a nearby farm or a private estate with woods and a lake."[90]

At fifteen he was writing poems in the manner of Kipling, "most of them about Zulus or the Wild West." At Mexborough Grammar School his teachers encouraged him to write; one of them, John Fischer, gave him a great deal of help. By the time he left school Hughes was a graceful, lyric poet. In 1948 he won an Open Exhibition to Cambridge—but first he had to do two years of National Service as a ground wireless mechanic in the RAF. He was stationed at an isolated three-man radio station in East Yorkshire where he had nothing to do but "read and reread Shakespeare and watch the grass grow."[91]

He went up to Pembroke College, Cambridge, in 1951. His supervisor was M. J. C. Hodgart, an expert in ballads, whom he found very sympathetic. Hughes, we are told, rarely attended lectures, but he occasionally went to hear F. R. Leavis whom he found highly entertaining.

There is a story about Hughes at Cambridge that will probably be told again and again.

At Cambridge he set out to study English Literature. Hated it. Groaned having to write those essays. Felt he was dying of it in some essential place. Sweated late at night over the paper on Dr. Johnson et al.—things he didn't want to read. One night, very late, very tired, he went to sleep. Saw the door open and someone like himself come in with a fox's head. The visitor went over to his desk, where an unfinished essay was lying, and put his paw on the papers, leaving a bloody mark; then he came over to the bed, looked down at Ted and said, "You're killing us," and went out the door.[92]

He belonged to none of the Cambridge clubs and was rejected by the Amateur Dramatic Club—"luckily," he says. However, he went to the theater frequently—there was a lot of good theater in Cambridge at the time, "almost an embryonic Royal Shakespeare Company." He was not fond of athletics—the only sport he practiced was archery. In his third year he switched from English to Archaeology and Anthropology. He graduated in June 1954, "the same month in which his first poem appeared in a Cambridge periodical." This was "The Little Boys and the Seasons," published in *Granta* under a pseudonym. It was, Keith Sagar observes, "a pleasing poem, but too much under the influence of Dylan Thomas for the true Hughes to show through."[93]

In the next two years Hughes worked as a rose gardener, night watchman in a steel works, zoo attendant, schoolteacher, and reader for the J. Arthur Rank film company. He lived in London or Cambridge and published a few poems in Cambridge poetry magazines.

He had begun at Mexborough Grammar with imitations of traditional English poetry.

> O lady, consider when I shall have lost you
> The moon's full hands, scattering waste,
> The sea's hands, dark from the world's breast,
> The world's decay where the wind's hands have passed,
> And my head, worn out with love, at rest
> In my hands, and my hands full of dust,
>   O my lady.[94]

The poems in his first book, *The Hawk in the Rain*, are full of echoes—in the 1950s the weight of older generations lay heavily on the young.

Among modern poets, Dylan Thomas was his favorite. Some of Hughes' writing at this time was so much like Thomas' in imagery and diction as to seem a parody.

> With whirling quarters, the axle cracked,
> Through that miracle-breached bed
> All the dead could have got back;
> With shriek and heave and spout of blood
>
> The huge-eyed looming horde from
> Under the floor of the heart, that run
> To the madman's eye-corner came
> Deafening towards light, whereon
>
> A child whimpered upon the bed . . .[95]

When he met Sylvia Plath he urged her to read Thomas. She had studied Thomas' poetry in her last year at Smith, but it hadn't taken. Now she set about reading it in earnest.

She was learning to see through Ted's eyes. "I cannot stop writing poems! They come better and better. They come from the vocabulary of woods and animals and earth that Ted is teaching me."[96] She read the poets he approved of, and wrote under their influence, "drunker than Dylan, harder than Hopkins, younger than Yeats." She wrote a poem about Ted and his love of nature.

> Loam-humps, he says, moles shunt
> up from delved worm-haunt;
> blue fur moles have; hafting chalk-hulled flint
> he with rocks splits open
> knobbed quartz; flayed colors ripen
> rich, brown, sudden in sunglint.[97]

Ted was incredible. He wore the same black sweater and corduroy jacket, the pockets "full of poems, fresh trout and horoscopes." She cooked for him on the gas ring. He was the first man she had known who really had a love of food. She cooked him "a nectar of shrimps Newburg with essence of butter, cream, sherry and cheese" which they had on rice with the trout. Afterwards he lay by the hearth groaning with utter delight, like a huge Goliath.

Ted had a wonderful sense of humor. He told her fairy tales and stories of kings and green knights. He had made up a fable about a little wizard named Snatchcraftington who looked like a stalk of rhubarb. He told her dreams, "marvelous colored dreams, about certain red foxes."

He said that he had never read poems by a woman like hers; they were strong and rich and full—"not quailing and whining like Teasdale or simple lyrics like Millay; they are working, sweating, heaving poems born out of the way words should be said. . . ."

She knew that within a year she would publish "a book of 33 poems" that would hit the critics violently in some way or another.

"Oh, mother," she wrote, "rejoice with me and fear not. I love you, and Warren, and my dear suffering granny and dear loving grampy with all my heart and shall spend my life making you strong and proud of me!"[98]

Everything conspired in her happiness—even the university. Her new supervisor in philosophy, Dorothy Krook, was very sympathetic. Under her supervision Sylvia read Plato, wrote a paper every week, and had lively discussions. "I am standing," she wrote, "at the juncture of Greek and Christian thought now, and it is significant to see what the mind of man has made, the significance of the development from the dialectical inquiries of Socrates to the Epistle of St. Paul."[99]

In a few years, she wrote Aurelia, the world would be marveling at Ted and herself; they both had "such strength and creativity and productive *discipline*." [100]

They were married on June 16, in London, at the church of St. George the Martyr. Aurelia Plath came over for the wedding. For the time being the marriage had to be kept secret to protect Sylvia's grant from the Fulbright Foundation and her place at Newnham College. In a letter to her brother she said that "the Victorian virgins" wouldn't see how she could concentrate on her studies with being married to such a handsome, virile man.[101]

Ted and Sylvia went to Spain on their honeymoon. There she started sketching again, making pen-and-ink drawings of the peasant market in Benidorm, three sardine boats on the bay with their elaborate lights, and the cliff headland with houses above the sea.[102] She was also writing prose, with difficulty, trying to get back the form she had when she wrote "Sunday at the Mintons." She was working on a story about a bull-fight and had an idea for a humorous story for *The Ladies' Home Journal*, to be called "The Hypnotizing Husband." Ted was doing the last chapter of a book for children. He was educating her daily, setting her exercises in concentration and observation. She though that his vision was photographic while hers tended to be an impressionistic blur.[103]

On their return to England they went up to Yorkshire where she met Ted's parents—"dear, simple Yorkshire folk, and I love them both." Ted had a rich uncle who drove them over to Wuthering Heights. To get there you had to go over the moors on foot. It was like being on the top of the world, "with all the purplish hills curving away, and gray sheep grazing with horns curling and black demonic faces and yellow eyes." They walked by black walls of stone and clear streams and came at last to the place, "a lonely, deserted black-stone house, broken down, clinging to the windy side of a hill." She began a sketch of the sagging roof and stone walls, and planned to come back on the first nice day and finish it.[104]

When Sylvia had been back at Cambridge for a while the secret of her marriage came out. Mary Ellen Chase, now retired from teaching at Smith, dropped in to see how Sylvia was doing—at Smith they thought of her as a prize pupil and were keeping an eye on her progress—and was offended to find that Sylvia had got herself a husband. And such a husband! When Miss Chase queried Ted about his willingness to earn a living as a teacher, he laughed the idea to scorn. He was going to be a writer, nothing else. Miss Chase reported back to Smith that Sylvia's husband had said, "God no, no! Well, maybe I will teach some day, but only as a last resort, if I am starving and find nothing else."[105]

This was educative for Sylvia. Moreover, Ted despised literary careerism; he was willing to do a program on the BBC or edit an anthology, but he did not intend to live in that clambering world.

It was his pagan side that delighted her especially. One night Ted came over to her room at Cambridge—this was before they were living together—after a drinking bout, bringing a bottle of wine. She had no corkscrew, so he went down the corridor, banged on the first door, and shouted, "Do you have a corkscrew?" The door was opened by a woman of strict principles, "moral watchdog" of the dormitory, who hated drink. She stared at Ted, expressing her disapproval. He stared back at her, then brought down the bottle on the doorknob, breaking it off at the neck. Then he walked back to Sylvia's room.

People who had known the old Sylvia who liked everything tidy would have been surprised to see how delighted she was with her bottle-smasher.

The great news was that Ted's book of poems had been accepted for publication in America, having won the Poetry Center award for a first book. No money, just publication by Harper's. The judges were W. H. Auden, Stephen Spender, and Marianne Moore.

America beckoned, and Sylvia began a campaign to make Ted "fall in love with America." Then, in March, she was offered a teaching job at Smith for $4,200 a year. With this prospect before them they could hardly wait to leave for the States—it looked like the Promised Land. Ted might even be willing to change his citizenship, though she would not try to persuade him.[106]

She took her exams in May. For the English Tripos she offered a manuscript of her poems. Then they got ready for the trip to the States —both of them, she wrote Aurelia, "delighted to leave the mean, mealy-mouthed literary world of England."[107]

They arrived in the last week of June. They went up to Wellesley, then to a cottage on the Cape where Sylvia did some reading to prepare for her teaching. In the autumn they moved to Northampton where they lived in an attic apartment—"another rugged beginning," says Mrs. Plath.

Sylvia's teaching went well—too well, for she found that she had no time to write. In spite of his dislike of the whole idea Ted accepted a teaching job at the University of Massachusetts. Then they both gave up teaching and moved into Boston. They lived in a rented apartment in Beacon Hill and did their writing. This was in the winter of 1958–

1959. Sylvia had a job at the Massachusetts General Hospital, writing up case histories.

It was during these months that Sylvia used to drop in on Robert Lowell's poetry seminar at Boston University. "I see her dim," says Lowell, "against the bright sky of a high window . . . willowy, long-waisted, sharp-elbowed, nervous, giggly, gracious—a brilliant tense presence embarrassed by restraint. Her humility and willingness to accept what was admired seemed at times to give her an air of maddening docility that hid her unfashionable patience and boldness."[108]

Anne Sexton, who audited the seminar, tells of going after class meetings with Sylvia and George Starbuck to the Ritz, where they would sit and talk in the lounge-bar. "Often, very often," she says, "Sylvia and I would talk at length about our first suicides. . . . We talked death with burned-up intensity, both of us drawn to it like moths to an electric light bulb. Sucking on it!" They were all three stimulated by their talk of suicide, "as if death made each of us a little more real at the moment."[109]

In the spring Ted was awarded a grant from the Guggenheim Foundation. They now planned, says Mrs. Plath, to have a child "whom Ted wished to be English-born," and so they decided to return to England. But first Sylvia wanted to see the country. In the summer of 1959, borrowing Mrs. Plath's car, they went on a cross-country camping tour.

When they came back East they stayed for two months at Yaddo, the writers' colony in Saratoga. Here Sylvia wrote several of the poems in *The Colossus*.

What most strikes the reader is her imagery. This is her gift—all the rest, the structure of the poem, her "mythology," she arrives at by hard work, but metaphors and similes rise in profusion: "The pears fatten like little buddhas."[110]

Aristotle says that the ability to think in metaphors is the distinctive mark of a poet. There is an opposite theory, held by Williams and the Objectivists, that metaphors are a distraction, but Plath seems not to have heard of it. In this she is very much a poet of the 1950s. After Auden came Dylan Thomas with his Freudian symbols, and Theodore Roethke with his "greenhouse" poems that suggest delving into the unconscious. Psychoanalyzing oneself and looking for associations were common in intellectual circles in the fifties; this appeared in poetry as the creation of metaphors, the more remarkable the better.

The title poem shows that Plath has been thinking psychoanalytically, no doubt as a result of her own case and the case histories she has been

typing. The speaker is addressing a dead father: he is the broken colossus. She says, "I shall never get you put together entirely." She
speaks of having labored thirty years to dredge the silt from his throat,
and concludes by saying that her hours are "married to shadow."

In the course of the poem she refers to "the blue sky of the Oresteia."
Both in her treatment of a Freudian theme and her use of Greek
tragedy Plath is awkward; these ideas have not been translated into her
own language of feeling. "The Colossus" was written at some time
between the summer of 1958 and the summer of 1959. Compare it with
poems in *Ariel* written three years later:

> This black boot has no mercy for anybody.
> Why should it, it is the hearse of a dead foot . . .
>
>   "Berck-Plage"

> A yew hedge of orders,
> Gothic and barbarous, pure German.
>
>   "'Little Fugue"

> I have always been scared of *you*,
> With your Luftwaffe, your gobbledygoo.
> And your neat moustache,
> And your Aryan eye, bright blue.
>
> Panzer-man, panzer-man, O You—
>   "Daddy"[111]

These, also, are references to the "colossus," Otto Plath, who had blue
eyes and spoke German, and whose foot was amputated (so that
through an inversion it looms as a "black boot"). The speaker of *Ariel*
may, indeed, be taking part in an Aeschylean tragedy, but she has
learned not to say so—instead, to show how it works, in actual life.

The dead father of *The Colossus* appears in "Full Fathom Five,"
"Moonrise," and "The Beekeeper's Daughter," as well as the title poem.
There are a number of references to death and suicide. The theme of
the Muse which will be important in later poems is launched with "The
Disquieting Muses" and "Moonrise."

> Lucina, bony mother, laboring
> Among the socketed white stars, your face
> Of candor pares white flesh to the white bone . . .[112]

Plath writes in cadences, lines with strong but irregular accents, and in
stanzas with frequent run-ons from one stanza to the next. The rhymes
the assonantal.

The black bull bellowed before the sea.
The sea, till that day orderly,
Hove up against Bendylaw.

The queen in the mulberry arbor stared
Stiff as a queen on a playing card.
The king fingered his beard . . .

"The Bull of Bendylaw"[113]

Sylvia Plath and Ted Hughes returned to England in December 1959, and moved into a flat in London near Primrose Hill. The following April Sylvia gave birth to a daughter whom they named Frieda Rebecca.

The Colossus was published in October by Heinemann. At the beginning of 1961 Sylvia had a miscarriage and an appendectomy. In August they moved to an old house in Devon.

All this interfered with writing; nevertheless, that August she published three poems and in September five more, work she had been doing over the past two years. She was not happy about it. "These poems," she wrote, "do not live: it's a sad diagnosis."[114] Some were about places in America, from her camping trip with Ted, and others were about places she had visited in England.

"I Am Vertical," reads the title of one poem, and it proceeds: "But I would rather be horizontal."

It is more natural to me, lying down.
Then the sky and I are in open conversation,
And I shall be useful when I lie down finally:
Then the trees may touch me for once, and the
flowers have time for me.[115]

The impression this makes is of a mind wearily going through the motions; she is dragging out the *grand guignol* props and using them yet once more to scare the public with her dying. But the writing lacks energy, even interest.

In November she received a grant to work on *The Bell Jar*. In January she gave birth to a son whom they named Nicholas Farrar. This was followed by a burst of energy: hearing a broadcast by Laura Riding on the BBC may have had something to do with it. In April she wrote "the first rush of late poems": "Little Fugue," "Crossing the Water," "An Appearance," "Among the Narcissi," "Pheasant," and "Elm."[116]

What followed is well known: how she found out that her husband was involved with another woman; how she went with him to Ireland, then came back alone to Devon, and they agreed to separate; how she moved with the children to London; how she wrote the last poems—twenty-six in October, the first month after the separation; and how, finally, she killed herself.

In *The Savage God* Alvarez argues that she did not mean to go through with it. The separation from her husband had brought back the grief and abandonment she felt as a child when her father died. The poems she wrote that winter were obsessed with death. She always had the fantasy of rejoining her father in death. But she had so much to live for now, the children, and her writing. So she determined to be rid of her obsession with death once and for all. This was to be accomplished by acting out a ritual death. As she said in a note for the BBC on "Daddy," the narrator had to "act out the awful little allegory" in order to be free of it. She sealed the door and window with towels, put her head in the oven, and turned on the gas. But this time the ritual was not interrupted: her *au pair* girl couldn't get into the house, and the man who lived in the apartment below was drugged by the gas seeping down and did not hear the knocking. So the attempt succeeded.[117]

"Dying," she wrote,

> Is an art, like everything else.
> I do it exceptionally well.
>
> I do it so it feels like hell.
> I do it so it feels real.
> I guess you could say I've a call.
>
> "Lady Lazarus"[118]

This is the Sylvia Plath everyone knows, with a "long, escalating drive toward suicide."[119] It is common to think of her as a woman bent on committing suicide and her poems as confessions.

M. L. Rosenthal labeled her a "confessional poet," along with Robert Lowell, Allen Ginsberg, Theodore Roethke, John Berryman, and Anne Sexton. The term, applied to poets as different as these, can mean very little—in fact, is misleading, for it does not take into account Lowell's deliberate self-portraiture, Ginsberg's "hallucinatory-mystical" experiments, Roethke's writings about nature, or Berryman's invention of "Henry." It misses the most important thing about Sylvia Plath, her conversion of life into art. The only poet whom Rosenthal's term defines adequately is Anne Sexton who, indeed, placed "the literal self . . . at the center of the poem" so as to reveal her "psychological vulnerability and shame."[120]

Plath writes about her life but her poems are works of art, the images going down to a level of feeling that is shared by others.

> I know the bottom, she says. I know it with my great tap root:
> It is what you fear.
> I do not fear it: I have been there.
>
> "Elm"[121]

The poems make connections with "the language of the tribe"; this is what distinguishes them from confessional writing.

Judith Kroll has this to say: "Sylvia Plath obviously sensed that if one were to experience imminent death, the inessential aspects of self and personal history could separate from and be regarded by the permanent true self, leaving a sense of eternity and unity with the world."[122]

If this is true, the "long, escalating drive toward suicide" was no such thing, but a wish to be moving on.

It is a hard point to make. Everything seems to be against it; the poems do appear to be in love with death, and people can hardly be blamed for reading them so. In her zeal to right the balance Kroll argues that society is mistaken in its values: ". . . it would be presumptuous to assume that one's actual suicide, or images of self-inflicted death in one's art, are inherently sick or morbid. Where a culture lacks a transcendent or sacramental dimension, death will be a taboo subject; people would rather not be reminded of it, and suicide in such a culture will be considered an embarrassment."[123]

But Plath did live in that culture and accept its norms—indeed, in some things she was very conventional—and if one reads her letters there can be no doubt that she thought that her first attempt at suicide was embarrassing, to say the least. There is every reason to think that if the second attempt had been interrupted she would have gone through the same cycle of shame and remorse, followed by a determination to live.[124]

For those who care about poetry the real interest is not in the circumstances of her death but the transformation of the skillful poet of *The Colossus* into the inspired poet of *Ariel*. What could have brought this about?

Anger was the cause. She had been very much in love with Ted Hughes—though not so adoring as her letters to her mother show. She wanted everyone back home to think that her husband was just perfect. But it was a good marriage, far better than most. She was Ted's equal, especially in her determination to succeed as a poet. Their quarrels were soon made up and forgotten.

Then Ted went off with another woman. He appeared to have abandoned her, just as her father had abandoned her by dying. She was cast down again in the darkness she had known as a child and young woman. A feeling of panic—she was loved by no one and utterly alone.

Then she became angry—at Ted of course, but also at herself for letting herself be taken in—by life. She had never really believed in it anyway.

At the end she stripped herself of illusions. When Alvarez saw her she was gaunt and pale; her hair, that she usually wore in a tight bun, hung straight to her waist and gave off a sharp smell like an animal's. She walked before him down the passage and up the stairs to her flat on the top two floors. The children had already been put to bed and the flat was silent. It had been painted recently, a chilly white. There was hardly any furniture, rush matting on the floor, a few books, "bits of Victoriana and cloudy blue glass on the shelves." The windows were curtainless, looking out on the cold night.[125]

In the poems she wrote at the end she was scarifying herself, purging from her style every drop of sentimentality. The images of her inner anguish poured forth and she gave expression to her thought in language that was hard, mocking, direct. She no longer had any patience—she wasn't thinking how to please. And still her writing took the forms of art.

She would show Ted Hughes. She was a poet in her own right, maybe even a better poet. She didn't need his approval or anyone else's. She could say anything she pleased, and it had an air of truth, the pressure of a life behind it. She could dispense with all of them—Ted, her mother, her father, people she had known at Cambridge and at Smith. She could even dispense with herself, she was that angry.

From her reading of Sir James Frazer's *The Golden Bough* and Robert Graves's *The White Goddess,* Sylvia Plath grew familiar with myths of the Mother Goddess who is the Muse of poetry, and came to think of her life as exemplifying the Muse. "There is a kinship or identity," says Judith Kroll, "between the White Goddess and all of the subsidiary heroines and goddesses who enact aspects of her myth, for these are all facets or versions of the same White Goddess. Graves writes, 'The daughters are really limited versions of herself—herself in various young-moon and full-moon aspects. . . . Plath's protagonist (in all her guises) is in a similar sense a facet or version of the Moon-muse."[126]

Through her association with the Muse, Sylvia Plath transcended her "personal history." The detached, mocking, cruel voice in the later poems became the voice of the Muse.

She worked consciously to make everything hang together and give her feelings a larger significance. Many poets have done as much: Blake, Yeats, Eliot, all have matched their experiences to mythology. And critics are pleased with authors who do so, for it gives them something to look up.

Yet, it can be a frigid enterprise unless there is a real need for such fusion. The myth must be brooded over until the poet believes it just as truly as he believes that he has had eggs for breakfast or is taking the 5:25 to White Plains. This is where poets fail and earn the derogatory term, "academic." One can see them turning the pages of Frazer or Graves or Murray.

This was how Sylvia Plath began—the wonder is that she changed into a true poet. The poet of *Ariel* seems to mean what she says. "Seems," because she is writing poetry—the meaning of a poem is never literal, it is always a fiction of some kind. The "seeming" consists of a passion for words. The poet of *Ariel* is filled with a passion for words.

Writing of this kind does not depend on mythology—it is original. This is why Sylvia Plath is such an important poet: she "transcends" *The Golden Bough* and *The White Goddess* just as she transcends her personal history.

Nowhere is this more evident than in the bee poems, written in October and November 1962, her period of greatest creativity.

In June of 1962 Sylvia Plath and Ted Hughes took up beekeeping on their place in Devon. They went to a local meeting together with the rector, the midwife, and other people interested in bees, to watch a Mr. Pollard transfer his queen cells from one hive into two others under the supervision of a bee man sent by the Government. They all wore masks, says Sylvia, describing the event to her mother, and it was thrilling.

Mr. Pollard let Ted and Sylvia have an old hive for nothing; they painted it white and green and ordered a swarm of "docile Italian hybrid bees." Mr. Pollard brought the bees over and installed them. The bees were furious from being in a box, and as Ted had only put a handkerchief over his head where the hat should go in the bee mask, the bees crawled into his hair and he went running off with a half-dozen stings. The hive was placed in a sheltered, out-of-the-way spot in the garden.

Sylvia was delighted to see the bees entering with pollen sacks full and leaving with them empty. At least, that was what she *thought* they were doing.[127]

She wrote six poems about bees. In *The Colossus*, "The Beekeeper's Daughter" evokes the myth of a dead king and dead season: "Father, bridegroom . . . The queen bee marries the winter of your year." The speaker in the poem does a curious thing: she kneels on the ground and looks down a hole where she sees "an eye / Round, green, disconsolate as a tear."[128] Then we remember that Sylvia Plath's father as a boy was called the Bee King, that he would track wild bees to their burrows in the earth and suck up wild honey through a straw. The poem depends, as many of her poems do, on a fusion of autobiography and myth.

Five of the bee poems are in *Ariel*. The first is like a dream—the speaker caught up in a ritual she does not understand. She is being met at the bridge by people she knows: the rector, the midwife, the sexton, the "agent for bees." They are protected with clothing while she has only a sleeveless "summery" dress that does not protect her. "They are smiling and taking out veils tacked to ancient hats."

The "secretary of bees" covers her with a silken garment. She thinks that none of the bees will notice her, will not smell her fear. The villagers put on head coverings and "breastplates" of cheesecloth. "Their smiles and their voices are changing." Then they lead her through a bean field:

> Strips of tinfoil winking like people,
> Feather dusters fanning their hands in a sea of bean flowers,
> Creamy bean flowers with black eyes and leaves like bored hearts.
> Is it blood clots the tendrils are dragging up that string?
> No, no, it is scarlet flowers that will one day be edible.

The villagers give her a "fashionable white straw Italian hat" and a black veil, making her one of them. They lead her to "the shorn grove, the circle of hives." Is it the hawthorn, she wonders, that smells so sick, "The barren body of hawthorn, etherizing its children?"

She wonders if some sort of separation is taking place. Confronted with an "apparition in a green helmet, / Shining gloves and white suit," she asks if this is the "surgeon" her neighbors are waiting for. Is it the butcher or the grocer or the postman, someone she knows?

She is rooted to the spot and cannot run. The gorse hurts her "With its yellow purses, its spiky armoury." If she started to run she would have to run forever.

The white hive is snug as a virgin,
Sealing off her brood cells, her honey, and quietly humming.

Smoke rolls and scarves in the grove.
The mind of the hive thinks this is the end of everything.
Here they come, the outriders, on their hysterical elastics.
If I stand very still, they will think I am cow parsley,
A gullible head untouched by their animosity,

Not even nodding, a personage in a hedgerow.

There follows the hunt for the old queen: the villagers open the chambers of the hive, looking for her. "Is she hiding, is she eating honey?" But the old queen is clever. "She is old, old, old, she must live another year, and she knows it."

Meanwhile, the "new virgins / Dream of a duel they will win inevitably." They dream of the "bride flight, / The upflight of the murderess into a heaven that loves her." But this does not come to pass —the villagers move the virgins. "There will be no killing. / The old queen does not show herself, is she so ungrateful?"

The poem concludes:

I am exhausted, I am exhausted—
Pillar of white in a blackout of knives.
I am the magician's girl who does not flinch.
The villagers are untying their disguises, they are
   shaking hands.
Whose is that long white box in the grove, what have
   they accomplished, why am I cold?[129]

Here again we see the two strains that run through Plath's writing, autobiography and myth. The old queen is like the priest-king at Nemi, described in *The Golden Bough*. He guards the sacred grove and the bough that represents or embodies his soul. The one who plucks the bough and kills the priest-king will take his place as guardian of the sacred grove until he is slain in his turn.

In "The Bee Meeting," however, the duel is not allowed to take place —"there will be no killing." The observer—"Pillar of white in a blackout of knives"—emerges from her dream state to see the villagers taking off their "disguises" and shaking hands. They seem to think that the "operation" has been a success. But, she asks, "Whose is that long white box in the grove, what have they accomplished, why am I cold?"

In a letter Sylvia Plath once tried to explain how she felt in the summer of 1953 when she tried to kill herself. She was discovered after three days lying on a ledge in the basement: "My brother," she says, "finally heard my weak yells, called the ambulance, and the next days were a nightmare of flashing lights, strange voices, large needles, an overpowering conviction that I was blind in one eye, and a hatred toward the people who would not let me die, but insisted rather in dragging me back into the hell of sordid and meaningless existence."[130]

There is an evident connection between the attempted suicide and the ritual in "The Bee Meeting." The villagers who assist at the "operation" are like the well-meaning people who "dragged" Sylvia Plath "back into the hell of sordid and meaningless existence." The ritual was supposed to go to the end but was not allowed to.

The speaker in "The Bee Meeting" describes herself as a "Pillar of white in a blackout of knives" and "the magician's girl who does not flinch." It seems, therefore, that she has been at the center of violence. She cannot be the old queen—her position as observer makes this clear. The old queen is in hiding. Therefore, the speaker must be the challenger of the old queen, and as the attempt has failed it is her body that lies in the white box. This is why she feels cold.

But we are told there would be no killing. There has not, in fact, been a killing. The poet has envisioned her death in the sacred grove, but there is a separation between art and life—or death.

Identifying the speaker with the challenger of the old queen seems the right solution when we recall poems in which Sylvia Plath thinks of herself as Electra.[131] When her father, Agamemnon, was slain by the queen and her paramour, Electra devoted herself to avenging his death. His memory belonged to her; she played the part that should have been played by the queen.

In her poems she was able to project images of the new life she wanted. The poem "Ariel" speaks of "the drive / Into the red / Eye, the cauldron of morning."[132] The poem "Stings" shows the queen reviving. We do not know whether she has been dead or asleep, but

> Now she is flying
> More terrible than ever she was, red
> Scar in the sky, red comet
> Over the engine that killed her—
> The mausoleum, the wax house.[133]

These are surrealist images; they make an impression that cannot be accounted for by looking to their sources in mythology or the life of the poet. The image is itself, a new thing.

Whose is that long white box in the grove, what
have they accomplished, why am I cold?[134]

Her art is complete and distinct from her life. This may not be the
renascence she wanted—in any case, it is what she achieved.

". . . if one is fortunate, one may come upon a young queen of the beautiful species *ternarius* . . . whose orange and yellow pile blends with the
colors of the male willow catkins just bursting into blossom. A bit
farther on, among the inconspicuous flowers of a female willow, one
is almost certain to find a queen of *B. terricola* in her splendid livery
of black, banded with yellow."

Otto Emil Plath, *Bumblebees and Their Ways*

Robert Lowell's Indissoluble Bride

ROBERT LOWELL was born into the class of people in Boston who used to hand down standards of ethics and culture to the rest of the country. James Russell Lowell, poet and ambassador to the Court of St. James's, was his great-great-uncle. On his mother's side he is descended from Edward Winslow, a Pilgrim Father who came over on the *Mayflower*. Edward Winslow's son was a famous killer of Indians and a governor of Plymouth Colony.

Thinking about his ancestors has given Lowell some disagreeable moments. The novelist Ford Madox Ford once told him that with his background he would never amount to anything as a poet—he would only be an ambassador or a president of Harvard.

If you were a Lowell you were expected to conform to a code of behavior; you went to certain schools, mixed with the best people, and made your mark.

But Robert Lowell's father was unable to make a mark of any kind. He served in the Navy, then he resigned and went to work for the Cambridge branch of Lever Brothers. But he had no business ability and drifted from one job to another, "a fish out of water." He seems to have had no character—none, at any rate, that would appeal to his wife and son. "Father," says Robert Lowell, ". . . was a mumbler. His opinions were almost morbidly hesitant, but he considered himself a matter-of-fact man of science and had an unspoiled faith in the superior efficiency of northern nations." On Sundays he did not go to church, thinking that this was not suitable for a Navy man; instead, he puttered around—for example, painting his name on garbage cans, followed by the letters "U. S. N."

On the other hand Lowell's mother, Charlotte Winslow Lowell, had definite opinions. She admired heroic men and disliked being married to a "weakling" who was only interested in "steam, radio, and 'the fellows.' " But though she took her son into her confidence he liked her none the better for it—both his parents got on his nerves. " 'Weela-waugh, we–ee–eelawaugh, weelawaugh,' shrilled Mother's high voice. 'But–and, but–and, but–and!' Father's low mumble would drone in answer."[1]

Young Bob attached himself to his Grandfather Winslow. "He was my Father," says Robert Lowell, "I was his son." One of the poems in *Life Studies* begins:

> "I won't go with you. I want to stay with Grandpa!"
> That's how I threw cold water
> on my Mother and Father's
> watery martini pipe dreams at Sunday dinner.
> . . . Fontainebleau, Mattapoisett, Puget Sound . . .
> Nowhere was anywhere after a summer
> at my Grandfather's farm.[2]

He tagged along with his grandfather on his farm; in the Indian Summer they would drive out of Boston to the family graveyard to rake the leaves, spending time together in perfect communion.

Lowell tells us that as a boy he had a passion for toy soldiers, and that he invented a romantic history for one Mordecai Myers, a relative of his Grandmother Lowell who had fought against the British. He imagined him to be "such a fellow as Napoleon's mad, pomaded son-of-an-innkeeper-general, Junot, Duc D'Abrantes. . . ." But Mordecai Myers turned out to have been thoroughly sober and respectable.

At the age of thirteen Lowell entered St. Mark's boarding school. There, together with a friend named Frank Parker, he began reading books and histories of art, "looking at reproductions, tracing the Last Supper on tracing paper, studying dynamic symmetry, learning about Cézanne, and so on." This study, he says, was rather close to poetry, "And from there I began." He read Elizabeth Drew or some such book on modern poetry that had free verse in it, "and that seemed very simple to do."[3]

He had wanted to be a football player, and won his letter but did not make the team. In his disappointment he turned to writing poetry. He had some luck, too, in having Richard Eberhart for a teacher. He did not take classes with Eberhart but went to see him. "He'd smoke honey-scented tobacco, and read Baudelaire and Shakespeare and Hopkins—it made the thing living—and he'd read his own poems."

He wrote "very badly" at first, but Eberhart was encouraging. It made all the difference to the beginner that someone he admired was himself a practicing poet. He tried writing blank verse and free verse, then writing in stanzas.

From St. Mark's he went to Harvard where, in his second year, he took courses in English, "the easiest sort of path." He paid a visit to Robert Frost and showed him a long poem he was writing on the First Crusade. Frost said that he lacked compression and showed him Collins's "How sleep the brave" as an example of a poem that was not too long. He talked about "the voice coming into poetry," and pointed to the line in Keats's *Hyperion* about the Naiad pressing a cold finger to her cold lips. There, he told Lowell, the writing came alive. This was a revelation; Lowell had admired the poem for its "big Miltonic imitation"— now he realized that this kind of writing could be diffuse and monotonous.[4] Then he tried his hand at short Imagistic poems in the manner of William Carlos Williams. A group of these were accepted by the editor of the Harvard *Advocate* and set up in galleys, but after Lowell left Harvard they were turned down.

He left at the end of two years. The reason was a quarrel with his father. From Lowell's account, in *Notebook*, he had been seeing a girl, and his father wrote to her father saying that she had visited Lowell in his rooms at college, alone. The girl gave Lowell the letter; he brooded over it, then "punctiliously" handed it to his father and knocked him down. "He half-reclined on the carpet; / Mother called from the top of the carpeted stairs. . . ."[5]

This was bad, but a solution presented itself. In Boston Lowell had come to know Merrill Moore, the psychiatrist and sonnet writer. Moore came from Tennessee where he had been one of the Fugitives who stood for Southern agrarian values and opposed the ways of the North: the city, the machine, and centralized government. Moore thought that Lowell ought to study with a poet, namely John Crowe Ransom who was then teaching at Vanderbilt. Then Lowell met Ford Madox Ford who was on his way South to visit Allen Tate and his wife in Tennessee, and Ford said, "Come and see me down there," so Lowell drove down to Nashville. He found Ford installed at the Tates' with his wife and secretary. "I think," Lowell says, "I suggested that maybe I'd stay with them. And they said, 'We really haven't any room, you'd have to pitch a tent on the lawn.' " So he went to Sears, Roebuck and bought a tent and rigged it on the lawn. The Tates were too polite to tell him that they had just been using a figure of speech. He stayed for two months and took his meals with the Tates.[6]

Then he went to Kenyon College in Gambier, Ohio, to study with Ransom who had moved there from Vanderbilt.

Getting to know Tate and Ransom worked a great change in Lowell. The "mob of ruling-class Bostonians"[7] thought of literature, if they thought of it at all, as a shabby and unprofitable occupation—certainly not fitting for a gentleman. Look at the recent example in the Lowells' own family, Amy Lowell, who smoked cigars! But in the view of Tate and Ransom there was nothing better than a poet, unless it were a critic.

They themselves were New Critics, deriving their attitudes from T. S. Eliot and Mallarmé and Flaubert and Baudelaire. New Critics were old Aesthetes writ large: they believed in the absolute self-sufficiency of the work of art. The poem was treated "primarily as poetry and not another thing." Poetry was not responsible to "life"; "le poème ... n'a d'autre but que de préparer son dénouement."[8]

The method of the New Criticism was rigorously empirical analysis of the text. The function of the critic was to "explicate" the text and not be distracted by the author's life or intention (the intentional fallacy), the history of the society in which he lived, the traditional genre of the work, or the effect it had upon the reader's emotions (the affective fallacy).

In reaction against the use of literature for political purposes, New Critics argued for the separation of art from politics. When Van Wyck Brooks and Archibald MacLeish attacked Tate and his circle for their apolitical stance, calling them "The Irresponsibles" and holding them partly to blame for the rise of Fascism, Tate replied with an argument in favor of the "universality" of the artist and against "expediency."[9] Yet Tate's views were political: he did not hesitate to express his contempt for modern democracy; he believed in an aristocracy such as had existed in the antebellum South, and like Pound he could only find fault with present conditions. Pound became a supporter of Mussolini—Tate did not go so far, but during the Second World War he described American flyers as "proconsuls of the air" and derided them for destroying traditional values:

> Dive, and exterminate
> The Lama, late
> Survival of old pain.
> Go kill the dying swan.[10]

Tate, Ransom, and their friends were an exclusive club. This was tremendously appealing to Lowell; he was an outsider to his family, a "morose and solitary" figure,[11] and here he suddenly found himself included and *they* were the outsiders. The Tates' house in Nashville and Ransom's house at Kenyon College were like beleaguered fortresses. When Tate or Ransom wrote a critical article it was possible to imagine that they were engaged in mortal battle with hordes of ignoramuses. "When I was twenty," says Lowell, "and learning to write, Allen Tate, Eliot, Blackmur, and Winters, and all those people were very much news. You waited for their essays, and when a good critical essay came out it had the excitement of a new imaginative work."[12]

Within two months of pitching his tent on the Tates' lawn Lowell had stopped writing free verse and was writing in rhyme. He had been "converted to formalism."[13]

At Kenyon he studied Greek and Roman classics as well as literature in English. The Greeks were entirely different from the English—"Greek wildness and sophistication all different, the women different, everything." Roman history had a "terrible human frankness" that wasn't customary in English—"corrosive attacks on the establishment, comments on politics and the decay of morals, all felt terribly strongly, by poets as well as historians."

His favorite English poetry was "the difficult Elizabethan plays" and the Metaphysicals, then the nineteenth century. He read nineteenth-century poetry with excitement and, at times, aversion—it was closer to his own writing than anything else.[14]

In 1940 Lowell underwent a religious conversion and entered the Roman Catholic Church. In the same year he married the novelist Jean Stafford, and graduated from Kenyon College *summa cum laude*, with a major in Classics. Then he taught English literature at Kenyon.

At this time, he tells us, he was reading Hart Crane "and Thomas and Tate and Empson's *Seven Types of Ambiguity*," and each poem he wrote was more difficult than the one before, and had more ambiguities. "Ransom, editing the *Kenyon Review*, was impressed, but didn't want to publish them. He felt they were forbidding and clotted." Finally Ransom did accept one poem, but for about three years Lowell's poems were rejected. He says, "I seemed to have reached a great impasse. The kind of poem I thought was interesting and would work on became so cluttered and overdone that it wasn't really poetry."[15]

In 1941–1942 he worked in New York as an editorial assistant at Sheed and Ward, a publishing house that specialized in Catholic books. The following year he taught at Louisiana State University; there he met Cleanth Brooks and Robert Penn Warren who were editing the

Southern Review and producing textbooks that would teach New Criticism to the next generation.

After Pearl Harbor he had tried to enlist in the Navy but had been rejected. By 1943 he had become a conscientious objector. He refused to report to his draft board. He wrote a letter to President Roosevelt, and sent copies to the newspapers, saying that the Lowells, like the President's family, had served in all wars since the Declaration of Independence, but he was opposed to the policy of bombing Germany and Japan into submission, and could not participate in a war that might leave Europe and China to the mercy of the U.S.S.R., "a totalitarian tyranny committed to world revolution."

For refusing to report he was sentenced to a year and a day in a Federal prison, of which he served five months.

Lowell has referred to this as his "seed time."

> I was a fire-breathing Catholic C. O.,
> and made my manic statement,
> telling off the state and president . . .[16]

Written long after the event, the lines show a fine irony—nevertheless it is true, this was his seed time. In these years he developed, under great pressure, into a poet. This was his heroic period. In later years he would frequently refer back to it. Knowing, as Wordsworth says, that he had once been strong gave him confidence and the power to judge men and events. It gave him authority.

In July 1944, he published his first book of poems, *Land of Unlikeness*, in an edition of 250 copies. There were twenty-one poems with an introduction by Allen Tate. "There is no poetry today," said Tate, "quite like this. T. S. Eliot's recent prediction that we should soon see a return to formal and even intricate metres and stanzas was coming true, before he made it, in the verse of Robert Lowell. Every poem in this book has a formal pattern. . . ."

There were two types of poetry in the book which had not yet been successfully united: a poetry of Christian symbolism that was satiric, pointing to "the disappearance of the Christian experience from the modern world," and, on the other hand, some shorter poems that were "richer in immediate experience than the explicitly religious poems." The latter were more dramatic, "the references being personal and historical and the symbolism less willed and explicit."

Tate ended with a prophecy: "unless, after the war, the small public for poetry shall exclude all except the democratic poets who enthusiastically greet the advent of the slave-society, Robert Lowell will have to be reckoned with." The present condition of material progress was a mask for social and spiritual decay, but the decay was not universal, and in Lowell's poetry, whether one liked the Catholicism or not, there was "at least a memory of the spiritual dignity of man, now sacrificed to mere secularization and a craving for mechanical order."[17]

Turning to the poems in *Land of Unlikeness* we find that they are full of violent and grotesque imagery:

> O mother, I implore
> Your scorched, blue thunderbreasts of love to pour
> Buckets of blessings on my burning head
> Until I rise like Lazarus from the dead . . .[18]

As Alan Williamson remarks, there is a tradition of sensuous and violent expression in Catholic mysticism, but the equation of the Virgin's milk with a thunderbolt cannot be explained by any Catholic doctrine. "It reminds one of Jung's description of a very early stage in human religious development at which the ultimately good, and ultimately evil, qualities are united in the same divinities—a stage which, Jung says, often resurfaces in a neurotic's conception of parental figures." Williamson concludes with a remark that describes *Land of Unlikeness* as a whole: "Lowell's imagination is preoccupied, to the deepest level, with the violence whose outward manifestation he totally condemns."[19]

The poems are heavy with meaning. A critic tells us that

"Dea Roma," a history of Rome from Augustus to the present, reinforces Catholicism as a condition for salvation. In the world of fading Christianity, Rome is still the Eternal City, and Christ still walks the waters of her rivers to the Celestial City of Heaven. In fact, like Dante, only from the "dry Dome" of St. Peter's can the souls of the faithful leave to meet Christ. This dry dome, Michelangelo's sublime masterpiece, which time has colored gold, complements the "golden" Statehouse dome of "The Park Street Cemetery."

These poems suggest that modern man should pay careful attention to the qualities which helped to save Arthur Winslow's soul. To them Lowell has added Catholicism, knowledge, imitation of Christ, and mysticism . . .[20]

This kind of reading proceeds on the assumption that all the ideas in poems are important. But ideas may only be pegs to hang poetry on, and this appears to have been the case with Lowell.

In "The Park Street Cemetery" he looks at the names of the founding fathers on the tombstones. They have bequeathed America their zeal for making war. Over against .them he sets the "Easter crowds / On Boston Common," the Irish who "hold the Golden Dome." The old

Protestant world of "Adams, / Otis, Hancock, Mather, Revere; Franklin's mother" is decaying, and Catholicism taking its place.[21]

He sees the Second World War as a struggle for empire, that is all.

> So, child, unclasp your fists
> And clap for Freedom and Democracy.
> No matter, child, if Ark Royal lists
> Into the sea;
> Soon the Leviathan
> Will spout American.
>
> "The Boston Nativity"[22]

Lowell's attitudes in *Land of Unlikeness* are so much like Pound's —contempt for democracy, belief that war is a swindle, et cetera—that it would not be surprising if he were also tainted with Pound's anti-Semitism, and in one place at least we find him sharpening a knife for the Jew.

> In Greenwich Village, Christ the Drunkard brews
> Gall, or spiked bone-vat, siphons his bilged blood
> Into weak brain-pans and unseasons wood:
> His auctioneers are four hog-fatted Jews.
>
> "Christ for Sale"[23]

How seriously are we to take Lowell's profession of faith? He appears to have been fascinated with Christian symbolism but to have had no understanding of the one rule that, we are told, includes all the rest: we are to love one another.

Lowell himself would say years later that the Catholicism had served to give his poems a form and bring them to a climax. "It's all to the good if a poem *can* use politics, or theology, or gardening, or anything that has its own validity apart from poetry. But these things will never *per se* make a poem."[24]

Then what does make a poem? It must be language, images, rhythm— the form of the thought.

In *Land of Unlikeness* the thought turns inward upon itself. Yenser puts it well: "The characteristic structural principle . . . is what Tate has called 'intension,' the network of ambiguities and contradictions generated beneath the surface of the poetry." Lowell's perceptions "are primarily of the relationships among words and phrases, not of the relationships among people and things. . . ." Lowell has an irresistible urge to create ambiguities, a compulsion to "tinker with commonplaces and to polish touchstones."[25]

Language of this kind calls for explication.

> This Easter, Arthur Winslow, five years gone,
> I come to bury you and not to praise
> The craft that netted a million dollars, late
> Mining in California's golden bays . . .[26]

The second line alludes to Mark Antony's speech in *Julius Caesar* for no good reason—making these allusions is like a nervous habit. Yenser points out that the words "craft," "netted," "dollars" and "golden bays" join "images drawn from fishing with the vocabulary of the capitalism which, among other things, Arthur Winslow represents."[27]

These were poems for critics, and Lowell's next book, *Lord Weary's Castle*, gave them all they could have hoped for. Randall Jarrell, a friend of Lowell—they had been at Kenyon together—reviewed both *Land of Unlikeness* and *Lord Weary's Castle*. He said, "When I reviewed Mr. Lowell's first book I finished by saying, 'Some of the best poems of the next years ought to be written by him.' The appearance of *Lord Weary's Castle* makes me feel less like Adams or Leverrier than like a rain-maker who predicts rain and gets a flood which drowns everyone in the country."[28]

About a third of the poems in *Land of Unlikeness* were carried over to *Lord Weary's Castle*. Lowell kept the more concrete poems—"That's what the book was moving toward: less symbolic imagery." And there was less gratuitous violence—he says, "I tried to take some of the less fierce poems. There seemed to be too much twisting and disgust in the first book."[29]

The reader of *Lord Weary's Castle* is gripped by the vitality in things. As Lowell says, he has turned away from symbolism and is focusing on concrete particulars. He is seeing and hearing intensely. As a result, things appear to be animated:

> The search-guns click and spit and split up timber
> And nick the slate roofs . . .[30]

> Listen, the hay-bells tinkle as the cart
> Wavers on rubber tires along the tar . . .[31]

> The beach increasing, its enormous snout
> Sucking the ocean's side . . .[32]

> The death-lance churns into the sanctuary, tears
> The gun-blue swingle, heaving like a flail,

> And hacks the coiling life out: it works and drags
> And rips the sperm-whale's midriff into rags,
> Gobbets of blubber spill to wind and weather . . .[33]

Lowell may be a pacifist, but as a writer he is aggressive—he seems to be grappling with the world in order to subdue it. The book is memorable for its energetic language and strong rhythms. The lines are rhymed as though to rivet them down. They march in iambic. Plosives give a sense of hammering energy:

> The empty winds are creaking and the oak
> Splatters and splatters on the cenotaph,
> The boughs are trembling and a gaff
> Bobs on the untimely stroke
> Of the greased wash exploding on a shoal-bell
> In the old mouth of the Atlantic . . .[34]

"The Quaker Graveyard in Nantucket" is a fair specimen of the book as a whole. It has often been discussed for its ideas, but the living tissue of the poem is its imagery. Lowell makes the sea rise up as if to overwhelm the reader. Like Rimbaud's "Bateau Ivre," "The Quaker Graveyard" evokes the upheaval of Creation, "When the Lord God formed man from the sea's slime. . . ."[35]

The poem begins with the apparition of a drowned sailor rising from the deep with "matted head and marbled feet." Lowell took this description of a drowned man from a book, Thoreau's *Cape Cod*.[36]

The poem is supposed to be an elegy for Lowell's cousin, Warren Winslow, who was drowned on Navy duty. But there is very little about Winslow; he serves merely to introduce the subject of the Quakers, the pursuit and dismemberment of the whale, and the coming punishment of the world. When Lowell asks, "Sailor, can you hear / The Pequod's sea wings . . . ," the sailor must answer yes, and the *Pequod* comes sailing in, with the story of Ahab and Moby Dick. The poem is now off and running; it is to be about literature, Lowell's favorite subject. He writes best when he writes about literature or those who make it, himself not least of all.

In Part III the Quakers who hunted the whale are condemned for their self-righteousness while engaged in a bloody and mercenary calling. In Part IV there is pity for the whale: "Spouting out blood and water as it rolls, / Sick as a dog. . . ." "Sick as a dog" is good; it domesticates the whale—a pet is being killed. We are told that the end of the whaleroad is to be "poured out like water"—we shall be punished for our materialism as the Quakers were when they drowned, the ribs of their ship stove in.

Part V shows the Day of Judgment "When the whale's viscera go and the roll / Of its corruption overruns this world." The poem mockingly asks what will men do then—will they persist in killing? Can the sword save them? There follows a vision of a whale being hacked to pieces in the very center or womb of things: "The death-lance churns into the sanctuary." The poem wields Apocalypse to Creation—the morning stars sing as the gulls fly around the sinking *Pequod*. The masthead with the red flag hammered to it is cast upon a beach. This section ends with the words, "Hide, / Our steel, Jonas Messias, in Thy side." The dying whale has become Christ crucified, the harpooner the soldier who thrust his spear into His side. The plea is for Christ by his dying to obtain forgiveness for the eternal, repeated cruelties of men.

Part VI is a calm following the vision of the end. We are on the road to Our Lady of Walsingham. The drowned sailor once visited the shrine at Walsingham. The statue of Mary near the altar has "no comeliness / At all or charm in that expressionless / Face with its heavy eyelids," and the absence of expression expresses God. "She knows what God knows." Though there is no cross now at Calvary, nor crib at Bethlehem—I take this to mean there are no signs and wonders—there is still the Church and, forced by the consequences of its evildoing, "the world shall come to Walsingham." Because it must.

In the conclusion the poem returns full circle to Nantucket with its memories of "supercilious, wing'd clippers" and reek of fish guts. The smell evokes both Creation and Apocalypse; the genesis of man is coeternal with his dying. But "The Lord survives the rainbow of His will." A difficult saying . . . perhaps it means that God is apart from nature and the working-out of history. Apart and exceedingly remote.[37]

Such is the argument of "The Quaker Graveyard in Nantucket." It can be made to appear a great deal more complicated—Williamson, for example, speaks of three kinds of religious vision in the poem: "the harsh moral fable of the withdrawal of God's mercy occasioned by man's persistence in evil"; the Christian Existentialist faith that the absence of conventional religious comforts may be the occasion for "the rebirth of a living relation"; and a vision that is animistic or pantheistic. "I feel pantheistic implications," says Williamson, "in the poem's strange linking images, which identify so many forces and beings with their natural enemies, with Satan and Jehovah, and with Christ; and in its vision of a formless primal matter, conjured up by science, but identified through the image of the heavy eyelids with the expressionless expression that knows God's will."[38]

This is taking "The Quaker Graveyard" as philosophy and theology, the critic assuming what the writer assumes, whereas in fact the poem makes a very different impression. The argument is obscure, but the imagery is immediate and vivid, and what it amounts to is a Grand Guignol or spook show, lavish with death and wounds. Many of Lowell's early poems are like this; there is something childish or pathological about them. Has anyone noticed, for example, how often a corpse is being burned, or someone is playing with fire?

Writing such as this is not a "criticism of life," for the writer is not well. "The Quaker Graveyard" looks forward to the end of the world —earth, sea, and the ships upon it. But as this prophet seems to have so little share in the life of the world, his judgment of it does not matter.

In spite of the references to religion, *Lord Weary's Castle* is not a religious book. Rather it is about death and the fear of dying. Arthur Winslow dies of cancer, "Wrestling with the crab— / The claws drop flesh upon your yachting blouse." Mary Winslow dies with "hideous baby-squawks and yells." Thousands of innocent people are killed in Europe by aerial bombardment. In a translation of Propertius, Lowell gloats over the corpse of Cynthia burning on its funeral pyre.

> . . . the sizzling grate
> Left its charred furrows on her smock
>   And ate into her hip.
> A black nail dangles from a finger-tip
> And Lethe oozes from her nether lip . . .

Jonathan Edwards watches the death of a spider in a fire and compares it to the burning of a soul in Hell. In "After the Surprising Conversions" the citizens of Concord hear a voice urging them to cut their throats, "Now! Now!"[39]

In Lowell's poetry there is no vision of grace such as Dante had, or of the ideal Beauty envisioned by Baudelaire. The Christian poet is repelled by the world because it is not Heaven. So is the Romantic; his inability to live in the world like a bourgeois shows that he is made for better things. But Lowell has no beliefs or illusions; he is entirely committed to a physical universe.

When he dreams it is not of Paradise or Cytherea but a Hôtel de Ville. A squall is blowing, filling the ledges with "a sort of rusty mire / Not ice, not snow. . . ." There are dragons made of pig iron that "grip / The blizzard to their rigor mortis."[40] In the imaginary worlds of his creation Lowell concentrates on things. The rougher the surface the better, for it gives him something to hold on to.

Lord Weary's Castle, awarded a Pulitzer Prize in 1947, established Lowell as one of the leading poets of the new, postwar generation—Richard Wilbur was the other. But Lowell's next book, *The Mills of the Kavanaughs* (1951), struck readers as disappointing. There were exceptions: Randall Jarrell said that "Mother Marie Therese" was the best poem Lowell had ever written, and "Falling Asleep Over the Aeneid" was ... better.[41] But, in general, people felt that the writing was too "literary"; the rhymes called attention to themselves and the narrative was clogged with unnecessary details. The long narrative poem, "The Mills of the Kavanaughs," became tangled right at the start; it was difficult to know whether the actions were in the present or the past, or what was important.

> "Our people had kept up their herring weirs,
> Their rum and logging grants two hundred years,
> When Cousin Franklin Pierce was President—
> Almost three hundred, Harry, when you sent
> His signed engraving sailing on your kite
> Above the gable, where your mother's light,
> A daylight bulb in tortoise talons, pipped
> The bull-mad june-bugs on the manuscript
> That she was trying to redeem our mills
> From Harding's taxes ...[42]

A "signed engraving," a kite, a bulb "in tortoise talons," these things are described in an attempt to show the actual process of thought; as Yenser says, *The Mills of the Kavanaughs* shows "an increased tendency ... to get the process of thought rather than its product into the poetry." This is fine—we would gladly do without the dogma of the early poems if it were replaced with a sense of what people think and feel. But the criticism that Yenser makes of *Lord Weary's Castle* is even more true of *The Mills of the Kavanaughs:* "The chief danger entailed by Lowell's method is simply that the poetry might acquire a homogeneous texture, that the very unity of a poem might preclude a structure. If every object is a potential icon, and if the primary means of developing action is through symbolic connections, then the logical end is a poetry in which each detail develops the action and all details are of equal weight."[43] In *The Mills of the Kavanaughs* the dogma that enabled Lowell to organize his early poems has ceased to function, and his thoughts are tangled in a web of details, all "of equal weight."

Lowell has said that his aim was not simply to tell a story; he was writing "an obscure, rather Elizabethan, dramatic and melodramatic poem." He wanted to get things he had actually experienced into the poem, in indirect ways. His model for this kind of writing was Robert Frost; Frost's plots were so carefully worked out that it almost seemed they were not there. "Like some things in Chekhov," the art was very well hidden.[44]

The title poem does represent "experience" to some extent, for Anne Kavanaugh and her dead husband are versions of Lowell's mother and father (his father died in 1950). The trouble is in the way Lowell chooses to tell the story. Anne Kavanaugh is thinking, and we hear her thoughts, but she thinks in rhyme, and in the twentieth century we find it impossible to believe that anyone thinks this way. So the effort Lowell puts into trying to recreate experience is destroyed by the form and language in which he writes.

The fault was common at the time; poets imitated the forms of the past. Lowell tells how, during a year he spent with Allen Tate, they set about writing "formal" poems. "We both liked rather formal, difficult poems, and we were reading particularly the Sixteenth and Seventeenth centuries. . . . It seems to me we took old models like Drayton's ode— Tate wrote a poem called 'The Young Proconsuls of the Air' in that stanza. I think there's a trick to formal poetry. Most poetry is very formal, but when a modern poet is formal he gets more attention for it than old poets did. Somehow we've tried to make it look difficult. . . ."[45]

It is curious to think of poets deliberately trying to make their poems "look difficult." Poetry cannot come of itself but must be wrung out, the language of poetry is not that in which people think but some other language modeled on dead authors. This concept of poetry is what is meant by the word "academic," and no one did more to establish it than Allen Tate and Robert Lowell. The success of *Lord Weary's Castle* encouraged other poets to write, in rhyme and meter and formal English, on themes taken from literature or mythology.

"The Mills of the Kavanaughs" is underpinned with mythology. Anne Kavanaugh sits in the garden of her husband's estate, playing solitaire opposite his grave. She meditates on the decline of the Kavanaugh fortune, and the traditions she has inherited, and begins to daydream. "The narrative," Staples says in his analysis of the poem, "is a mixture of remembered incidents in her life and a symbolic commentary, largely phrased in Ovidian allusions, by which she endeavours to

interpret these events." He adds that "In terms of the outer framework
of the poem, the action is confined to her imagination."[46] Indeed it is,
and this is another trouble with the story: nothing happens, though
Anne Kavanaugh rows out on the pond and it may be she intends to
drown herself.

The basic myth is that of Demeter and Persephone—a statue of
Persephone by the millpond points the reader in this direction. In Anne
Kavanaugh's daydream, four periods of her life are ordered in terms of
the four seasons. As Staples points out, much of the detail is taken from
Ovid. Anne Kavanaugh's first meeting with her husband is based on
Metamorphoses, V. 391–401. "Similarly, stanza 8 recapitulates Persephone's abduction by Pluto in the pool of Cyane; stanza 11 describes her
restoration to earth, and stanza 17 Pluto's assertion of his right to reclaim
his bride at the end of the growing season."[47]

There are other details borrowed from myth, but this may be enough
to show what Lowell is hoping to do: to make his emotions cohere and
give them a point by attaching them to Ovid. The Catholic underpinning
is no longer sufficient—he does not believe in it. Perhaps he never
really did. In order to structure his poems he will now use mythology.
It has served Yeats in many poems, Eliot in *The Waste Land*, Pound in
the *Cantos*, and Joyce in *Ulysses* and *Finnegan's Wake*. A generation
has been taught by these masters to look for archetypes, patterns of
mythology, the Jungian "racial unconscious" that is said to underlie
the surface of appearances. This was the new way, Eliot said in a
review of *Ulysses*, to organize a narrative; Joyce had discovered in "the
continuous parallel between contemporaneity and antiquity" a way of
shaping the futility and anarchy of modern life.[48] After the Second
World War, when the generation trained by New Critics to accept the
ideas of Eliot came to maturity, writers frequently used a plot based
on myth to give their work a deeper significance. This lasted until the
end of the 1950s when certain writers—Ginsberg, Mailer, Lowell himself
—swung in the opposite direction, to writing of a personal, autobiographical kind.

The Mills of the Kavanaughs deals obsessively with thoughts of
violence. Consider, for example, the epigraph of the last poem in the
book: "Thanksgiving night, 1942: a room on Third Avenue. Michael
dreams of his wife, a German-American Catholic, who leapt from a
window before she died in a sanatorium. . . ." Or consider the much-
praised "Falling Asleep over the Aeneid," in which an old man dreams
that he is Aeneas at the funeral of Pallas, and that he will soon be

strangling some prisoners, "gagged Italians," who will then be burned on pyres.

I suspect that before he wrote this description of a hecatomb Lowell had read Flaubert's *Salammbo,* and when I see, in "Thanksgiving's Over," a celluloid parrot that is taken for the Holy Ghost, I am sure he had been reading "Une Coeur Simple." Lowell's imagination is stimulated by reading; literature appears more present to him than life itself —exotic, hotly colored—while matters within the ordinary range of human contact and feeling seem to escape his attention.

He taught English at Boston University. And spent some time in mental hospitals. From this time forward, mental illness will be a theme of Lowell's writing—apparently it has been a recurring condition.[49]

In 1959 he published a book of poems that appeared to be a radical departure from his previous work and caused a sensation in literary circles.

An English poet recalls that no one was taking any notice of poetry until *Life Studies* came along, then the place woke up.[50] They might have been reading Ginsberg—*Howl* preceded *Life Studies* by three years —but Ginsberg was not taken seriously. Lowell, on the other hand, had a reputation; therefore the critics took note of a new movement in American poetry. The term "confessional" was applied by M. L. Rosenthal; over in England A. Alvarez said "extremist."

Lowell has spoken of the changes that led up to his writing *Life Studies.* He had always been interested in two different kinds of writing. One kind would be represented by Tolstoi: "his work is imagistic, it deals with all experience, and there seems to be no conflict of the form and content." Poetry could conceivably bring over "that kind of human richness in rather simple descriptive language." Another kind of poetry would be marked by "compression, something highly rhythmical and perhaps wrenched into a small space."[51] This was what he had been writing in *Lord Weary's Castle.* Though he does not say so, in *The Mills of the Kavanaughs* he had made the mistake of trying to get "Tolstoyan" material into formal, rhymed verse, and the content and form worked against each other.

Critics may find excuses for an author who is in favor, but the author, if he is at all honest, knows when he has failed. Lowell speaks of the forties and fifties as "a sort of Alexandrian age" when poets were very proficient at writing skilfully in form, "yet the writing seems divorced from the culture somehow."[52] He felt that he could not get enough of his experience into tight metrical forms. After *The Mills of the Kavanaughs* he set about learning to write the kind of poetry "in rather simple descriptive language" that would express "human richness."

Elizabeth Bishop showed him the way; she was "a sort of bridge between Tate's formalism and Williams' informal art."[53] Bishop was interested in rendering details accurately—so was he. Another point of contact was her poetry of landscapes; he, too, liked to give a sense of character by showing the landscape it inhabited.

He learned something from W. D. Snodgrass, who was one of his students. Snodgrass had lived in Iowa City and attended writing work-ships at the University. He wrote poems that expressed the miseries of postwar America as they were felt by students. "The poems are about his child, his divorce, and Iowa City, and his child is a Dr. Spock child." All this grubby, depressed material, as Lowell says, was handled "in expert little stanzas."[54]

He set about retraining his style by writing prose. He felt that the best style for poetry was none of the many styles in English, but some-thing like the prose of Chekhov or Flaubert.[55] He had come a long way from his tutelage at the hands of Tate when they would vie with each other in imitating the masters of English verse.

A poetry-reading tour took him to the West Coast where he heard the San Francisco poets reading their poems aloud. They soon let him know where he stood: though he might be a big name in the East, there were a dozen poets in North Beach who were just as good. He felt uncomfortable when he found himself reading aloud—and tried to please them by making his poems more simple. If he had a Latin quota-tion he would translate it into English. If adding a couple of syllables in a line made it clearer he would add them, and made other changes impromptu as he read.[56]

So he developed a new style, conversational, intimate, "open." The verse is more or less free: the lines vary in length, the meter is irregular, and rhyme when it occurs is unobtrusive. The poetry sounds like a man speaking—one who has a passion for accuracy:

> a Rocky Mountain chaise longue,
> its legs, shellacked saplings.
> A pastel-pale Huckleberry Finn
> fished with a broom straw in a basin
> hollowed out of a millstone . . .[57]

Accuracy such as this implies an affection for the world—or gives the illusion. The narrator is a man of the world; the messianic clamor of

Lord Weary's Castle has been replaced by a quiet, observant humor. He has a history of mental illness and does not try to conceal it—reliable when he talks about himself as well as others.

This is not "confession," it is a way of writing. To read *Life Studies* as a straightforward account of Lowell's life is to overlook the art with which the poems are constructed. According to M. L. Rosenthal, "Robert Lowell's poetry has been a long struggle to remove the mask, to make his speaker unequivocally himself."[58] It would be truer to say that the struggle has been to develop a *persona* and to forge a style, and now at last he has succeeded.

Speaking of "Skunk Hour," one of the poems in *Life Studies*, Lowell says that he began to feel that real poetry came "not from fierce confessions, but from something almost meaningless but imagined." He was haunted by the image of a blue china doorknob. He had never used the doorknob, nor did he know what it meant, but it started the train of images in the opening stanzas.[59]

This is a description of a process of evoking the unconscious. The doorknob performs the function of a *mandala*, the circle used in Tibetan Buddhism as an aid in meditating, the aim being to detach the self from its relations with the world. For an artist, however, the aim would be, by releasing the mind from its preoccupations, to disengage the will and so enable the unconscious—or whatever one wishes to call that part of one's being that is not amenable to one's will but seems to have a will of its own—to rise to the surface.

Lowell's discovery of the unconscious as an aid in writing came as a result of the psychiatric disorder from which he suffered and the therapy he underwent in order to control it. His blue china doorknob, something "almost meaningless but imagined," is like the image a therapist chooses from his patient's speech as he associates freely, in order to pursue it and see where it leads. It is a thread into the unconscious; tugged at, it brings other images in its train.

Lowell uses the method to recreate his childhood and the lives around it. In the house on Revere Street "the vast number of remembered *things* [Lowell's emphasis] remains rocklike. Each is in its place, each has its function, its history, its drama. There, all is preserved by that motherly care that one either ignored or resented in his youth. The things and their owners come back urgent with life and meaning—because finished, they are endurable and perfect."[60]

The resemblance to Proust is striking—it was so that the narrator of *La Recherche du Temps Perdu* set about recovering the past. Things are the repositories of an affection that one was too preoccupied to notice. One was too selfish, the equivalent in Proust of original sin. But there may come a day when the veil is lifted, and it is a thing that lifts it—things have the power to evoke, by shape or taste or smell, a time that has been lost. The senses are the house of memory, sought not for its own sake, but because to remember is to love.

"Well-adjusted" people think that people with "artistic temperament" are always dreaming of other worlds and imagining unreal things. This is not so—it is life these neurotics dream of. It is as hard for them to find the way there as it would be for a member of the Yale Club to enter Aladdin's cave. So they have a passion for facts: Proust writes to a woman of his acquaintance asking what dress she wore on a certain occasion, and Lowell pushes through the doors of "91 Revere Street." We wish to feel and express the affection we did not feel at the time—for time without affection is time lost. But with the lifting of the veil we are able to live again in a new way; this is the "philosophic mind" Wordsworth speaks of. And if we are artists we are able to point the way to others.

This is what is happening in *Life Studies*, not "fierce confessions." Lowell is discovering his "true self," to use Proust's term for the author as he appears in his work, and this is very different from his personal life.[61] The work depends on this "true self," manifested in style, and one part is connected to another through the style—for example, by the relation of words and images, a device Lowell may have come upon in a review by Randall Jarrell of Williams' *Paterson, Book One.* Jarrell said that the organization of *Paterson* was musical; Williams would introduce a theme that stood for an idea, repeat it in varied forms, develop it alongside other themes, and recur to it again and again, echoing it for ironic or grotesque effects in thoroughly incongruous contexts. Sometimes this would be done with great complication and delicacy. As an example, Jarrell showed how Williams used exclamatory phrases to prepare the reader for a bird call.[62]

Similarly, in *Life Studies* Lowell frequently repeats a theme. The "mustard spire" in "A Mad Negro Soldier Confined at Munich" is echoed two sections later in the description of Ford Madox Ford who was "mustard gassed voiceless some seven miles / behind the lines," and is further developed in "To Delmore Schwartz" where Lowell recalls that "the antiquated / refrigerator gurgled mustard gas / through your mustard-yellow house." The purpose of this linking imagery, Yenser remarks, is to link one alienated figure with another; and, also, Lowell wishes to associate war, madness, and art.[63] The episodes, therefore, are connected in the most natural way by association, the working of thought itself.

This kind of linking makes it possible to read *Life Studies* as one long poem. It is instructive to compare it with another long American poem, Hart Crane's *The Bridge*. Crane, like Lowell, had written short poems heavy with symbolism. In *The Bridge* he undertook to write a long poem. But there is always a danger for a lyric poet in trying to write extended narrative; as R. P. Blackmur says, Crane "used the private lyric to write the cultural epic" and he went astray.[64] His writing, line by line, was too obscure to convey a general narrative. Moreover, he chose a symbol, Brooklyn Bridge, to give his poem meaning; but it is too rigid a structure—it creaks and groans at every rivet. The reader has to wait for Crane to go through the ponderous motions of trying to make a piece of iron signify something.

Life Studies, on the other hand, is as fluent as life and thought. The narrator seems to be thinking aloud. But, as I have said, this is not confessional writing, and Lowell has suggested the difficulty of the struggle he went through in transforming life into art. "It's a terrible struggle, because what you really feel hasn't got the form, it's not what you can put down in a poem."[65]

There is a kind of symbolism with which many readers are familiar: Freudian psychology. Lowell uses it in order to explain the relationship of the narrator to his parents and provide *Life Studies* with the equivalent of a plot.

The narrator sees his mother as having been dominated by her father:

> Terrible that old life of decency
> without unseemly intimacy
> or quarrels, when the unemancipated woman
> still had her Freudian papa and maids!

No wonder that such a woman cannot really love her husband and instead, tries to pre-empt the love of her son. "Often," says the narrator, "with unadulterated joy, / Mother, we bent by the fire / rehashing Father's character."[66]

Lowell has said elsewhere that his life may have been determined in every respect by his relations with his parents. In one of the poems in *History*

> now more than before fearing everything I do
> is only (only) a mix of mother and father,
> no matter how unlike they were, they are—[67]

Williamson remarks that many of Lowell's attitudes can be seen as reactions to this "unusual family romance": Lowell's pacifism, yet "helpless fascination with power and violence"; his sympathy for bodily weakness; his love and hatred of perfectionists, revolutionists, tyrannicides. And perhaps his refusal to accept adult responsibility stems from this, "the feeling of being pushed into a premature adulthood."[68]

To the narrator of *Life Studies* his grandfather is everything that his own father is not—"manly, comfortable, / overbearing. . . ."[69] And his grandfather returns this affection:

> My Grandfather found
> his grandchild's fogbound solitudes
> sweeter than human society.
> . . . .
> He was my Father. I was his son.[70]

Yet the grandfather can be cruel and terrifying:

> My Uncle was dying at twenty-nine.
> "You are behaving like children,"
> said my Grandfather,
> when my Uncle and Aunt left their three
>   baby daughters,
> and sailed for Europe on a last honeymoon . . .
> I cowered in terror.
> I wasn't a child at all—
> unseen and all-seeing, I was Agrippina
> in the Golden House of Nero . . .[71]

Though here he is canceled out by the grandfather's power, at times the child allies himself with it. He borrows his grandfather's cane, which is carved with the names of Norwegian mountains he has scaled, and using this, "more a weapon than a crutch," probes in the ooze for newts. Captured and imprisoned in a tobacco can, the mature newts lose their spots and lie "grounded as numb / as scrolls of candied grapefruit peel." The child identifies himself with a young newt, "neurasthenic, scarlet / and wild in the wild coffee-colored water." The poem concludes:

> In the mornings I cuddled like a paramour
> in my Grandfather's bed,
> while he scouted about the chattering greenwood stove.[72]

"Like a paramour" . . . truly, this writing calls for psychoanalysis. The child and his grandfather share an illicit, wicked secret. They know about pleasure. They may be "neurasthenic," but note that the coffee-

colored water in which the newts are captured is also "wild"—civilization and its discontents—so that one may as well be neurotic; in fact,
the neurotic may be better adapted to survive than "mature" newts who
lose their spots and sink to the bottom of the can. But the young newt
continues to rage, rebellious, like the old man.

Life Studies, like Proust's novel, may be read as the study of the
decline of a class. The failures of the narrator in his personal life reflect
the failure of his parents and the old ruling class from which they came.
Yenser finds four kinds of disintegration in *Life Studies:* in Part One,
disintegration of the old order in religion and politics; in Part Two, "91
Revere Street," decay of love between individuals and in the family—
to be continued in Part Four; in Part Three, the isolation of the artist;
and in Parts Three and Four, the breaking-down of the individual
through destructive behavior or outright insanity.

The gloom, however, is not unrelieved. "Over against these centrif-
ugal forces, especially in the last two parts of *Life Studies,* Lowell sets
the ability of man, or rather of individual men, to absorb the shock of
cultural disintegration."[73]

As in Proust, these individuals—Ford, Santayana, Delmore Schwartz,
Hart Crane, and the narrator—are artists. It is art that will redeem the
fallen world.

Here, once more, we find that Lowell is like the poet he admired when
he was beginning to write: Ezra Pound. In spite of all the efforts
that have been made to present Pound as an important thinker on social
questions, an expert in economics, and a historian, the basis of his
thought is aestheticism. He remains an exponent of those views, current
in London about 1910, that may be traced back to Dowson and other
poets of the Nineties, and the Pre-Raphaelites, and further back to
Gautier and Flaubert. If Pound wanted to change the system of banking,
it was in order that artists might be free to do as they liked.

Lowell, too, sees everything as either serving art or failing to serve
it. *Life Studies* is a portrait of the artist as a young man. Indeed, if
Lowell's work as a whole has an underlying theme, it is this—not a
concern with history, as some readers, and Lowell himself, seem
to think, but a "portrait of the artist."

If they were considered as social criticism, and not as part of this
portrait, the poems would not be convincing. Consider, for example,
"Memories of West Street and Lepke." The narrator is living, in the
"tranquilized fifties," on Boston's "hardly passionate Marlborough
Street." Life is thoroughly tame—even the man who scavenges in the

back-alley trash can is a "young Republican" and has "two children, a beach wagon, a helpmate."

The narrator recalls his own passionately dedicated "seed-time"—he is positively ironic about it: "I was a fire-breathing Catholic C. O., / and made my manic statement, / telling off the state and president. . . ."

This brings us to his term in the West Street jail along with other misfits: "a Negro boy with curlicues / of marijuana in his hair," and a man named Abramowitz who is a vegetarian—he wears rope-soled shoes and prefers to eat fallen fruit. There are also two Hollywood pimps, Bioff and Brown. Abramowitz tries to convert them to his diet and they react violently:

> Hairy, muscular, suburban,
> wearing chocolate double-breasted suits,
> they blew their tops and beat him black and blue.

Here we may pause to see the social significance. Abramowitz is a crank. The Hollywood pimps, on the other hand, with their "chocolate double-breasted suits," are perfectly square; they represent the ideals of suburban America. Though they are criminals—perhaps because they are criminals—they are far more representative of America than the religious vegetarian Abramowitz.

The point is hammered home with Lepke Buchalter, the "czar" of Murder Incorporated, who is in jail waiting execution for his part in the murders. "Incorporated" is the key word: murder is a business like any other. This, too, like the pimping of Bioff and Brown, is done in the American spirit of free enterprise. Then we are shown that Lepke is a patriot, with his "two toy American / flags tied together with a ribbon of Easter palm."

The poem concludes with a striking picture of Lepke approaching execution day:

> Flabby, bald, lobotomized,
> he drifted in a sheepish calm,
> where no agonizing reappraisal
> jarred his concentration on the electric chair—
> hanging like an oasis in his air
> of lost connections . . .[74]

Lepke with his American flag stands for America, and we are to take it that America has lost its connections and is drifting toward an end. The atom bomb, perhaps.

Williamson calls "Memories of West Street and Lepke" a great political poem.[75] But for one to take writing seriously as political one must believe the statements in it to be true, and only paranoia could see two convicted criminals, Bioff and Brown, as representative of the middle class, or Murder Incorporated as representative of American foreign policy. The poem expresses the despair that many of us, at one time and another, have felt about conditions; this is perfectly understandable as an expression of the narrator's point of view, but it cannot be taken seriously as a picture of life.

The strongest impression the poem makes is the sketch of Lepke. The narrator is drawn toward him irresistibly until he finds himself looking through Lepke's eyes. The electric chair hanging in the air is a stroke of genius—it concentrates the mind wonderfully. The poem could conceivably be a plea for the abolition of capital punishment, but it is neither politics nor history—it is far too personal. It is not so concerned with these matters as with the predicament of the man who has lost his connections—Lepke and the author himself who, lounging all day in pajamas on Marlborough Street, might as well be incarcerated on West Street with the others.

The point becomes urgent when we consider Lowell's later writing, especially in the work titled *History*.

In 1961 Lowell published a collection of translations and reworkings of other men's poems that he called *Imitations*. Of the poets he dealt with, Baudelaire and Rimbaud seem closest to his own concerns: Baudelaire in his power to transcend lust and decay through his art, Rimbaud in his view of childhood as a time of primitive innocence.

In his rewriting of Baudelaire, Lowell seems not to see, or prefers to ignore, the nobility Baudelaire strove for and the calm that lies at the center of his work. Where Baudelaire writes:

> Ainsi, qu'un débauché pauvre qui baise et mange
> Le sein martyrisé d'une antique catin,
> Nous volons au passage un plaisir clandestin
> Que nous pressons bien fort comme une veille orange.

Lowell writes:

> Like the poor lush who cannot satisfy,
> we try to force our sex with counterfeits,
> die drooling on the deliquescent tits,
> mouthing the rotten orange we suck dry.[76]

Baudelaire presents his grotesque metaphor in elevated language; "le sein martyrisé" evokes a state of religious exaltation. Lowell does the opposite: his vulgar slang debases the actors: "poor lush . . . deliquescent tits."

Lowell is using Baudelaire for his own purposes. Pound did the same thing with his Propertius; the difference is that Pound departed further from the original, so that we have a new Propertius. Lowell sticks fairly close to Baudelaire, and yet he makes these changes. The result is neither translation nor an original piece of writing.

Not all the *Imitations* are like this. Some are good, especially when Lowell is dealing with an author with whom he has little in common so that he does not feel that he has to go him one better. This rendering of Leopardi, for example:

> I hear the rasp of shavings,
> and the rapping hammer
> of the carpenter working all night
> by lanternlight—
> hurrying and straining himself
> to increase his savings
> before the whitening day . . .[77]

The same year, Lowell published a translation of Racine's *Phèdre*. As with Baudelaire he did not hesitate to distort the meaning of the original. Phèdre's words to Theseus, "Au défaut de ton bras prête-moi ton épée"—"If you will not strike me yourself, lend me your sword"—are rendered in Lowell: "I want your sword's spasmodic final inch."[78]

But it appears that Lowell could do no wrong, and a Bollingen committee awarded him the prize for translation.

His reputation was now at its peak. Everything he turned his hand to seemed to succeed. When he wrote verse plays they were performed, and his *Benito Cerino*, a version of Melville, was awarded a prize as the best Off-Broadway play of 1964. His new book of poems, *For the Union Dead*, was favorably reviewed. "I envy Lowell," said a writer in *The Hudson Review*. "Everywhere I go among literary people I meet only others who envy Lowell."[79]

He must not have met Robert Bly. According to Bly most of the poems in *For the Union Dead* were bad. Lowell was surrounded by flatterers, people like Jason Epstein, Stephen Marcus, and A. Alvarez, "perfect examples of the alienated establishment intellectual," and he seemed to share their worn-out fatigued vision of things.

Bly said that as Lowell had no new ideas he had filled his poems with pointless excitement, taking up the notion that the artist must be extreme at all costs. In his *Imitations* he had inserted "violent anal or explosive images" into quiet, meditative poems—those of Montale, for example—and now he was doing the same thing to his own verse. "He is pretending," Bly said, "to have *poetic* excitement, when all he has to offer is *nervous* excitement." He concluded with the observation that American readers were "so far from standing at the center of themselves" that they could not tell when a poet was counterfeiting and when he was not; Lowell was being praised for qualities that he did not possess, and this could not fail to "draw him farther from himself."[80]

This criticism shows that a new critical spirit was in the air, at the furthest remove from the New Criticism. It was not enough to show how poems were put together, one must also consider their psychological or spiritual meaning. But when we turn from Bly's criticism to the poetry he is criticizing, we notice a disturbing fact: *For the Union Dead* is not the book he says it is. The tone is sad rather than violent. The book opens with two poems set in Maine, the first describing a lobster town, "White frame houses stuck / like oyster shells / on a hill of rock," and evoking the sadness of two people, a man and woman:

> One night you dreamed
> you were a mermaid clinging to a wharf-pile,
> and trying to pull
> off the barnacles with your hands.
>
> We wished our two souls
> might return like gulls
> to the rock. In the end
> the water was too cold for us.[81]

There is nothing strained or melodramatic about this poetry—it seems to be telling the truth.

In the second poem, "The Old Flame," the narrator recalls how he and his wife were snowbound, "simmering like wasps / in our tent of books!"

> Poor ghost, old love, speak
> with your old voice
> of flaming insight
> that kept us awake all night.
> In one bed and apart,
>
> we heard the plow
> groaning up hill—
> a red light, then a blue,
> as it tossed off the snow
> to the side of the road.[82]

This is a poetry of feeling, the unhappiness of the characters again being represented by objects in the outer world. There are other poems of this quality in *For the Union Dead*, for example, "The Mouth of the Hudson" and "Night Sweat." In "Night Sweat" Lowell describes the litter of his desk, his staying up all night, the gray coming of dawn, and he ends with a funny description of sexual intercourse: "absolve me, help me, Dear Heart, as you bear / this world's dead weight and cycle on your back." There is often some humor in Lowell's writing, or lurking in the vicinity.[83]

The title poem does deal with violence, but it is not all in Lowell's imagination. There really was a Colonel Shaw who led a regiment of Negro soldiers in the Civil War and died at the head of his troops. Lowell speaks of this not for the sake of "pointless excitement" but to make a point: "He rejoices in man's lovely, / peculiar power to choose life and die. . . ."

There may very well have been a "commercial" photograph on Boylston Street that showed "Hiroshima boiling / over a Mosler Safe, the 'Rock of Ages.' "[84] And the Negro schoolchildren the narrator sees on television are probably trying to enter a desegregated school against violent opposition. The violence Lowell writes about does exist and would be difficult to ignore. Bly's criticism may apply to Lowell's early poems, but not *For the Union Dead*. It is true that Lowell used to revel in images of pain and death—the early poems were continually threatening annihilation. But now he seems less fearful; he has come to terms with his own weakness and is able to show concern for others.

If we were to hear *For the Union Dead* read aloud we might think it was written in free verse, for the lines follow patterns of speech rather than meter; but, in fact, most of the poems are in stanza and rhyme. Lowell appears to be moving away from the greater freedom of *Life Studies*. He has said that he has always been divided between two different kinds of verse, one that would be simple and descriptive and another kind that would be "highly rhythmical and perhaps wrenched into a small space."[85] In *For the Union Dead* he began returning to the second kind.

He had never really renounced it. *Life Studies* had been a departure from his early, formal training. At the time he had needed a kind of verse that would allow him to speak more freely. The age, also, required it: in the wake of the Beat poets and the writers of Projective Verse, audiences of young people had sprung up, and they had new expectations. Poetry must sound spontaneous; to strive for perfection of language and form, to *revise*, was to reveal a damning insincerity.

(When we speak of these poets and their followers, we are speaking of only a segment of the population. Thousands of young people were

not at all revolutionary—they were pumping gas or planning to be
doctors or engineers. There were still poets who followed English
models and thought highly of Auden. But these were not the ones
who were heard from and publicized in the media; like the happy
families that Tolstoy assures us have no history, these seem to have
had none either.)

To the young who were making news, the most important fact of
their lives was the war in Vietnam—they did not want to be drafted.

Poets came to their aid. Some had been protesting against the war
from the start, that is, the Tonkin Bay Resolution. They spoke from
platforms and took part in peace marches. The war-protest movement
began in California, then spread across the country; and every other
college campus had its poetry reading against the war in Vietnam.

In June of 1965 Lowell was invited by President Johnson to a White
House Festival of the Arts. Some well-known writers attended—Saul
Bellow, for example—but Lowell refused, as a protest against the war.
The gesture received maximum publicity. A dozen other writers sent a
signed telegram to the President supporting Robert Lowell. The President was said to be greatly angered. He had called the signatories
traitors to their country.

Two years later Lowell took part in the March on the Pentagon.
Norman Mailer wrote a book about it, paying particular attention to
Lowell. The account is marred by Mailer's preoccupation with himself—
"There are days," he says, "when I think of myself as being the best
writer in America."

He sees Lowell as an aristocrat with an inborn air of superiority.
Lowell is solicitous, however, of people who may be useful to him—
for instance, he sends postcards to other writers praising their work.
Above all, Lowell is a poet, that is, Mailer's idea of a poet: someone
whose nerves are not strong.

Lowell is described as sitting "in a mournful hunch on the floor,
his eyes peering over his glasses to scrutinize the metaphysical substance
of his boot, now hide? now machine? now, where the joining and to
what? foot to boot, boot to earth. . . ." Lowell presents a "disconcerting
mixture of strength and weakness" that must make him sensationally
attractive to women. There is a force in him that is almost insane; he
would die for any one of a number of causes "with an axe in his hand
and a Cromwellian light in his eye." Obviously he has been spoiled by
everyone for years, yet he seems to need the spoiling: "These nerves—
the nerves of a consummate poet—were not turned to any battering."[86]

On this occasion Lowell read a poem to the crowd, "Waking Early Sunday Morning," from his new book. The choice of this poem shows something about Lowell—it was thoroughly unsuitable to the occasion. The thoughts were those of the closet, not the podium:

> I watch a glass of water wet
> with a fine fuzz of icy sweat,
> silvery colors touched with sky,
> serene in their neutrality—

The audience listened respectfully. Most of them cared nothing for poetry, but they were gratified. Lowell was a celebrated poet, this was "where it was at." And it was within their power to give their approval or withhold it. There was nothing anyone could say or do to win their favor if they chose to withhold it.

When he finished they started to clap. A few people stood. Others were rising to their feet. The movement became general. The ones who were still seated looked around them, then they too stood.

When we look at the poem they were applauding it is clear that poetry readings have little to do with reading poetry. "Waking Early Sunday Morning" begins with a wish to "break loose, like the chinook." But as it goes on we understand that the speaker is not going to break loose. Nor is he going to go to Church, for he is not one of the Faithful. Instead, he will putter around the house and yard:

> . . . put old clothes on, and explore
> the corners of the woodshed for
> its dregs and dreck: tools with no handle,
> ten candle-ends not worth a candle . . .

Readers of *Life Studies* will recognize Commander Lowell's way of spending a Sunday. The poem goes on to say that God no longer seems to take an interest in human affairs. The church with its spire and flagpole is "like old white china doorknobs, sad, / slight, useless things to calm the mad." There are satirical lines about the war-heavy state, "Hammering military splendor, / top-heavy Goliath in full armor." On the other hand, peace may be no better if it brings "no true / tenderness, only restlessness, / excess, the hunger for success."

The only strong statement appears to be in the twelfth stanza: "O to break loose. All life's grandeur / is something with a girl in summer. . . ."

It draws to an end with lines that have the classic sound of resignation.

> Pity the planet, all joy gone
> from this sweet volcanic cone;
> peace to our children when they fall
> in small war on the heels of small
> war . . .[87]

It is difficult to see what the crowd at the Pentagon could have heard in this to encourage them. A poem that said it was resigned to having children die in wars around the globe—what could this have to say to war protesters, Civil Rights marchers, and other political activists? This was counsel of despair, if ever there was.

Moreover, with its carefully tuned couplets the poem was listening to itself and indifferent to their existence.

But, of course, they weren't aware of this. They had Lowell there in person—and they had one another. When they rose in a body to applaud it was themselves they were applauding.

If anyone had been paying attention he might have asked the question one reader asked when the book came out: "Why has Lowell moved progressively away from the simplicity of *Life Studies* toward a new formalism?"[88] One part of the answer is that Lowell had been trained to write in traditional forms and *Life Studies* was a wrench from this. The rest of the answer is that he was ahead of his time.

After the antiwar demonstrations, and Black Power, and the Weathermen who proclaimed themselves revolutionaries and terrorists, there would be a swing back to conservatism. The 1970s have been compared to the years under Eisenhower—conservatism in politics and the arts. Lowell in his poems anticipated the conservative reaction. *Near the Ocean*, published in 1967, would not have come amiss in 1975—or in 1950.

The form of this poetry is the message: iambic tetrameter, rhymed— we are in for a period of conservative reaction. In the United States people do not take art seriously, yet even here the forms of art are connected to politics and social change. The free lines Whitman wrote went hand in hand with Democracy, the unbuttoned, expansive manners of day laborers and the unlimited profits envisioned by Jay Gould and James Fisk and the House of Morgan. When Lowell writes

> Great ash and sun of freedom, give
> us this day the warmth to live,
> and face the household fire. We turn
> our backs, and feel the whiskey burn.[89]

the rhymes tell us that the sixties and their hope of freedom are at an end. We are returning to business as usual and the life of the family—every man in his house with his wife and child. There is nothing the individual can do in the face of the power wielded by government and the great corporations. The horror of nuclear war waits beneath the horizon. In the meantime we shall watch the children turn cartwheels, and listen to a recording.

Liberals are in retreat from political activism because it is violent. They are back at Dover Beach:

> Ah, love, let us be true
> To one another! for the world, which seems
> To lie before us like a land of dreams,
> So various, so beautiful, so new,
> Hath really neither joy, nor love, nor light,
> Nor certitude, nor peace, nor help for pain;
> And we are here as on a darkling plain
> Swept with confused alarms of struggle and flight,
> Where ignorant armies clash by night.[90]

Love is the opiate of the intellectuals. *Near the Ocean* prophesies this reversion, a trumpet that sounds retreat. The notes are weak and rueful.

In 1967 Lowell began writing sonnets without rhymes. He arranged them in sequences and gave the sequences names: "Harriet" (the name of his daughter), "Long Summer," "Searchings," "Five Dreams," et cetera. Between the sequences single sonnets were left to stand alone. The whole work, extending to 156 pages of verse, was published in 1969 under the title *Notebook 1967–68*. In an afterword he said that the poems had been written as one poem, "jagged in pattern but not a conglomeration or sequence of related material." It was neither a chronicle nor an almanac—"many events turn up, many others of equal or greater reality do not." It was not a diary or confession, not "a puritan's too literal pornographic honesty, glad to share private embarrassment, and triumph." The poem covered a certain period of time, from one summer to the following summer. The plot rolled with the seasons. "Accident threw up subjects, and the plot swallowed them—famished for human chances."

He went on to speak of his concept of poetry. He leaned heavily to the rational but was devoted to surrealism. "Surrealism can degenerate into meaningless clinical hallucinations, or worse into rhetorical machinery, yet it is a natural way to write our fictions."

The meter he had chosen, "fourteen lines unrhymed blank verse sections," was fairly strict at first and elsewhere, but often corrupted in single lines to the freedom of prose. Even with this license he feared that he might have failed to avoid the "themes and gigantism" of the sonnet.[91]

The reader must wonder why the sonnet form is used at all if it is not accompanied by rhyme. The appeal of sonnets, for those who like them, is in the skill with which the thought is expressed in a limited space and a pattern of rhyme. But no skill is needed to write fourteen lines without rhyme. At the same time the arbitrarily determined length prevents the poem from finding its own shape. Lowell has made the worst of both worlds: the writing is neither ingenious nor free. He seems to be using too many words and still does not seem to have found the right ones. "I no longer know the difference between prose and verse," he told Carne-Ross in 1968.[92] This appears to be true, but not in the self-gratulatory way he intended.

There are poems in *Notebook* that we have seen before, now altered to fit. For example, "Night Sweat" from *For the Union Dead* reappears with the second half missing. "Accident," Lowell says, "threw up subjects, and the plot swallowed them," but it is not a plot that is doing the swallowing, it is his determination to fit everything he knows into poems fourteen lines long. He seems determined to out-Wordsworth Wordsworth.

A more immediate influence was his friend Berryman. Lowell was impressed with Berryman's *77 Dream Songs*—he couldn't praise them enough: "I think *Dream Songs* is one of the glories of the age, the most heroic work in English poetry since the War. . . ."[93] The *Dream Songs* were written in a regular form: each poem had three stanzas and each stanza had six lines. This regularity was striking in an age of free verse. The long poems of the age, Pound's *Cantos*, Williams' *Paterson*, and Olson's *Maximus*, were written in free verse of one kind and another. In the face of this Berryman's determination to write stanzas was provocative, practically an innovation.

Now, Lowell was competitive, he would not be outdone, and who could tell, after an age of free verse a new age of formalism might be in the making, with stanza and rhyme, sonnets, villanelles. If the army were retreating from Moscow in its own footsteps, if modernism were in full retreat, then here, too, his place would be at the front.

He may also have thought that a regular form would make his thoughts coherent.

There was another appealing aspect of Berryman's performance. He seemed to have broken loose; he managed to talk about himself and speak his mind by putting his thoughts in the mouth of a speaker named

"Henry." The voice ranged from melancholy to manic glee—he had learned how to write falsetto. He was able to be self-pitying, to be boastful, to have something to say about everything and everybody without being held to account. The *Dream Songs* were like singing in the shower.

And Lowell hankered to break loose. When he wrote *The Mills of the Kavanaughs* he tried to talk about his life indirectly; in *Life Studies* he had shown some scenes from his life. Now he would speak his mind once and for all, put everything in its place as though he were writing for a future biographer. But unlike Berryman and his "Henry," in *Notebook* Lowell comes out with his reminiscences and observations in his own voice. It reads like a series of brief lectures or essays— there is nothing dramatic about it.

Notebook is different from *Life Studies*. The poems in *Life Studies* read like fiction. In *Life Studies* the life of the author is used to make narrative poems; in *Notebook*, on the other hand, the poetry is used to explain the life of the author as though this had some evident importance in itself.

Copying from life is not enough to make a work of art. Rousseau in his *Confessions* describes certain incidents that have formed his character. The character is important because it is original, a new way of feeling; on the basis of this Rousseau will undertake to judge men and society. Wordsworth in *The Prelude* describes moments of experience that have given him insight into the workings of the universe. Similarly, Proust describes certain moments in which he perceived a reality that lies behind appearances. In each case the artist-hero has used his life as a basis for a philosophy or way of looking at things. But there is no philosophy in *Notebook*, no meaning to Lowell's life as a whole. We do not see the "growth of a poet's mind" nor are we granted a sudden revelation of how things hang together. All that we have are poems about things that have happened to the poet and his thoughts on various subjects. The only possible connection is that these incidents and ideas have occurred to this particular man.

A common error of writers when their creative energy is low is to fall back on "subject matter." Thus, the Victorian poets wrote thousands of lines of blank verse about historical "personages," and there are stretches of Pound's *Cantos* where there is no sound of verse, only of a man talking about history and economics. The more that poets lose touch with the life of verse, which originates in feelings, the more they have to explain, and as Lowell has no feeling for the writing itself we find him talking about more things, expanding his *Notebook* in an attempt to get everything in and make a whole. But there is no whole, only life, and the account of this life lacks a form, the joy in itself that distinguishes verse from prose.

Lack of feeling is at the root of the trouble. Lowell seems detached— his sonnets, as I have said, read like essays. But it is the involvement of a poet, as he writes, that involves the reader. It is almost a physical thing, what is meant by the word "imagination." "The word is predominantly used in cases where, carried away by enthusiasm and passion, you think you see what you describe, and you place it before the eyes of your hearers."[94]

Poetry is not just looking back. Nor does it consist of comments on life. It is a form of present life. "Art does not seek to describe but to enact."[95]

A poet of Lowell's intelligence could not apply himself to writing sonnets without writing some good ones—this, for example, titled "Elizabeth":

> An unaccustomed ripeness in the wood;
> move but an inch and moldy splinters fall
> in sawdust from the aluminum-paint wall,
> once loud and fresh, now aged to weathered wood.
> Squalls of the seagulls' exaggerated outcry,
> dimmed out by fog . . . Peace, peace. All day the words
> hid rusty fish-hooks. Now, heart's ease and wormwood,
> we rest from all discussion, drinking, smoking,
> pills for high blood, three pairs of glasses—soaking
> in the sweat of our hard-earned supremacy,
> offering a child our leathery love. We're fifty,
> and free! Young, tottering on the dizzying brink
> of discretion once, we wanted nothing,
> but to be old, do nothing, type and think.[96]

But the feeling is muffled by echoes of literature. The poet of *Life Studies* and *For the Union Dead* has lapsed from a muscular, nervous, colloquial style into what might be called "accomplished" verse—a language that has long been dead for poetry in the United States, though it is still being written in England.

As this is a language critics know, it is not surprising to see a front-page review in the *New York Times* praising *Notebook*, and for the thing it most evidently does not have, a sense of order. "When one of our best poets . . . ," says the reviewer, "writes down all the patterns of his mind, he seems to be saying they are fragments of order. The poet—in all modesty, in all vanity—creates order, if at all, by arrangement."[97]

It may have been reviews such as this that encouraged Lowell to continue his arrangements and rearrangements. He extracted poems from *Notebook* and made a new book, *For Lizzie and Harriet*, dealing with his personal life. He took a large number of poems from *Notebook*, added about eighty more, and called it *History*. He has said that the composition of *Notebook* was jumbled and that he hoped to clear it up and "cut the waste marble from the figure."[98]

Lowell died yesterday. His picture was on the front page of this morning's *Times*. The death was sudden and unexpected. The obituary must have been written some years ago for there was no mention of his divorce from Elizabeth Hardwick and marriage to Caroline Blackwood, and the son born of this marriage. There was no mention of his residence in England during recent years.

He was sixty years old, and he had been writing new poems. They were nearly as good as the poems in *Life Studies* and *For the Union Dead*, and of the same kind—he had recovered his feelings for poetry and the shape of the poem. I had just written a review of his new book, *Day by Day*, at the conclusion of which I advised him to forget about plot and rhyme (something he said made me think he believed that plot and rhyme were necessary for imaginative writing in verse). I advised him to reread Flaubert and Chekhov and immerse himself again in experience. He might yet, I concluded, write poems that would astonish us all.

And then, this morning. . . . One feels very foolish giving advice to the dead.

It seems belated now to speak of the books he made out of *Notebook*. He placed his thoughts in categories and called it *History*, but there was no plan to the work as a whole and whole eras and continents were omitted. In Lowell's history a "Blizzard in Cambridge" has its place but India and China are missing. The "Pacification of Columbia" looms as large as the battle of Verdun. There is no mention of Copernicus, but Allen Tate and Elizabeth Bishop each have two pages.

There is no need to dwell on the distortions of this work. It is a boy's view of history—there was always something boyish about Lowell, playing with toy soldiers in the attic, envisioning some final, Napoleonic victory while listening for the sounds of the grown-ups quarreling downstairs. In his fantasies there were only great men and brilliant events. From his poems most of mankind are absent, and this is to be expected, for what could he have known of the lives of the poor, the unlucky, the obscure?

He was spoiled, as Mailer said, and protected by his friends, of whom he had many in influential places. As a result, he was not often criticized adversely. On one occasion a magazine sent out a book by Lowell to be reviewed. When the review came in it was unfavorable. The reviewer was paid and the review never appeared. No doubt this was not the only instance of the kind.

But Lowell was self-critical. It is one of the advantages of being ambitious. He was never satisfied, and sooner or later he would discover his mistakes. Attempting to group poems from *Notebook* thematically and so create a single, important "epic" poem was a mistake, and he saw that it was; he gave up writing sonnets and went back to the kind of poetry he had been writing in *Life Studies* and *For the Union Dead*: narratives drawn from life but transformed into art.

Day by Day has the realism we had come to recognize as Lowell's specialty. There are not as many strong images as in the early books, but the ear for language is there, for the movement of verse and the curve of an emotion that will fill a poem and bring it to an end. He is, once more, in control of his experience. He again confronts his parents, and revisits his school, and speaks of men and women he has known. He goes back to the mental hospital with a humor that must be all his own—no one else has written so truthfully, and yet in so detached a manner, about mental disorder.

There is one constant theme throughout, his life as a poet. I have said that ideas may only be pegs to hang poetry on—Lowell's best peg was his life as a poet. He once said, in a poem that he removed from *Day by Day* before it went to press, that writing had been his "indissoluble bride" for thirty years. He may have decided to leave this poem out because what it said came too close to home. He loved poetry with all his heart, and knew how destructive this could be.

This is why I have ended with him. To understand Lowell is to understand what happened in a generation of American poets from the Second World War to the present.

He came to maturity during the postwar period. *Lord Weary's Castle* expressed his alienation and turning away from the world into which he had been born, the capitalist Puritanism of New England. The poems made gestures in the direction of religion, but what was most assured about this poetry was its formal excellence.

By the mid-fifties poets were rediscovering the free-verse experiments of Pound and Williams. They began to express their thoughts directly; Lowell's *Life Studies*, written in a direct, conversational manner, continued the story of his alienation, at the same time portraying the life devoted to art as a possible solution. Younger poets looked back to Blake and Whitman, and the sound of prophecy was heard again. In the 1960s, with the struggle for Civil Rights and the war in Vietnam poets became political. Radical views and direct personal utterance went hand in hand.

By the end of the sixties the experiments of the previous decade had hardened and produced their own orthodoxies. Direct personal writing had become a habit of literal reporting. Lowell's *Notebook* shows the prevailing temper of these years—the hope that the facts about oneself, if they are told sincerely, will have some significance. The personality of the individual is everything and art is confined to expressing this.

At this point Lowell appeared to have come to a standstill and to be repeating his own history. The hero of *Life Studies* had been a representative man, or at least a representative poet. The life presented as *History* was only Robert Lowell's.

Lowell's stasis was typical of the seventies. American poets were intent on expressing their personal views, and no two spoke alike.

Afterword

If one considers the impersonality of the modern bureaucratic state it is likely that, more and more, poetry will be written to express the life of an individual.

In order to do so it will narrow its scope. Personal writing cannot have the epic dimension, the grandeur of a Trojan war or a fall from Paradise. The personal voice does not speak for society at large or a belief held in common. Here and there a poet may subscribe to some form of mysticism, but in general the poet who writes about his experiences must be content to be a naturalist, believing, in Wordsworth's terrible phrase, that this world is where we find our happiness or not at all.

To most people living in the West, poetry has become almost exclusively a means of self-expression. This is bound to continue until the aim of education is changed, and this must wait on changes in society as a whole. Only then will what poets write and what the people think come together.

For the time being we do not have that poetry—we are stuck with our sweating selves, and worse. By the worse I mean "confessional" writing. One hears the author speaking of the most intimate details of his life, one sees the figure weeping, and then one remembers that this is all taking place before the camera. As a novelist said at the beginning of the century, "I have always suspected, in the effort to bring into play the extremities of emotions, the debasing touch of insincerity."[1] The confessional writer is at all times aware of the profit to be made from exhibiting his soul; there is nothing that he or she will not trot out for your inspection. Everything is for sale: furniture, rags, bundles of personal letters, everything.

In contrast to this, what I have called the personal voice is an expression of character. And character is something made. The self that appears in the novel or poem has been constructed according to certain aesthetic principles. This version of the self is not intended to direct attention upon the author but to serve the work of art. The purpose is to create a symbolic life, a portrait of the artist that will have meaning for others and so create a feeling of community, if only among a few thousand.

Until the birth of the larger community it appears that the best we can do is to live as individuals as happily as we can. Poetry that describes the effort may bind a few thousand souls in sympathy with one another. The books of poets create sub-societies of people bound together by something much closer to their heart's desire than the noise of the world.

In the absence of vision we gather around the lives of men- and women who have lived to some purpose.

Notes

FOREWORD

1 Ford Madox Ford, "On Impressionism," *Critical Writings of Ford Madox Ford*, ed. Frank MacShane (Lincoln: University of Nebraska Press, 1964), p. 42.
2 Ibid., p. 43.
3 Wallace Stevens, "To Richard Eberhart . . . Jan. 20, 1954," *Letters of Wallace Stevens*, ed. Holly Stevens (London: Faber and Faber, 1967), p. 815.
4 Susan Sontag, *Against Interpretation and Other Essays* (New York: Dell, 1966 reprint), p. 4.
5 Charles Olson, "Projective Verse," *Selected Writings* (New York: New Directions, 1966), p. 24.
6 Emerson, "The Poet."
7 Olson, p. 19.
8 Denise Levertov, "Notebook Pages," *The Poet in the World* (New York: New Directions, 1973), p. 19.
9 John Dewey, *Art as Experience*.
10 William Carlos Williams, "Prologue to KORA IN HELL," *Selected Essays of William Carlos Williams* (New York: Random House, 1954), p. 11.
11 "Starting from Paumanok."
12 Louis Simpson, "Rolling Up," *American Poetry in 1976*, ed. William Heyen (Indianapolis: Bobbs-Merrill, 1976), p. 332.

THE COLOR OF SAYING

1 Dylan Thomas, "Once It Was the Colour of Saying," *The Poems of Dylan Thomas* (hereafter cited as *Poems*), ed. Daniel Jones (New York: New Directions, 1971), p. 144.
2 Paul Ferris, *Dylan Thomas* (New York: Dial Press, 1977), p. 36.
3 Caitlin Thomas, *Leftover Life to Kill* (Boston: Little Brown, 1957), pp. 56-57.

4 Ferris, pp. 40–41.

5 Daniel Jones, *My Friend Dylan Thomas* (London: J. M. Dent, 1977), p. 15.

6 Thomas, "Poetic Manifesto," *Texas Quarterly* (Winter 1961); reprinted as "The Answers Called 'Poetic Manifesto' (1951)" in Andrew Sinclair, *Dylan Thomas: Poet of His People* (London: Michael Joseph, 1975), p. 227.

7 Jones, p. 15.

8 Ferris, pp. 43–44.

9 Ibid., p. 47.

10 Ibid., p. 48.

11 Thomas, "The Hunchback in the Park," *Poems*, p. 171.

12 Ferris, pp. 44–45.

13 Thomas, "The Peaches," *Portrait of the Artist as a Young Dog* (New York: New Directions, 1968), pp. 2, 3 (hereafter cited as *Portrait*).

14 Jones, p. 11.

15 Ferris, p. 53.

16 Ibid., p. 33.

17 Thomas, "Extraordinary Little Cough," *Portrait*, p. 47.

18 Ibid., "The Peaches," p. 13.

19 Caitlin Thomas, p. 52.

20 W. J. Turner, "Romance."

21 F. W. Harvey, "Ducks."

22 T. S. Eliot, "The Waste Land."

23 John Drinkwater, "Birthright."

24 Rupert Brooke, "The Old Vicarage, Grantchester."

25 Henry Newbolt, "The War Films."

26 Wilfred Owen, "Exposure."

27 Thomas, "Modern Poetry" from *Swansea Grammar School Magazine*, Vol. 26, no. 3 (December 1929), pp. 82–84; in *Dylan Thomas: Early Prose Writings*, ed. Walford Davies (London: J. M. Dent, 1971), pp. 83–86.

28 Ferris, p. 316.

29 Ibid., p. 50.

30 Thomas, "The Song of the Mischievous Dog," *Poems*, p. 221.

31 P. E. Smart, *The Spread Eagle* in "Introduction," *The Notebooks of Dylan Thomas*, ed. Ralph Maud (New York: New Directions, 1966), p. 11 (hereafter cited as *Notebooks*).

32 Thomas, "The Elm," *Poems*, p. 226.

33 Thomas, *Notebooks*, p. 51.

34 Ibid., p. 250.

35 "A letter ... of October 1933" quoted in "Introduction," *Notebooks*, p. 27.

36 Letter to Charles Fisher, February 1935, *Selected Letters of Dylan Thomas*, ed. Constantine Fitzgibbon (New York: New Directions, 1965), p. 151 (hereafter cited as *Selected Letters*).

37 Elder Olson, *The Poetry of Dylan Thomas* (Chicago: University of Chicago Press, 1954), p. 64.

38 Letter to Herman Peschmann, 1st February 1938, *Selected Letters*, p. 186.
39 Ferris, p. 241.
40 Thomas, "Where Tawe Flows," *Portrait*, p. 61.
41 Jones, p. 31.
42 Ibid., pp. 22–28.
43 Thomas, "Just Like Little Dogs," *Portrait*, p. 57.
44 Ibid., pp. 54–60.
45 Ferris, pp. 73–74.
46 Ibid., p. 82.
47 Thomas, "One Warm Sunday," *Portrait*, p. 102.
48 Thomas, *Notebooks*, pp. 155–56, 168; "After the Funeral," *Poems*, 136–37.
49 Ferris, p. 78.
50 Letter to Daniel Jones, August 1935, quoted by Ferris, p. 62.
51 Letter to Pamela Hansford Johnson, 11 November 1933, *Selected Letters*, pp. 63–64.
52 Ibid., mid September 1933, p. 21.
53 Ibid., late October 1933, p. 40.
54 Ibid., late October 1933, p. 35.
55 Ibid., 9 May 1934, p. 122.
56 Thomas, *Notebooks*, pp. 231–33.
57 Maud, "Introduction," *Notebooks*, p. 29.
58 Ferris, pp. 95–96. Ferris's life of Dylan Thomas is an indispensable source. I have drawn on it for facts; the interpretations are my own.
59 Letter to Trevor Hughes, 12 January 1934, *Selected Letters*, p. 87.
60 Maud, "Introduction," *Notebooks*, pp. 28–30.
61 André Breton, "Manifesto of Surrealism" (1924).
62 Thomas, *Notebooks*, pp. 257–58.
63 Henry Treece wrote an article on Thomas's work with the title, "Is Dylan Thomas a Hoax?" It angered him greatly.
64 Thomas, *Notebooks*, p. 258.
65 Letter to Trevor Hughes, 12 January 1934, *Selected Letters*, p. 87.
66 Letters to Pamela Hansford Johnson, week of July 5, 1934 and 20 July 1934, *Selected Letters*, pp. 136, 140.
67 Letter to Geoffrey Grigson, May 1934, *Selected Letters*, p. 112.
68 Letter to Glyn Jones, early December 1934, *Selected Letters*, p. 150.
69 Letter to Edith Sitwell, 2 September 1936, *Selected Letters*, pp. 176–77.
70 Ferris, p. 145.
71 Thomas, "Over Sir John's Hill," *Poems*, p. 201.
72 Letter to Vernon Watkins, 15 July 1937, *Selected Letters*, p. 182.
73 Ferris, p. 149.
74 Letter quoted by Ferris, p. 151.
75 John Malcolm Brinnin, *Dylan Thomas in America* (London: J. M. Dent, 1957), p. 126.
76 Caitlin Thomas, p. 157.
77 Ibid., p. 55.
78 Letter to James Laughlin, March 28, 1938, *Selected Letters*, pp. 193–94.
79 Letter to Henry Treece, July 1939, *Selected Letters*, p. 233.

80 Letter to Rayner Heppenstall, November 2, 1939, *Selected Letters*, pp. 242–44.
81 Letter to Henry Treece, 6 or 7 July 1935, *Selected Letters*, p. 204.
82 Letter to Edward Marsh, 14 September 1939, *Selected Letters*, pp. 238–39.
83 Letter to Oscar Williams, July 30, 1945, *Selected Letters*, p. 277.
84 Ibid., p. 279.
85 *New Lives: An Anthology*, ed. Robert Conquest (New York: St. Martin's Press, 1956), p. xii.
86 Kingsley Amis, *A Case of Samples: Poems* (New York: Harcourt Brace, 1957), p. 53.
87 John Wain, "Dylan Thomas: A Review of His Collected Poems" in *Dylan Thomas*, ed. C. B. Cox (Englewood Cliffs, N.J.: Prentice-Hall, 1966), p. 11.
88 Brinnin, pp. 146–47.
89 Letter to John Malcolm Brinnin, November 23, 1949, *Selected Letters*, pp. 333–34.
90 Letter to James Laughlin, November 23, 1949, *Selected Letters*, p. 336.
91 Brinnin, p. 10.
92 Ibid., pp. 13–15.
93 W. H. Auden, "Writing," *The Dyer's Hand* (New York: Random House, 1962), p. 27.
94 Olson, p. 23.
95 Ibid., p. 22.
96 William Blake, "Introduction," *Songs of Experience*.
97 Jane Kramer, *Allen Ginsberg in America* (New York: Random House, 1970), p. 108.
98 Thomas, "Especially When the October Wind," *Poems*, p. 98.
99 Theodore Roethke, "Prognosis," *The Collected Poems of Theodore Roethke* (Garden City, N.Y.: Doubleday, 1966), p. 5. .
100 Roethke, "The Long Winter," *Collected Poems*, p. 196.
101 Caitlin Thomas, p. 60.
102 Brinnin, p. 120.
103 Ibid., pp. 140–41.
104 Thomas, "Do Not Go Gentle into That Good Night," *Poems*, p. 207.
105 Thomas, "Fern Hill," *Poems*, p. 195.
106 Thomas, "On Reading One's Own Poems," *Quite Early One Morning* (New York: New Directions, 1954), pp. 174–75.
107 Thomas, "After the Funeral," *Poems*, p. 137.

"THE EYE ALTERING ALTERS ALL"

1 Alexander Pope, "Epistle to Dr. Arbuthnot."
2 Robert Frost, "Once by the Pacific," *Complete Poems of Robert Frost* (New York: Holt, Rinehart and Winston, 1964), p. 314.

3   Mark Van Doren, "Sonnets . . . 1935," *Selected Poems* (New York: Henry Holt, 1954), p. 75.
4   Jack Kerouac, *Visions of Cody* (New York: McGraw-Hill, 1972), p. 265.
5   John Tytell, *Naked Angels* (New York: McGraw-Hill, 1976), p. 50.
6   Tytell, p. 55.
7   Ibid.
8   Ibid., p. 57.
9   Kerouac, *Visions of Cody*, p. 187.
10 Tytell, p. 57.
11 Kerouac, *On the Road* (New York: Signet, 1957), p. 9.
12 Kerouac, *The Town and the City* (New York: Harcourt Brace Jovanovich, 1950), p. 365.
13 William Carlos Williams, *Paterson* (New York: New Directions, 1963), p. 204.
14 The letter is included in Jane Kramer's *Allen Ginsberg in America* (New York: Random House, 1970), p. 166.
15 Aaron Latham, "The Columbia Murder that Gave Birth to the Beats," *New York* (19 April 1976), p. 41.
16 Salvador Dali, *The Unspeakable Confessions of Salvador Dali* (New York: William Morrow, 1976), p. 17.
17 He was soon released on parole, however. In later years he was a reporter for United Press. Latham, pp. 41–53.
18 Kramer, pp. 117–19.
19 Tytell, p. 85.
20 Ibid., pp. 85–86. Here as elsewhere Tytell endorses Ginsberg's point of view. This is true of others who have written about Ginsberg: Jane Kramer and Morris Dickstein. They appear to have fallen under the spell of Ginsberg's "paranoia criticism."
21 Kramer, pp. 120–21.
22 Tytell, pp. 86–87.
23 Kramer, p. 121.
24 Allen Ginsberg, "Dakar Doldrums," *The Gates of Wrath* (Bolinas, Calif.: Grey Fox Press, 1972), p. 5.
25 Ginsberg, *Allen Verbatim*, ed. George Ball (New York: McGraw-Hill, 1974), pp. 136ff.
26 Ginsberg, "A Western Ballad," *Gates of Wrath*, p. 11.
27 Ginsberg, *Allen Verbatim*, p. 138.
28 Ibid., p. 20.
29 Ginsberg, "Howl," *Howl and Other Poems* (San Francisco: City Lights, 1956), p. 17.
30 Ginsberg, "This Is the Abomination," *Columbia Review*, Vol. 26 (May 1946), p. 162.
31 Ginsberg, "Prose Contribution to Cuban Revolution," *Poetics of the New American Poetry*, Donald Allen and Warren Tallman, eds. (New York: Grove Press, 1973), p. 337.
32 Kramer, p. 123.

33 Ginsberg, "Stanzas: Written at Night in Radio City," *Gates of Wrath*, p. 20.
34 Kramer, p. 126.
35 Ibid., pp. 124–30. I have followed Kramer closely, paraphrasing her descriptions.
36 Tytell, p. 95.
37 Ibid., pp. 94–96.
38 Ginsberg, *The Visions of the Great Rememberer* (Amherst, Mass.: Mulch Press, 1974), p. 34.
39 Ginsberg, *Allen Verbatim*, p. 150.
40 Williams, *Paterson*, p. 204.
41 Ginsberg, *Journals*, ed. Gordon Ball (New York: Grove Press, 1977), p. 11.
42 Ibid., pp. 7–8, 12.
43 Ginsberg, *Allen Verbatim*, p. 144.
44 This is different from the account in Kramer (p. 134). According to Ginsberg in Kramer's version, following the newspaper interview he visited Williams regularly. The letter in *Paterson*, however, states that there was an interval of two years. Here as elsewhere Ginsberg's own account of his activities is confusing.
45 Williams, *Paterson*, pp. 204–206.
46 Ginsberg, "This Bricklayer's Lunch Hour," *Empty Mirror* (New York: Corinth, 1961), p. 41.
47 Kramer, pp. 134–35.
48 Ginsberg, *Allen Verbatim*, p. 142.
49 Ginsberg, *Notes After an Evening with William Carlos Williams* (Portents—17, 1970), n.p.
50 Williams, "Introduction," *Empty Mirror*, p. vii.
51 Ginsberg, "After All, What Else Is There to Say?" *Empty Mirror*, p. 13.
52 Ginsberg, "The Trembling of the Veil," *Empty Mirror*, p. 15.
53 Ginsberg, "An Atypical Affair," *Empty Mirror*, p. 47.
54 Ginsberg, "Hymn," *Empty Mirror*, p. 32.
55 Ginsberg, "Paterson," *Empty Mirror*, p. 51.
56 Tytell, pp. 234–35.
57 Ginsberg, "Prose Contribution . . ." *Poetics*, p. 338.
58 Kramer, pp. 187–88.
59 Ginsberg, "Craft Interview with Allen Ginsberg," *New York Quarterly*, (Spring 1971), p. 29.
60 Ginsberg, "A Meaningless Institution," *Empty Mirror*, p. 16.
61 Ginsberg, "Paterson," *Empty Mirror*, pp. 52–53.
62 Charles Tart, "The Effects of Marijuana on Consciousness," *Altered States of Consciousness* (New York: John Wiley, 1969).
63 Ginsberg, *Allen Verbatim*, pp. 145–46.
64 Ginsberg, *Visions*, pp. 14, 15.
65 Ibid., p. 10.
66 Tytell, p. 99.
67 Ginsberg, *Journals*, p. 13.

68 Ibid., p. 17.
69 Ibid., p. 47.
70 Kramer, p. 41.
71 Ginsberg, *Journals*, p. 59.
72 Ibid., pp. 71–76.
73 Letter to Mark Van Doren, 19 May 1956, cited by Tytell, p. 100.
74 Kramer, pp. 42–43.
75 Gordon Ball, "Reader's Guide," *Journals*, p. xx.
76 Ginsberg, *Journals*, p. 92.
77 Ibid., p. 94
78 Letter to Mark Van Doren, 19 May 1956, cited by Tytell, p. 100.
79 Tytell, p. 104.
80 John Hollander, "Poetry Chronicle," *Partisan Review* (Spring 1957), pp. 296–303.
81 Letter to John Hollander, cited by Kramer, pp. 163–77.
82 Ginsberg, "Howl," *Howl*, p. 9.
83 Kramer, p. 168.
84 Ginsberg, "A Supermarket in California," *Howl*, p. 23.
85 Ibid., "Sunflower Sutra," pp. 28–29.
86 Ibid., "America," pp. 33–34.
87 Tytell, p. 215.
88 Ibid., pp. 214–15.
89 Ginsberg, "Kaddish," *Kaddish and Other Poems* (San Francisco: City Lights, 1961), p. 29.
90 Ibid., p. 17.
91 Ibid., p. 18.
92 Delmore Schwartz, however, in his prose tale, "In Dreams Begin Responsibilities," had anticipated the tone and even the characters of "Kaddish."
93 Gustave Flaubert, "Letter to Louise Colet (1852)," *Selected Letters*, trans. Francis Steegmuller (New York: Farrar, Straus and Giroux, 1954), pp. 127–28.
94 Henry Miller, *The Rosy Crucifixion, Book One: Sextus* (New York: Grove Press, 1965), pp. 47–48.
95 Ginsberg, "Advice to Youth" (talk to students at Kent State University), *Allen Verbatim*, p. 107.
96 T. S. Eliot, "Tradition and the Individual Talent," *The Sacred Wood* (London: Methuen, 1966 reprint), p. 58.
97 Kramer, p. 174.
98 Morris Dickstein, *Gates of Eden* (New York: Basic Books, 1977), p. 16.
99 Ginsberg, "Kral Majales," *Planet News* (San Francisco: City Lights, 1968), pp. 89, 90.
100 Ginsberg, "Interview with Allen Ginsberg," *Free Lance*, Vol. 6, no. 1 (Washington University, 1967), p. 16.
101 Ibid.
102 Ginsberg, *Visions*, p. 35.

103 Ginsberg, "Interview," *Free Lance*, p. 16. Though not a quote this is a transcription of Ginsberg's conversation as reported in the interview.
104 Ginsberg, "Craft Interview," *New York Quarterly*, p. 34.
105 Ibid., pp. 35–37.
106 Ginsberg, "Scenes Along the Road," *Photographs of the Desolation Angels,* compiled by Ann Charters with three poems and comments by Allen Ginsberg (Potents/Gotham Book Mart, 1970), pp. 49–50.

BLACK, BANDED WITH YELLOW

1 The following account of the lives of Otto and Aurelia Plath is based on Aurelia Schober Plath's "Introduction" to *Letters Home by Sylvia Plath* (New York: Harper & Row, 1975), pp. 3–13 (hereafter cited as *LH*).
2 Sylvia Plath, "Ocean 1212-W," *The Art of Sylvia Plath*, ed. Charles Newman (Bloomington: Indiana University Press, 1971), pp. 266–72 (hereafter cited as Newman).
3 Ibid., pp. 268–69.
4 Ibid., p. 272.
5 Matthew Arnold, "The Forsaken Merman," quoted by Plath in "Ocean 1212-W" in Newman, p. 267.
6 Ted Hughes' word, and the title of an excellent book: Judith Kroll, *Chapters in a Mythology: The Poetry of Sylvia Plath* (New York: Harper & Row, 1976).
7 Wallace Stevens, "Disillusionment of Ten O'Clock."
8 Peter Orr, ed., *The Poet Speaks* (London: Routledge and Kegan Paul, 1966) quoted in Eileen Aird, *Sylvia Plath: Her Life and Work* (New York: Harper & Row, 1975), p. 5.
9 George Stade, "Introduction" to Nancy Hunter Steiner, *A Closer Look at Ariel: A Memory of Sylvia Plath* (New York: Popular Library, 1973), p. 24.
10 Plath, *The Bell Jar* (New York: Harper & Row, 1971), pp. 42–43, 94.
11 In conversation with the author.
12 "Introduction," *LH*, p. 34.
13 Ibid., p. 35.
14 November 13, 1949, diary entry quoted in "Introduction," *LH*, p. 40.
15 Ibid., p. 35.
16 Steiner, p. 52.
17 Letter dated May 12, 1953, *LH*, p. 113.
18 November 13, 1949, diary entry quoted in "Introduction," *LH*, p. 40.
19 Ibid.
20 Her mother's description of the image Sylvia wanted to project, *LH*, p. 45.
21 "Introduction," *LH*, p. 34.
22 Letter dated September 29, 1950, *LH*, pp. 46–48.

23 Letter dated October 31, 1950, *LH*, p. 56.

24 Letter dated November 15, 1950, *LH*, p. 59.

25 Letter dated November 11, 1950, *LH*, p. 58.

26 Edna St. Vincent Millay, *Collected Poems* (New York: Harper & Brothers, 1956), pp. 3–13.

27 Letter dated June 12, 1952, *LH*, p. 87.

28 Letter dated October 8, 1951, *LH*, pp. 75–80.

29 Letter dated November 15, 1950, *LH*, p. 59.

30 Letter dated November 19, 1952, *LH*, pp. 97–99.

31 Letter postmarked March 21, 1953, *LH*, pp. 107–108.

32 Letter dated April 28, 1953, *LH*, p. 110.

33 Poem dated April 30, 1953, *LH*, p. 110.

34 Letter dated December 28, 1953, *LH*, p. 129.

35 As of this date: July 1977.

36 Poem dated April 16, 1954, *LH*, p. 136.

37 W. H. Auden, "The Quest," *Collected Poems* (New York: Random House, 1976), p. 225.

38 *Times Literary Supplement* (London) no. 3010 (November 6, 1959), p. 29.

39 Plath, *The Bell Jar*, p. 69.

40 Auden, "Musée des Beaux Arts," *Collected Poems*, p. 147.

41 Plath, "Two Views of a Cadaver Room," *The Colossus* (New York: Vintage, 1968), pp. 5–6.

42 The 1959 edition.

43 Allen Ginsberg, *The Visions of the Great Rememberer* (Amherst, Mass.: Mulch Press, 1974), p. 34.

44 Letter dated February 2, 1955, *LH*, p. 157.

45 Steiner, p. 60.

46 Aurelia Schober Plath's comment, *LH*, p. 123.

47 Steiner, p. 61.

48 Plath, *The Bell Jar*, p. 20.

49 *Mademoiselle* (August 1953), p. 358.

50 Plath, *The Bell Jar*, p. 52.

51 Plath, "Ocean 1212-W" in Newman, p. 272.

52 Undated letter (late June 1953?), *LH*, p. 120.

53 Plath, *The Bell Jar*, p. 22.

54 Aurelia Schober Plath's comment, *LH*, p. 123.

55 Ibid., pp. 124–26.

56 Ibid., p. 134.

57 Steiner, pp. 57, 64.

58 Plath, *The Bell Jar*, p. 90.

59 Edward Butscher, *Sylvia Plath: Method and Madness* (New York: Seabury Press, 1976), p. 129.

60 Steiner, p. 75.

61 A friend of the author.

62 Plath, *The Bell Jar*, p. 260.

63 Stade, "Introduction," Steiner, p. 37.

64 Aurelia Schober Plath's letter to Harper & Row (1970) quoted by Lois Ames, "Sylvia Plath: A Biographical Note" in *The Bell Jar* (New York: Bantam, 1972), p. 215.
65 Sylvia Plath quoted by Aurelia Schober Plath in her letter to Harper & Row (1970) quoted by Ames, *The Bell Jar* (Bantam edition), p. 214.
66 Butscher, pp. 129–30.
67 Quoted by Butscher, p. 163. I have not wanted to look up the original.
68 Letter dated October 15, 1954, *LH*, p. 146.
69 See Kroll's *Chapters in a Mythology.*
70 Plath, "Ariel," *Ariel* (New York: Harper & Row, 1965), p. 27.
71 Letters dated April 16, April 21, April 23, 1955, *LH*, pp. 168–69, 171.
72 Letter dated October 9, 1955, *LH*, p. 186.
73 Letter dated October 5, 1955, *LH*, p. 185.
74 Letter dated October 18, 1955, *LH*, p. 190. But Brooke said "ten to three."
75 Letter dated October 24, 1955, *LH*, p. 191.
76 Letter dated October 29, 1955, *LH*, p. 193.
77 Letter dated November 22, 1955, *LH*, p. 198.
78 Letter dated January 7, 1956, *LH*, pp. 203–205.
79 Letter dated January 17, 1956, *LH*, p. 208.
80 Ibid.
81 Letter dated January 25, 1956, *LH*, p. 211.
82 Letter dated January 29, 1956, *LH*, pp. 212–13.
83 Letter dated March 3, 1956, *LH*, p. 221.
84 Letter dated April 19, 1956, *LH*, p. 234.
85 Hughes, "The Jaguar," *The Hawk in the Rain* (New York: Harper & Brothers, 1957), p. 15.
86 Poem dated March 9, 1956, *LH*, pp. 225–26.
87 Hughes, "The Rock," *Writers on Themselves* (BBC 1964), quoted by Keith Sagar in *The Art of Ted Hughes* (London: Cambridge University Press, 1975), p. 6.
88 Hughes, "Capturing Animals," *Poetry Is* (New York: Doubleday, 1970), p. 10.
89 Sagar, p. 7.
90 Ibid.
91 Ibid., 7–8.
92 David Porter, "Beasts / Shamans / Baskin: The Contemporary Aesthetics of Ted Hughes," *Boston University Journal* (Winter 1975), quoted by Sagar, p. 8.
93 Sagar, p. 9.
94 Hughes, "Song," *Hawk in the Rain*, p. 2.
95 Ibid., "Childbirth," p. 40.
96 Letter dated April 25, 1956, *LH*, p. 235.
97 Poem dated April 25, 1956, *LH*, p. 238.
98 Letter dated April 29, 1956, *LH*, pp. 243–44.
99 Letter dated May 9, 1956, *LH*, p. 251.
100 Letter dated May 18, 1956, *LH*, p. 254.

101 Letter dated June 18, 1956, *LH*, p. 257.

102 Ibid.

103 Letters dated July 25, August 2, 1956, *LH*, pp. 265–67.

104 Letter dated September 2, 1956, *LH*, p. 269.

105 Professor Gigian, quoted by Butscher, p. 207.

106 Letter dated April 28, 1957, *LH*, p. 309.

107 Letter dated June 17, 1957, *LH*, p. 317.

108 Robert Lowell, "Preface," *Ariel*, ix.

109 Anne Sexton, "The Barfly Ought to Sing" in Newman, pp. 174–75.

110 Plath, "The Manor Garden," *Colossus*, p. 3.

111 Plath, "The Colossus," *Colossus*, pp. 20–21; "Berck-Plage," "Little Fugue," "Daddy," *Ariel*, pp. 21, 70–71, 50.

112 Plath, "Moonrise," *Colossus*, p. 65.

113 Plath, "The Bull of Bendylaw," *Colossus*, p. 27.

114 Plath, "Stillborn," *Crossing the Water* (New York: Harper & Row, 1971), p. 20.

115 Plath, "I Am Vertical," *Crossing the Water*, p. 12.

116 Kroll, xv.

117 A. Alvarez, *The Savage God* (London: Wiedenfeld and Nicolson, 1971), pp. 30–32.

118 Plath, "Lady Lazarus," *Ariel*, pp. 6–7.

119 M. L. Rosenthal, *The New Poets* (New York: Oxford University Press, 1967), p. 83.

120 Rosenthal, pp. 27, 29.

121 Plath, "Elm," *Ariel*, p. 15.

122 Kroll, p. 169.

123 Ibid., p. 166.

124 She speaks of an attempt to kill herself by drowning, which would make three, but this seems to have been half-hearted.

125 Alvarez, pp. 25–26.

126 Kroll, p. 60.

127 Letter dated June 15, 1962, *LH*, p. 457.

128 Plath, "The Beekeeper's Daughter," *Colossus*, pp. 73–74.

129 Plath, "The Bee Meeting," *Ariel*, pp. 56–58.

130 Letter dated December 28, 1953, *LH*, p. 131.

131 E.g., "Electra on Azalea Path," *The Hudson Review*, XIII, iii (Fall 1960), 414–15.

132 Plath, "Ariel," *Ariel*, p. 27.

133 Ibid., "Stings," p. 63.

134 Ibid., "The Bee Meeting," p. 58.

ROBERT LOWELL'S INDISSOLUBLE BRIDE

1 Robert Lowell, "91 Revere Street," *Life Studies* (New York: Farrar, Straus and Cudahy, 1959), pp. 11–46.

2 Lowell, "My Last Afternoon with Uncle Devereux Winslow," *Life Studies*, p. 59.

3 Frederick Seidel, "An Interview with Robert Lowell" in *Robert Lowell: A Portrait of the Artist in His Time*, ed. Michael London and Robert Boyers (New York: David Lewis, 1970), p. 264 (hereafter cited as *RL: A Portrait*).

4 Ibid., pp. 280–81.

5 Lowell, "Charles River," *Notebook* (New York: Farrar, Straus and Giroux, 1970), p. 67.

6 Seidel, "An Interview" in *RL: A Portrait*, p. 282.

7 Lowell, "Commander Lowell," *Life Studies*, p. 72.

8 Valéry quoted by Stephen Yenser in *Circle to Circle: The Poetry of Robert Lowell* (Berkeley: University of California Press, 1975), p. 33.

9 Alan Williamson, *Pity the Monsters: The Political Vision of Robert Lowell* (New Haven: Yale University Press, 1974), p. 14.

10 Allen Tate, "Ode to Our Young Proconsuls of the Air," *The Swimmers and Other Selected Poems* (New York: Charles Scribner's Sons, 1970), p. 95.

11 Lowell's own description. Seidel, "An Interview" in *RL: A Portrait*, p. 281.

12 Seidel, "An Interview" in *RL: A Portrait*, p. 263.

13 Ibid., p. 282.

14 Ibid., pp. 278–79.

15 Ibid., p. 265.

16 Lowell, "Memories of West Street and Lepke," *Life Studies*, p. 85.

17 Allen Tate, "Introduction" to Lowell, *Land of Unlikeness* (Cummington, Mass.: The Cummington Press, 1944), n.p.

18 Lowell, "A Prayer for My Grandfather to Our Lady," *Land of Unlikeness*, n.p.

19 Williamson, pp. 16–17.

20 Jerome Mazzaro, *The Poetic Themes of Robert Lowell* (Ann Arbor: University of Michigan Press, 1965), p. 32.

21 Lowell, "In the Park Street Cemetery," *Land of Unlikeness*, n.p.

22 Ibid., "The Boston Nativity," n.p.

23 Ibid., "Christ for Sale," n.p.

24 Seidel, "An Interview" in *RL: A Portrait*, p. 276.

25 Yenser, pp. 21, 18, 20.

26 Lowell, "In Memory of Arthur Winslow," *Land of Unlikeness*, n.p.

27 Yenser, pp. 19–20.

28 Randall Jarrell, "The Kingdom of Necessity" in *RL: A Portrait*, p. 27.

29 Seidel, "An Interview" in *RL: A Portrait*, pp. 265–66.

30 Lowell, "The Exile's Return," *Lord Weary's Castle and The Mills of the Kavanaughs* (New York: Meridian Books/Harcourt, Brace and World, 1961), p. 3.

31 Ibid., "The Holy Innocents," p. 4.

32 Ibid., "The Quaker Graveyard in Nantucket," p. 11.

33 Ibid., p. 12.

34 Ibid., p. 20.

35 Ibid., p. 14.

36 See Hugh B. Staples, "The Quaker Graveyard in Nantucket" in *Robert Lowell: A Collection of Critical Essays,* ed. Thomas Parkinson (Englewood Cliffs, N.J.: Prentice-Hall, 1968), pp. 65, 70.

37 Lowell, "The Quaker Graveyard in Nantucket," *Lord Weary's Castle,* pp. 8–14.

38 Williamson, p. 46.

39 Lowell, "In Memory of Arthur Winslow," "Mary Winslow," "The North Sea Undertaker's Complaint," "The Dead in Europe," "The Ghost," "Mr. Edwards and the Spider," "After the Surprising Conversions," *Lord Weary's Castle,* pp. 19, 25, 33, 64, 50, 58–59, 60–61.

40 Lowell, "The Exile's Return," *Lord Weary's Castle,* p. 3.

41 Jarrell, *"The Mills of the Kavanaughs"* in *RL: A Portrait,* p. 39.

42 Lowell, "The Mills of the Kavanaughs," *The Mills of the Kavanaughs* (New York: Harcourt, Brace and Company, 1951), p. 3.

43 Yenser, pp. 83, 61.

44 Seidel, "An Interview" in *RL: A Portrait,* pp. 289–90.

45 Ibid., p. 266.

46 Staples, *Robert Lowell: The First Twenty Years* (New York: Farrar, Straus, 1962), p. 57.

47 Staples, *Robert Lowell,* p. 59.

48 T. S. Eliot, *"Ulysses,* Order and Myth," *The Dial* (November 1923).

49 There are poems about it in his most recent collection, *Day by Day* (New York: Farrar, Straus and Giroux, 1977).

50 Daniel Weissbort in conversation with the author.

51 Seidel, "An Interview" in *RL: A Portrait,* p. 267.

52 Ibid., pp. 269–70.

53 Stanley Kunitz, "Talk with Robert Lowell," *The New York Times Book Review* (4 October 1964), pp. 34–39.

54 Seidel, "An Interview" in *RL: A Portrait,* p. 271.

55 Lowell, "On 'Skunk Hour' " in Parkinson, p. 132.

56 Seidel, "An Interview" in *RL: A Portrait,* p. 268.

57 Lowell, "My Last Afternoon with Uncle Devereux Winslow," *Life Studies,* p. 60.

58 M. L. Rosenthal, "Robert Lowell and the Poetry of Confession" in *RL: A Portait,* p. 45.

59 Lowell, "On 'Skunk Hour' " in Parkinson, pp. 133–34.

60 Lowell, "91 Revere Street," *Life Studies,* pp. 12–13.

61 Proust, *Contre Sainte-Beuve.*

62 Jarrell, "Poets," *Poetry and the Age* (New York: Alfred A. Knopf, 1955), p. 226.

63 Yenser, pp. 120–21.

64 R. P. Blackmur, "New Thresholds, New Anatomies: Notes on a Text of Hart Crane," *Language as Gesture* (New York: Harcourt, Brace and Company, 1952), pp. 305–306.

65 Seidel, "An Interview" in *RL: A Portrait*, p. 291.
66 Lowell, "During Fever," *Life Studies*, pp. 79–80.
67 Lowell, "Mother, 1972," *History* (New York: Farrar, Straus and Giroux, 1973), p. 115.
68 Williamson, p. 74.
69 Lowell, "My Last Afternoon with Uncle Devereux Winslow," *Life Studies*, p. 60.
70 Ibid., "Dunbarton," p. 65.
71 Ibid., "My Last Afternoon with Uncle Devereux Winslow," p. 63.
72 Ibid., "Dunbarton," pp. 65–67.
73 Yenser, pp. 122–23.
74 Lowell, "Memories of West Street and Lepke," *Life Studies*, pp. 85–86.
75 Williamson, p. 78.
76 Lowell, "To the Reader," *Imitations* (New York: Noonday/Farrar, Straus and Giroux, 1961), p. 46.
77 Ibid., "Saturday Night in the Village," p. 27.
78 Lowell and Jacques Barzun, *Phaedra and Figaro* (New York: Farrar, Straus and Cudahy, 1961), p. 45.
79 Hayden Carruth, "A Meaning of Robert Lowell" in *RL: A Portrait*, p. 225.
80 Robert Bly, "Robert Lowell's *For the Union Dead*" in *RL: A Portrait*, pp. 73–76.
81 Lowell, "Water," *For the Union Dead* (New York: Farrar Straus and Giroux, 1965), p. 4.
82 Ibid., "The Old Flame," pp. 5–6.
83 Ibid., "Night Sweat," pp. 68–69.
84 Ibid., "For the Union Dead," pp. 71–72.
85 Seidel, "An Interview" in *RL: A Portrait*, p. 267.
86 Norman Mailer, *The Steps of the Pentagon* in *RL: A Portrait*, pp. 243–58.
87 Lowell, "Waking Early Sunday Morning," *Near the Ocean* (New York: Farrar, Straus and Giroux, 1967), pp. 15–24.
88 Hayden Carruth, "A Meaning of Robert Lowell" in *RL: A Portait*, p. 241.
89 Lowell, "Fourth of July in Maine," *Near the Ocean*, p. 34.
90 Matthew Arnold, "Dover Beach."
91 Lowell, "Afterthought," *Notebook 1967–68* (New York: Farrar, Straus and Giroux, 1969), pp. 159–60.
92 D. S. Carne-Ross, "Conversation with Robert Lowell," *Delos*, I (1968), 166, quoted by Philip Cooper, *The Autobiographical Myth of Robert Lowell* (Chapel Hill: University of North Carolina Press, 1970), p. 145.
93 Untitled reply to the editors of *The Harvard Advocate*, CIII (Spring 1969), 17; quoted by Cooper, p. 143.
94 Longinus, *On the Sublime.*
95 Charles Olson, "Human Universe," *Selected Writings*, ed. Robert Creeley (New York: New Directions, 1966), p. 61.
96 Lowell, "Elizabeth," *Notebook 1967–68*, p. 4.

97 The reviewer was William Meredith. The statement appears on the jacket of the expanded *Notebook* (1970).
98 Blurb on the jacket of *History*.

AFTERWORD

1 Joseph Conrad, *A Personal Record*.

Bibliography

DYLAN THOMAS: WORKS

Adventures in the Skin Trade. New York: New Directions, 1964.

Deaths and Entrances. London: J. M. Dent, 1946 (1965 reprint).

Dylan Thomas: Letters to Vernon Watkins, ed. Vernon Watkins: London: J. M. Dent and Faber and Faber, 1957.

Early Prose Writings, ed. Walford Davies. London: J. M. Dent, 1971.

The Notebooks of Dylan Thomas, ed. Ralph Maud. New York: New Directions, 1966.

The Poems of Dylan Thomas, ed. Daniel Jones. New York: New Directions, 1971.

Portrait of the Artist as a Young Dog. New York: New Directions, 1968.

A Prospect of the Sea, ed. Daniel Jones. London: J. M. Dent, 1972.

Quite Early One Morning. New York: New Directions, 1954.

Selected Letters of Dylan Thomas, ed. Constantine Fitzgibbon. New York: New Directions, 1965.

Under Milk Wood. New York: New Directions, 1954.

DYLAN THOMAS: SECONDARY SOURCES

Ackerman, John. *Dylan Thomas: His Life and Work.* London: Oxford University Press, 1964.

Brinnin, John Malcolm. *Dylan Thomas in America.* London: J. M. Dent, 1957.

Cox, C. B., ed. *Dylan Thomas: A Collection of Critical Essays.* Englewood Cliffs, N.J.: Prentice-Hall, 1966.

Ferris, Paul. *Dylan Thomas.* New York: Dial Press, 1977.

Fitzgibbon, Constantine. *The Life of Dylan Thomas.* Boston: Little Brown, 1965.

Fraser, G. S. *Dylan Thomas.* London: Longman Group, 1957 (1972 reprint).

Holbrook, David. *Dylan Thomas and Poetic Dissociation.* Carbondale: Southern Illinois University Press, 1964.

———. *Dylan Thomas: The Code of Night.* London: Athlone Press, 1972.

———. *Llareggub Revisited.* London: Bowes and Bowes, 1962.

Jones, Daniel. *My Friend Dylan Thomas*. London: J. M. Dent, 1977.

Jones, T. H. *Dylan Thomas*. New York: Barnes and Noble, 1966.

Kershner, Jr., R. B. *Dylan Thomas: The Poet and His Critics*. Chicago: American Library Association, 1976.

Kidder, Rushworth M. *Dylan Thomas: The Country of the Spirit*. Princeton: University of Princeton Press, 1973.

Kleinman, H. H. *The Religious Sonnets of Dylan Thomas*. Berkeley: University of California Press, 1963.

Maud, Ralph. *Entrances to Dylan Thomas' Poetry*. Pittsburgh: University of Pittsburgh Press, 1963.

Murdy, Louise Baughan. *Sound and Sense in Dylan Thomas's Poetry*. Paris: Mouton, 1966.

Olson, Elder. *The Poetry of Dylan Thomas*. Chicago: University of Chicago Press, 1954.

Sinclair, Derek. *Dylan Thomas*. London: Neville Spearman, 1964.

Thomas, Caitlin. *Leftover Life to Kill*. Boston: Little Brown, 1957.

Tindall, William York. *A Reader's Guide to Dylan Thomas*. New York: Farrar, Straus and Giroux, 1973.

Treece, Henry. *Dylan Thomas*. London: L. Drummund, 1949 (1977 reprint).

ALLEN GINSBERG: WORKS

Allen Verbatim, ed. George Ball. New York: McGraw-Hill, 1974.

"Craft Interview with Allen Ginsberg." *New York Quarterly* (Spring 1971), pp. 12–40.

Empty Mirror. New York: Corinth, 1961.

The Gates of Wrath. Bolinas, Calif.: Grey Fox Press, 1972.

Howl and Other Poems. San Francisco: City Lights, 1956.

"Interview with Allen Ginsberg." *Free Lance*. Vol. 6, no. 1 (Washington University, 1967), pp. 15–20.

Journals, ed. Gordon Ball. New York: Grove Press, 1977.

Kaddish and Other Poems. San Francisco: City Lights, 1961.

Notes After an Evening with William Carlos Williams. Portents—17, 1970(?).

Photographs of the Desolation Angels 1944–1960, compiled by Ann Charters with three poems and comments by Allen Ginsberg. Potents/Gotham Book Mart, 1970.

Planet News. San Francisco: City Lights, 1968.

Reality Sandwiches. San Francisco: City Lights, 1963.

"This Is the Abomination." *Columbia Review*, Vol. 26 (May 1946), pp. 159–63.

The Visions of the Great Rememberer. Amherst, Mass.: Mulch Press, 1974.

ALLEN GINSBERG: SECONDARY SOURCES

Dickstein, Morris. *Gates of Eden: American Culture in the Sixties*. New York: Basic Books, 1977.

Kerouac, Jack. *On the Road*. New York: Signet, 1957.
———. *The Town and the City*. New York: Harcourt, Brace, Jovanovich, 1950.
———. *Visions of Cody*. New York: McGraw-Hill, 1972.
Kramer, Jane. *Allen Ginsberg in America*. New York: Random House, 1970.
Latham, Aaron. "The Columbia Murder that Gave Birth to the Beats." *New York* (19 April 1976), pp. 41–53.
Tart, Charles. "The Effects of Marijuana on Consciousness," *Altered States of Consciousness*. New York: John Wiley and Sons, 1969.
Tytell, John. *Naked Angels: The Lives and Literature of the Beat Generation*. New York: McGraw-Hill, 1976.

SYLVIA PLATH: WORKS

Ariel. New York: Harper and Row, 1965.
The Bell Jar. New York: Harper and Row, 1971.
The Colossus and Other Poems. New York: Vintage-Random House, 1968.
Crossing the Water. New York: Harper and Row, 1971.
Letters Home by Sylvia Plath, ed. Aurelia Schober Plath. New York: Harper and Row, 1975.
Winter Trees. London: Faber and Faber, 1971.

SYLVIA PLATH: SECONDARY SOURCES

Aird, Eileen. *Sylvia Plath: Her Life and Work*. New York: Harper and Row, 1973.
Alvarez, A. *The Savage God*. London: Weidenfeld and Nicolson, 1971.
Butscher, Edward. *Sylvia Plath: Method and Madness*. New York: Seabury Press, 1976.
Kroll, Judith. *Chapters in a Mythology: The Poetry of Sylvia Plath*. New York: Harper and Row, 1976.
Newman, Charles, ed. *The Art of Sylvia Plath*. Bloomington: Indiana University Press, 1971.
Sagar, Keith. *The Art of Ted Hughes*. London: Cambridge University Press, 1975.
Steiner, Nancy Hunter. *A Closer Look at Ariel: A Memory of Sylvia Plath*. New York: Popular Library, 1973.

ROBERT LOWELL: WORKS

Day by Day. New York: Farrar, Straus and Giroux, 1977.
The Dolphin. New York: Farrar, Straus and Giroux, 1973.
For Lizzie and Harriet. New York: Farrar, Straus and Giroux, 1973.
For the Union Dead. New York: Farrar, Straus and Giroux, 1965.

History. New York: Farrar, Straus and Giroux, 1973.

Imitations. New York: Noonday/Farrar, Straus and Giroux, 1961.

Land of Unlikeness. Cummington, Mass.: The Cummington Press, 1944.

Life Studies. New York: Farrar, Straus and Cudahy, 1959.

Lord Weary's Castle and The Mills of the Kavanaughs. New York: Meridian-Harcourt, Brace and Co., 1961.

Near the Ocean. New York: Farrar, Straus and Giroux, 1967.

Notebook 1967–1968. New York: Farrar, Straus and Giroux, 1969.

Notebook, rev. ed. New York: Farrar, Straus and Giroux, 1970.

Phaedra and Figaro (with Jacques Barzun). New York: Farrar, Straus and Cudahy, 1961.

Prometheus Bound. New York: Farrar, Straus and Giroux, 1967.

Selected Poems. New York: Farrar, Straus and Giroux, 1976.

The Mills of the Kavanaughs. New York: Harcourt, Brace and Co., 1951.

The Old Glory, rev, ed. New York: Farrar, Straus and Giroux, 1968.

ROBERT LOWELL: SECONDARY SOURCES

Cooper, Philip. *The Autobiographical Myth of Robert Lowell.* Chapel Hill: University of North Carolina Press, 1970.

Cosgrave, Patrick. *The Public Poetry of Robert Lowell.* London: Victor Gollancz Ltd., 1970.

Crick, John. *Robert Lowell.* Edinburgh: Oliver S. Boyd, 1974.

Fein, Richard J. *Robert Lowell.* New York: Twayne Publishers, 1970.

Jarrell, Randall. *Poetry and the Age.* New York: Alfred A. Knopf, 1955.

Kunitz, Stanley. "Talk with Robert Lowell," *New York Times Book Review* (4 October 1964), pp. 34–39.

London, Michael, and Robert Boyers, eds. *Robert Lowell: A Portrait of the Artist in His Time.* New York: David Lewis, 1970.

Martin, Jay. *Robert Lowell.* Minneapolis: University of Minnesota Press, 1970.

Mazzaro, Jerome. *The Poetic Themes of Robert Lowell.* Ann Arbor: University of Michigan Press, 1965.

Parkinson, Thomas, ed. *Robert Lowell: A Collection of Critical Essays.* Englewood Cliffs, N.J.: Prentice-Hall, 1968.

Staples, Hugh B. *Robert Lowell: The First Twenty Years.* New York: Farrar, Straus, 1962.

Williamson, Alan. *Pity the Monsters: The Political Poetry of Robert Lowell.* New Haven: Yale University Press, 1974.

Yenser, Stephen. *Circle to Circle: The Poetry of Robert Lowell.* Berkeley: University of California Press, 1975.

GENERAL

Allen, Donald and Warren Tallman, eds. *The Poetics of the New American Poetry.* New York: Grove Press, 1973.

Amis, Kingsley. *A Case of Samples: Poems.* New York: Harcourt Brace, 1957.

Auden, W. H. *Collected Poems.* New York: Random House, 1976.

––––––. *The Dyer's Hand.* New York: Random House, 1962.

Blackmur, R. P. *Language as Gesture.* New York: Harcourt Brace, 1952.

Conrad, Joseph. *A Personal Record.* New York: Harper and Brothers, 1912.

Dali, Salvador. *The Unspeakable Confessions of Salvador Dali.* New York: William Morrow, 1976.

Dewey, John. *Art as Experience.* New York: Minton, Bach, 1934.

Eliot, T. S. *The Sacred Wood.* London: Methuen, 1960 reprint.

Emerson, Ralph Waldo. *The Complete Writings of Ralph Waldo Emerson.* New York: H. W. Wise, 1929.

Ford, Ford Madox. *The Critical Writings of Ford Madox Ford,* ed. Frank MacShane. Lincoln: University of Nebraska Press, 1964.

Frost, Robert. *The Complete Poems of Robert Frost.* New York: Holt, Rinehart and Winston, 1964.

Hall, Donald, ed. *Contemporary American Poetry.* London: Penguin Books, 1962.

Heyen, William, ed. *American Poetry in 1976.* Indianapolis: Bobbs-Merrill, 1976.

Hughes, Ted. *The Hawk in the Rain.* New York: Harper and Brothers, 1957.

––––––. *Poetry Is.* Garden City: Doubleday, 1970.

Hynes, Samuel. *The Auden Generation: Literature and Politics in England in the 1930s.* New York: Viking Press, 1977.

Jenkins, Alan. *The Thirties.* New York: Stein and Day, 1976.

Leavis, F. R. *The Common Pursuit.* New York: New York University Press, 1964.

Levertov, Denise. *The Poet in the World.* New York: New Directions, 1973.

MacDiarmid, Hugh. *Collected Poems.* New York: Macmillan, 1967.

Mailer, Norman. *Armies of the Night.* New York: New American Library, 1968.

Maxwell, D. E. S. *Poets and the Thirties.* London: Routledge and Kegan Paul, 1969.

Mersmann, James F. *Out of the Vietnam Vortex: A Study of Poets and Poetry Against the War.* Lawrence: University Press of Kansas, 1974.

Millay, Edna St. Vincent. *Collected Poems.* New York: Harper and Brothers, 1956.

Miller, Henry. *The Rosy Crucifixion: Book One, Sextus.* New York: Grove Press, 1965.

Olson, Charles. *Selected Writings,* ed. Robert Creeley. New York: New Directions, 1966.

Roberts, Michael, ed. *New Country.* London: Hogarth, 1933.

Roethke, Theodore. *Collected Poems.* Garden City: Doubleday, 1966.

Rosenthal, M. L. *The New Poets.* New York: Oxford University Press, 1967.

Schmidt, Michael. *British Poetry Since 1960.* Oxford: Carcanet Press, 1972.

Sontag, Susan. *Against Interpretation and Other Essays.* New York: Dell, 1966.

Stevens, Wallace. *Letters of Wallace Stevens,* ed. Holly Stevens. London: Faber and Faber, 1967.

Tate, Allen. *The Swimmers and Other Selected Poems.* New York: Charles Scribner's Sons, 1970.

Tolley, A. T. *The Poetry of the Thirties.* New York: St. Martin's Press, 1976.

Van Doren, Mark. *Selected Poems.* New York: Henry Holt, 1954.

Williams, William Carlos. *Paterson.* New York: New Directions, 1963.

———. *Selected Essays.* New York: Random House, 1954.

Wouk, Herman. "A Doubled Magic," *University on the Heights.* Garden City: Doubleday, 1969.

Index